SIBLINGS
IN THE HANDS OF AN ANGRY GOD

Brothers and Sisters through Mythology and the Dominance of Females in Human Morality

Wilson Jeremiah Moses

an imprint of Sunbury Press, Inc.
Mechanicsburg, PA USA

an imprint of Sunbury Press, Inc.
Mechanicsburg, PA USA

FIRST OXFORD SOUTHERN EDITION: November 2025

Set in Adobe Garamond Pro | Interior design by Crystal Devine | Cover by Lawrence Knorr | Edited by Sarah Peachey.

Publisher's Cataloging-in-Publication Data
Names: Moses, Wilson Jeremiah, author.
Title: Siblings in the hands of an angry God : brothers and sister through mythology and the dominance of females in human morality / Wilson Jeremiah Moses.
Description: First trade paperback edition. | Mechanicsburg, PA : Oxford Southern, 2025.
Summary: Since the beginning, sibling incest has retained a role in storytelling. Here is a fresh perspective on Adam and Eve, Hansel and Gretel, Isis and Osiris, and even Grimms' fairy tales, among others. The protagonists in nearly all these stories are female, and the stories contain the narrative elements of withholding knowledge and a resistance to an authority. And it's the sisters, not the brothers, who take charge.
Identifiers: ISBN : 979-8-88819-281-8 (paperback).
Subjects: LITERARY & CRITICISM / Fairy Tales, Folk Tales, Legends & Mythology | LITERARY CRITICISM / Subjects & Themes / Women | SOCIAL SCIENCE / Folklore & Mythology.

Designed in the USA
0 1 1 2 3 5 8 13 21 34 55

For the Love of Books!

CONTENTS

"The Rebuke of Adam and Eve" by Domenichino (1626)

INTRODUCTION

THIS STUDY, rooted in the piously titillating legend of Adam and Eve, is, despite its biblical source, neither a theological treatise nor a study in ancient languages. It is an essay in the history of ideas that assembles a number of myths and fairy tales concerning brothers and sisters in the hands of powerful and arbitrary adult authority—without any moral preachments or prescriptions, although readers cannot be prevented from imposing their own. From my earliest childhood, the nursery tale of Adam and Eve's was a chamber of horrors: the fear of punishment, the fear of fear itself, the shame of weakness, the awareness of vulnerability, the limitations of knowledge, the duplicity of friends, the ignorance of teachers, the secrets of parents, and the dread of abandonment. Childhood was no Paradise; it was a dark forest filled with beasts of terror, with anger, frustration, guilt, and discontent internally generated by my own innate infantile depravity.

Legends such as the stories of Adam and Eve, Hansel and Gretel, and other nightmares of babes in the woods once reached the ears of youngsters from parents, Sunday school teachers, or other children. Today's children are exposed to myths and fables through animated productions; they are not limited to fairy tales and Bible stories received by word of mouth. But I first heard stories of the God who "made man from clay" and "rained down fire on sinners" from my father's mother, who cared for me in Chicago when I was four, during my mother's sixteen-month hospitalization in Detroit due to tuberculosis. Grandma's garden was peaceful and pleasant, with a cherry tree, raspberry bushes, and a strawberry patch, where I once saw my father hacking furiously at something on the ground, and then lifting it lifeless on his hoe.

"Never touch a snake," said my father to my sister and me. And shouldn't a good father warn his children that serpents are dangerous? Evil was present throughout the environment, from sexually precocious schoolboys with worms in their heads. During the fourteen months my two younger sisters and I lived with my grandmother, other children occasionally came and went. One of them, Vincent, was living with her when I arrived, and we shared a bedroom for a while. He was my own age, four years old, and he got me into trouble right away with his example of stealing cherries, and egging me on to shout at the top of my voice, "Mother Forker!"

I could easily imagine what a colorful person this "Mother Forker" must be, based on an illustration in my Mother Goose book, from which my mother had read to me the nursery rhyme "Hey Diddle Diddle," about the cat and the fiddle and the dish that ran away with the spoon. I'd seen a picture of an anthropomorphic spoon, so why not an anthropomorphic fork named Mother Forker? And I saw nothing wrong with proclaiming her fame.

"God is going to rain down fire on Vincent," said my grandmother shortly after he ruined a watermelon on the vine by thrusting a stick into it. By this time, I had soured on Vincent, but my juvenile sense of justice told me it was not right for a big man in the sky to rain down fire on a little boy. Angry and resentful, I wanted to climb onto the rooftop with a stick and strike at that Evil Genius. Still, my grandmother's God seemed almost as fabulous as Mother Forker. Throughout my childhood, I maintained an Orwellian state of mind, simultaneously believing and disbelieving in Him—just as I "believed" and disbelieved in Santa Claus, described by my mother as a good-natured peddler with a thick German accent who responded with a jolly "Ho! Ho! Ho!" and a firm "No! No! No!" to her suggestions that he adjust his prices.

My conception of God was a Santa Claus with muscles, like the one by Michelangelo in the art history books that Mom provided after we got back home. Jesus looked like Billy Graham as quarterback, his arm raised to throw a pass. Iconographers surmise that Michelangelo's conception of the Holy Ghost is represented by the finger of God that almost touches the finger of Adam. This seems reasonable enough, but perhaps the trinitarian doctrine was as problematic for Michelangelo as it was centuries later for John Adams, America's erudite founding father, who, at the mature age of eighty-six, expressed his bafflement in a letter to his daughter-in-law Louisa Catherine Johnson Adams on November 15, 1821.

> The doctrine of the Trinity is a part of an immense system of doctrines of too inormous faith for me to digest.—The imputation of Adam's Sin to all his Posterity. There merit of eternal punishment for it.—The damnable State in which we are all born—The necessity of an infinite sacrifice in the blood and death of Almighty God, as an atonement to myself for this guilt in a very few elected by his mere will to shew the glory of his power—But I must stop for the present . . .

Unlike Adams, I am actually eager to practice "the willing suspension of disbelief." I accept the Bible as "true" in a mythic sense, and I even enjoy reading it as literally as possible. I can see no point in discrediting or falsifying mythologies, whether biblical, Greek, Germanic, Egyptian, or Mesopotamian, no more than I would in beheading or castrating the Grimm fairy tales. My friends and relatives explain to me, sometimes with exasperation, that the Bible is a collection of fairy tales. I have suspected as much since sixth grade, and even before a Sister of Saint Dominic reassured me that some Bible stories are allegorical—but with the caveat that while parts of the Bible may be symbolic or metaphorical, neither the fathers of the church nor their successors in the Vatican ever tampered with or distorted their moral content. Over the years, I have examined several Bibles, some bearing the *imprimatur* and *nihil obstat.* And I've read a few commentaries leading me to the opinion of most scholars that whoever first anthologized the Bible's several books felt no need to force them into consistency or agreement. Nor did they feel the necessity to endow the Bible with any consistent moral instruction.

I have been amazed by several wonders in my eighty years, some happy, some tragic, and some I still find stupefying—the decline of *de jure* segregation, the American withdrawal from Vietnam, the dissolution of the Soviet Union, the 9/11 terrorist attacks, a Black president in the White House, and Communist China's taking "the Capitalist Road." I have lamented the loss of Gregorian chant in Roman Catholic ritual while less appealing aspects of medieval culture are maintained. Rome's inflexibility on the ordination of women remains an oddity, since, in my experience, it was women, the Sisters of Saint Dominic, in beautiful white habits, invested with power, authority, and considerable independence, who preached and interpreted the doctrine of original sin. That responsibility was and remains far too important to be relegated to male preachers alone.

White Catholic women watered the seeds of guilt planted by my grandmother's Christian Black Nationalism, keeping the knowledge of Adam and Eve's nakedness alive in my consciousness, simultaneously stimulating and repressing my sinful curiosity. Repression was my teachers' "necessary and proper" responsibility, for as Freud said, "There would be no prospect of curbing the sexual life of adults if the ground had not been prepared for it in childhood." Pious women were charged with preparing that ground, reinforcing the taboos on forbidden games, kissing, cuddling, and sinful curiosity. Since the dawn of history, this task has traditionally been assumed by mothers, grandmothers, nuns, and women storytellers who have terrified and titillated children with the old wives' tale of Adam and Eve caught naked in the garden.

Adam and Eve were expelled from the Garden of Eden by an angry God, jealous "lest they take also from the tree of life and eat, and live forever." Their story has counterparts in classical myths, medieval romances, and folkish fables of brother-sister dyads who suffer at the hands of angry gods, heartless parents, cold stepmothers, ogres, or witches. The tale of Hansel and Gretel, cast out by cruel parents and derived of food, is most known of these stories, but the fable of Adam and Eve is an equally grim fairy tale of a naive brother and sister thrust into a cruel world. It fits neatly into the Aarne-Thompson-Uther Motif Index of Folk Literature category ATU 450—tales of "babes in the woods."

Adam and Eve have been viewed as children by various priestly and scholarly authorities, which I cite in this study. I also refer to ancient and modern traditions that have seen them as a brother and sister. Adam and Eve were no less siblings than Yama and Yami, the progenitors of the human race in Indo-Iranian mythology. The words "brother" and "sister" are employed as terms of endearment in the Bible's Song of Songs and in the amatory poetry of Egypt and Mesopotamia. Ancient lyrists presented the mutual devotion of brother and sister as a metaphor for erotic love at its most sublime. The non-divorceable brother-sister bond, a union that cannot be put asunder, symbolizes eternal love and finds expression in the ancient legend of Isis and Osiris, the Egyptian divinities, who are both brother and sister and husband and wife.

The sibling incest taboo is universal, except in cases of divine incest, royal incest, and the presumed intimacy of opposite-sex twins, who, in some folklore, are said to have been lovers in the womb. All three criteria are met by Isis and Osiris, the sacred twins of ancient Egyptian religion, the epitome of sibling love and marital devotion. They set the pattern of brother-sister marriage practiced by Egyptian royalty, both in ancient times and later under the Greek dynasty of the Ptolemnies. In the myths and legends of many ancient peoples, the human race sprang from the loins of one sibling pair, like Adam and Eve, formed of the same bone and flesh. Their sons took their daughters as wives, according to ancient rabbinical authority, and the fathers and learned doctors of the Christian faith did not challenge that view. Cain and his wife were twins according to some ancient legends.

The book of Genesis states that the prophet Abraham claimed Sarah as both his wife and his sister, saying, "indeed she is my sister; she is the daughter of my father, but not the daughter of my mother; and she became my wife." The mythical King Arthur embraced his sister Morgana and begat his nemesis, Mordred, his nephew and his son. The Arthurian myth was wildly popular in medieval France, and this tantalizing tale of royal incest likely inspired the unfounded legend that Charlemagne conceived the hero Roland with his sister, Gisele. In various tales regarding incestuous children, King Aeolus appeared in the works of Homer, Ovid, and Euripides. John Gower knew these fables well and added unique moral embellishments in his tale of Canace, Machaire, and Aeolus, their wrathful father.

Additional medieval authors were drawn to the ancient classical and biblical legends that revolved around the sacred and profane amours of siblings. *Geste Romanorum* and Hartmann von Aue's "Gregorius" told the tale of a fictional incest committed by the fictional royal parents of the equally fictitious Pope St. Gregory of the Rock. Hartmann gave the story a happy ending, with the brother, the sister, and their Christlike child ascending into heaven. Likewise, the romantic poet Percy Shelley had his sibling lovers escorted by a divine child, presumably their own, into Elysium at the end of their saga. The Grimm brothers alluded to the story of Adam and Eve in numerous variant tales of brother and sister exiled to the dark forest—sometimes only for a season, but in one instance, having them live happily ever after in quasi-marital happiness.

Within the exile narrative of Hansel and Gretel, one episode contains a veiled metaphor for incest avoidance. The prudent and resourceful Gretel assumes control in this instance, just as she controls the plot at other points. Eve takes control of all human history when she grasps the Fruit of Knowledge and hands it to Adam.

One objective of this book is to celebrate the tradition of female assertiveness in brother-sister narratives after the pattern established by the Adam and Eve legend. Eve, the defiant, disobedient female, represents anarchy, but her quest for knowledge represents historical progress and civilization. In a traditional pious framework, her legitimate desire for knowledge must be dismissed as childish curiosity. One medieval drama, *The Play of Adam,* represents her merely as the dupe of Satan. Her challenging words to Adam, lifted from that play, are quoted in Thomas Mann's novel *Der Erwählte* [*The Chosen One*], where two "*schlimmen Kinder*" [bad children], an adolescent prince and princess, who ultimately follow their incestuously conceived son into sainthood, are deliberately modeled on Adam and Eve.

Prominent theologians have called Jesus and Mary "the new Adam and Eve." Others have identified the brother and sister in the Song of Songs as Jesus and Mary. The ultra-conservative Pope Pius XII, speaking *ex cathedra,* declared them the new Adam and Eve, as he pontificated the doctrine that they are the king and queen of heaven. This book acknowledges the religious mysticism surviving in the myth of Adam and Eve, and the literary manifestations of their counterparts who sprang up independently but spontaneously in ancient times, external to biblical tradition. I have mentioned the mythology of the Egyptian divinities, in which Isis, the sister, assumes a dominant and protective role over Osiris, her male sibling, as Gretel does in struggling against her brother's oppressor.

It would be wrong to ignore those legends in which sisters are tragic victims of an imbalance of power—clearly the fate of Eve, who is exiled and punished along with Adam. Orthodox Christianity has no praise for Eve's heroic character as the anima or genetrix who takes control of the narrative. Women are not supposed to seize control, and yet they stubbornly insist on doing so. The pattern of female agency pops up irrepressibly in Western folklore and literature, from ancient times through the Middle Ages, the Renaissance, the Enlightement, and the Romantic movement. It persists into our own times.

Carl Jung, the eventually errant disciple of Sigmund Freud, presents a fleeting glimpse of Eve as the *anima,* the creative force in civilization, but Otto Rank, a more faithful Freud disciple, obsessed with the Oedipus complex, could never conceive of Eve as Adam's dominant sister or the force of independence and dynamism; she could only be the passive object of masculine desire. In Rank's system, a sister was merely a mother surrogate, never an archetypal symbol in her own right. Freudianism, at its most rigid, directs incest discourse mainly to the inter-generational examples of Oedipus—or Antiochus, the legendary king of Antioch, who is engaged in an incestuous relationship with his daughter.

In the disciplines of medicine, social work, and law enforcement, most discussions of incest are dominated by the responsibilities of those fields in the prevention of child abuse. In literary history, there is less pressure to conflate the pathology of incest as paternal abuse with the more ambiguous, if nonetheless unacceptable discourse, of sibling romance. The distinction has been observed by medieval scholar Elizabeth Archibald, and its importance emphatically iterated by the contemporary novelist Laure-Marie Lapouge. It is particularly evident in the poetic and social theory of Percy B. Shelley, who regarded paternal incest with horror in his play *The Cenci* but idealized sibling incest approvingly in his long poem, "Laon and Cythna." His editors nonetheless forced him to expurgate the work and give it a new title, "The Revolt of Islam."

The female sibling may sometimes be charged with adult responsibilities. She may supplant the wicked or negligent mother and assume a quasi-parental role as the brother's guide or protectress. The roles are rarely reversed; the sister is usually more catalytic and energizing than her passive brother. In some tales, a little sister may evolve into a surrogate mother, or she may simultaneously play the roles of wife or seductress. As I have noted elsewhere, mythologies characteristically allow their models to embody or to reconcile several contradictory archetypes.[1] Circumstances beyond their control place the brother and sister in physical and/or spiritual isolation, engendering exceptional closeness, a mutual sense of interdependency, and sometimes even an antisocial disposition. Often, and with good reason, as in Doris Lessing's 1999 novel, *Mara and Dann*, the siblings adopt the rebellious attitude of "us against the world."

Kindred myths and fairy tales may deviate from one another in accidental details, but the essentials of brother-sister exile narrative are easily seen in the core myth of the Adam and Eve story. The narrative elements of food deprivation, the withholding of knowledge, and resistance to an authority that either issues or represents a death threat are recurrent. The element of an insuperable imbalance of power between the children and the adult figures is also recurrent in these tales. In numerous versions of these fables, animals play determining roles. A serpent tempts Eve; Hansel and Gretel learn of the enchanted house of sweets from a talking bird, and they return home by crossing a river on the back of a duck. One version of their story has them escaping their stepmother at the counsel of their dog, who accompanies them. This version, reproduced at the electronic *Märchenlexikon* (edition amalia), notes that stories of the ATU 450 type compare to the Greek myth of Phrixus and Helle—a brother and sister who take flight from a wrathful goddess on the back of a ram.

A more familiar Greek myth involving sibling exiles, an unenthusiastic stepmother, and a somewhat less sympathetic animal is the legend of Artemis and Apollo, the divine children of Zeus and the titaness Leto. These siblings begin their lives as fugitives from the wrath of the goddess

Hera, who is both the wife and sister of Zeus. The outraged Hera finds herself against her will in the position of a non-consenting and understandably resentful stepmother, and she sends the serpentine python to destroy the children who are reminders of Zeus's infidelity.

Without actually marrying them, the unknown author of the Homeric Hymns placed Artemis and her twin brother, Apollo, in an eternally intimate relationship. As we shall see, the ancient lyrist bound them together as tightly as any other sibling couple on Olympus. The perpetual chastity of Artemis was a gift of the Greeks; her primeval roots are oriental and associated with fecundity and lactation. Her virginity was seemingly forgotten at times by the Romans, who syncretized her with a sexualized version of Diana and with their several moon goddesses—a matter noted by Cicero in *De Natura Deorum*.[2] Artists, poets, and mythographers since Homeric times have been tempted to suggest that Artemis and Apollo were consorts, as I illustrate elsewhere (for example, in the iconography of German Renaissance painter Lucas Cranach, who presented the divine siblings in his characteristically erotic style, mingling their Christian and pagan attributes and making them indistinguishable from Adam and Eve).

While Adam and Eve's legend bears the impact of a child's fear of detection by parental authority, it is also fraught with adult emotions—the humiliation of being "caught," the fear of retribution, the horror of ostracism. It is a moral fable of greater universality than the putative cognate, to which academic historians often compare it, the Sumerian-Babylonian epic of Gilgamesh and Enkidu, which is fragmentary, lengthier, and more complicated. It depicts titanic struggles between gods and demigods, while Adam and Eve seem like ordinary human adolescents. *The Epic of Gilgamesh* may be archetypal, but it is remote from everyday experience, the ordinary misdeeds of curious and disobedient children. The story of Adam and Eve could well have originated at the campfires of Cro-Magnons or Neanderthals and passed down for ages before it was transcribed at some obscure date between the twelfth and fifth centuries BCE to survive with several variations in the Abrahamic religions. Gilgamesh—which may or may not be more ancient—has little, if any, surviving religious significance. It was a "lost and buried book" until its rediscovery in the mid-nineteenth century BCE, and its fragments are still being pieced together from clay tablets in the British Museum and more recently discovered fragments in remote archeological sites.[3]

The story of Adam and Eve is a concise, "familiar," "homey" moral fable with a terrifying outcome, while the poignant *Epic of Gilgamesh* is lengthy, other-worldly, complicated, and not easily summarized. Modern scholars have pieced it together from several incohesive elements, some of them superficially resembling stories in Genesis. Unlike Genesis, however, it is not a narrative of creation, for it begins with Gilgamesh ruling as king over a city called Uruk, where the population complains of his cruelty. In response, the gods send a hairy savage named Enkidu to tame him, but after a wrestling match, the two become lovers. According to some accounts, they destroy a sacred tree, and the gods commission a sex goddess to subdue Gilgamesh. When she is unsuccessful, the gods send down the Bull of Heaven to challenge them, but they impiously slay the Bull. Enkidu is punished with death, and the heartbroken Gilgamesh "sees the maggot dripping from his nose." This legend, due to its elements of a sacred tree, a seductive female, a serpent, a deluge, and a life-giving plant, has led generations of scholars to hypothesize that the *Epic of Gilgamesh* is the likely source for some elements of the Bible's Genesis mythology.[4]

It had become commonplace for professors of art, literature, and comparative religion to exaggerate the similarities between Genesis and the *Epic of Gilgamesh* by the time I entered university in the mid-twentieth century, and it was conventional to imply that Mesopotamian epics were likely sources of biblical myths and legends. But the story of Adam and Eve is fundamentally different from that of Gilgamesh and Enkidu, whose wrestling never resulted in a pregnancy.

The foundation myth of ancient Egypt, the story of Isis and Osiris, resembles the story of Adam and Eve in that it is the epic of a man and wife contesting the will of a powerful oppressor. Sir James G. Frazer's *The Golden Bough* touched suggestively on similarities between Bible stories and several other "vegetation myths" related to "dying and reviving gods." The Egyptian saga features a villain who disrupts the happiness of a primal pair, Isis and her brother, Osiris, who, like Adam, is threatened with death. Osiris is slain and dismembered by his tyrant brother, Seth, but resurrected by Isis after she wanders the world, gathering up his various components. She seizes control of her divine brother's severed penis and spikes herself with it to conceive Horus, a powerful and terrifying god with the head of a hawk, who anticipates Jesus Christ's descent into hell to bind up an evil spirit. Plutarch did not acknowledge the Judeo-Christian cognates to which Frazer alludes, although he surmised that Artemis and Apollo were the Greek counterparts of Isis and Osiris. They had some potential as a procreative pair, for, like Isis and Osiris, they were presumably lovers in the womb. However, unlike their Egyptian counterparts, they never produced offspring, which was probably just as well, for while they were beautiful in form and fair of face, their personalities were not invariably charming.[5]

The primal story of a brother and sister in the hands of an angry God or some other implacable adult is the archetype of such brother-sister exile stories as the fairy tales of Giambattista Basile and the Grimm brothers. Core elements are in the legend of Hansel and Gretel and the variant tale of the seven brothers, *Le Petit Poucet,* recounted by Charles Perrault. They fall into ATU 327B—tales of abandoned children. The Grimms collected numerous fables of the type, centered on an outcast brother and sister, and among them, at least twenty-one variants of Hansel and Gretel, the most familiar of their "*Brüderchen und Schwesterchen,*" or "little brother and sister" tales. All of these Grimm brother-sister pairs dwell at least temporarily in the dark forest. In some of these variants, a surrogate brother is provided in order for the sister to conceive a child, but in all of them, the siblings remain together at the end and live happily ever after.

But while some of these stories have happy endings, others do not. The most characteristic sister-brother exile narratives, whether in classical myths, medieval legends, the Age of Enlightenment, or the Romantic Movement, do not end happily. Richard Wagner fashioned a tale from elements of ancient Germanic mythologies in which twin siblings, Siegmund and Sieglinde, fall in love, conceive a child, and flee into the forest, but Wagner could not allow incestous siblings to live happily ever after. Correctly anticipating the squeamishness of his audiences, he decided his characters must suffer, and thus he had Wotan, their father, under pressure from his wife, Fricka—their righteously wrathful and understandably unenthusiastic stepmother—withdraw his protection from his children who must perish in the wilderness.

Homer alludes in the *Illiad* to the divine brother-sister incest of Zeus and Hera, and presents brother-sister marriages in the *Odyssey*, where Aeolus—perhaps a demigod, but certainly a favorite of the gods—married each of his six sons to each of his six daughters and had them all living happily. Euripides and Ovid revised the story and depicted Aeolus, outraged at the incest of only two of his children, driving the son into exile, the daughter to suicide, and condemning their baby to death by exposure in the wilderness. Aeolus's punishment and exile of his children parallels the story of Adam and Eve. John Milton, a profound classicist, could hardly have been unaware of the similarities when he attempted "to justify the ways of God to man" in *Paradise Lost,* but Mary Shelley rejected this justification with a specific allusion to Milton when she reconfigured and accused his God as Doctor Frankenstein.

Ovid, in classic antiquity, reframed the story as a tragedy, with a focus on only two of Aeolus's children, and John Gower, in the late Middle Ages, repeated Ovid's version, mingling Christian moralizing with pagan embellishments and portraying the siblings as adolescents with the natural impulses of Adam and Eve. He adopted one useful convention of Ovid by allowing his Eve to write a poignant letter in her own defense. In several striking instances in the Christian literature of the Middle Ages, the sister figure is presented as an avatar of Eve—dominant, seductive, and headstrong, most notably in the medieval play *Le Mystère d'Adam.* Throughout the Middle Ages, we occasionally catch sight of daughters of Eve, who are pragmatic, tenacious, and resourceful. This is evident in several versions of *La vie du pape Saint Grégoire, ou La légende du bon pécheur,* where, after being impregnated by her physically stronger but morally weaker brother, the sister takes control of the situation at the moment when she reveals to him her pregnancy. Hartmann von Aue's "Gregorius" retold this story of a brother and sister who suffered mightily for becoming lovers but were ultimately redeemed by the piety of the mother and the suffering of their son, who is the fruit of their incestuous union.

With the eighteenth-century Enlightenment and Romantic movements, the literary handling of sibling incest underwent modification. Montesquieu romanticized and heroized the marriage of a brother and sister in his short story "Apheridon and Astarte." Percy B. Shelley idealized brother-sister romance in "Laon and Cythna" but was pressured into revising the story by converting the protagonists into mere childhood sweethearts, albeit raised from infancy as if they were siblings. The heroine, Cythna, is abducted and victimized by a tyrant, but she progresses into a symbol of defiance and revolution. The story has a remarkable, if inadvertent and seldom recognized, antecedent in the conclusion of Hartmann's *Gregorius,* for in both epics, the siblings are eventually united in Paradise.

"Apollo, God of Light, Eloquence, Poetry and the Fine Arts with Urania, Muse of Astronomy" by Charles Meynier (1798)

– CHAPTER ONE –

DIVINE INCEST, ROYAL INCEST, AND THE SIBLING EXILE NARRATIVE

SIBLING EXILE narratives can be located and analyzed in any of several recognized categories of the Aarne-Thompson-Uther Motif Index of Folk Literature. The present study focuses on categories ATU 327, "Tales of Abandoned or Exiled Children," and ATU 450-59, "Brother and Sister." The siblings are children evolving into adults, who escape, or attempt to escape, from an abusive parent. In the Grimm variations on this theme, the siblings are sometimes exiled by a cruel parent; in others, they voluntarily take flight. The sibling exile narrative does not require that the siblings be a brother and sister who have committed some original sin. Hansel and Gretel, for example, have broken no laws, although Gretel does share some rebellious characteristics with Eve. She equally shares a rebellious nature with Charles Perrault's *Le Petit Poucet,* who is sent into exile with his several brothers. This leads to the observation that the exiled siblings in a fairy tale do not necessarily have to be a brother and sister, nor is it necessarily that they be caught naked, hiding in the bushes from an angry father.[1]

Fables of siblings in exile need not adhere rigidly to the ATU categories. Apollo and Artemis are born in exile, the children of Leto, a fugitive Titaness in flight from the wrath of Hera, the jealous wife of Zeus, their father. Other narratives of exiled, abandoned, or fugitive siblings often involve a sister's search for and rescue of a brother or several brothers: "The Maiden Who Seeks Her Brothers," "The Six Swans," "The Twelve Wild Ducks," and "The Seven Ravens." The variants included in the Grimm collections may feature a protecting or guardian sister, like Gretel, who becomes the savior or guardian of her brother. The most famous sibling narrative from ancient Egypt tells of the wanderings of Isis in search of her brother-husband, the murdered and dismembered Osiris, whose body she eventually retrieves and resuscitates.

Not every sibling exile narrative requires that the sister be an inferior duplicate who leads the brother astray. It does not require that a brother and sister be caught naked and ashamed or that their tribulations result from any misdeed. Hansel and Gretel are model children, innocent of wrongdoing, nakedness, or shame. They have committed no "original sin" and display no "happy fault."[2] Their sole disobedience is in their attempts to frustrate their parents' plans by persistently returning from their exile in the forest, although eventually, they become as guilty as Adam and Eve of pilfering sweets.

Sometimes the exile narrative involves the separation of brother and sister in the flight of one from the other. Ovid's "Metamorphoses" presents the tragic tale of Caunis, a brother who flees into exile, driven by the incestuous advances of his sister, Byblis. Ovid presents a lesser-known variant on that theme, which is not included in the "Metamorphoses"—Macareus is exiled after impregnating his sister, Canace; both siblings languish in their separation from one another until they are driven to suicide. In their tragedies, Aeschylus, Sophocles, and Euripides tell the story of Orestes, who returns from exile, having taken flight at the advice of his sister, Electra. His fate is to be driven into exile a second time, pursued by the Eumenides.

Elements of the brother-sister narrative in Wagner's opera *Lohengrin* are evident from the start as Elsa von Brabant is about to stand trial, falsely accused of murdering her younger brother, Gottfried, who mysteriously disappeared during their wanderings in the forest. In the course of the drama, there is no interaction between brother and sister since Gottfried does not appear until the final scene, where his disappearance and exile are finally explained. The opera's dramatic opening centers on Elsa's deliverance from the murder charge by a mystic champion, Lohengrin, who arrives mysteriously from an undisclosed "foreign land." The crusader for African American civil rights, W. E. B. Du Bois, alluded to Wagner's opera several times directly in his short story, "The Coming of John." In this iteration, a brother returns from his travels in foreign lands to become his sister's champion. Wagnerian mythology and the themes of exile and deliverance dominate Thomas Mann's novel *Der Erwählte,* which is based on the medieval legend of a fictitious Pope Gregory, a tale of forbidden love, where the brother exiles himself by embarking on a Crusade, then dies of grief, unable to endure separation from his sister. Variations on exiled and fugitive siblings are presented throughout numerous versions of the brother and sister fairy tales recorded by the Grimm brothers.

Mythologies represent efforts to reconcile the irreconcilable, the contradictions of the human condition that are irrepressible in every culture and civilization. The story of Adam and Eve as presented in Jewish and Christian Bibles cannot be disentangled from pagan mythology, although the story is not necessarily derived from it. The date of its first telling cannot be established, but the testing and banishment of Eden's primeval children has more in common with Zeus or the cruel and vindictive Sky-Father of Wagnerian mythology than he does with the "Powerful Goodness, bountiful Father, merciful Guide" invoked by Enlightenment deist Benjamin Franklin in his daily prayers.[3] The story of Adam and Eve endures because it echoes the universal resentment of authority and the child's sense of unfairness in an unequal relationship.

Several of the Grimm fairy tales address the universal problem of a child's outrage at the abuse of inequality of parental power—problematic because the child's natural resentment of arbitrary authority must be repressed in the process of maturation and social adjustment. Grimm fairy tales include twenty-one variants in the outrageously abandoned brother and sister category, with cognates in the folklore of Russia, Jamaica, and the Philippines. Hansel and Gretel are like Adam and Eve, babes in the woods, placed in a world of danger by an invincible authority. Their reactions to their exile reveal paradoxical impulses endemic to human nature—the need for security and the yearning for independence.

In the several variants of the Hansel and Gretel story, we see a brother and sister retreating to a solitary house in the woods where they dwell, at least for a season, "alone and happy." It is a cruel fact of human history that not every child is along for the security of Eden, but it is the human condition to wander into a dark forest, where they must learn to be resourceful, and defiant to the point of mercilessly slaying the ogre.

THE ONLY MORAL LESSON OF GENESIS: MIGHT MAKES RIGHT

It is widely acknowledged that no surviving "Urtext" or original text of the Genesis creation myth exists in its original language or languages. The persons who created and preserved the Genesis fables conceived a God driven by want, need, and desire. He makes known his needs through arbitrary commandments and acts of will. He says, "Let there be light," governing by will, not reason. In the words of Bach's oratorio, "*Was Gott tut dass it wohlgetan,* well done, and perfectly justified."[4] Nonetheless, God is at liberty to change his mind. He may decide not to kill Adam on the day he bites the apple, He may soften the harshness of his curse on Cain, and He may "repent that he ever made man." For the Lord of Creation's wants or needs are repeatedly frustrated. An act of will implies a need to act in order to fulfill a lack, a want, or a desire. The Lord of Creation craves the submission of Eve, and she refuses him his heart's desire.

The fable of Adam and Eve is a tragedy played out by characters who have not seen the complete script of their drama and lack the knowledge of its plot and final outcome. Adam is commanded to limit his knowledge and is threatened with death, but Genesis does not record that Eve ever received any such threat or command. Genesis offers no explanation for its gratuitous element of shame in nakedness. The moral of the story would have been conveyed just as well without that provocative reference. Its moral lessons are "might makes right" and "curiosity killed the cat," which could just as easily be conveyed with a boy, a girl, an apple, and a vengeful father. The story requires neither a serpent nor any mention of nakedness. All it requires is that Adam and Eve, in their desire for knowledge, eat the apple and that they be punished for doing so.

ADAM AND EVE'S CHILDLIKE INNOCENCE AND PUBESCENT *INZESTSCHEU*

"Before they ate the apple, Adam and Eve were babies," said Professor George Nakhnikian in his Introduction to Philosophy course at Wayne State University in the fall of 1960. On that morning, I was unaware that his opinion was neither original nor heterodox, and Nakhnikian, who once alluded to his upbringing in the Orthodox Church, most likely knew he was reiterating the position of several second-century Christian authorities. Joel Edmund Anderson points out that the apostolic father, Clement of Alexandria, referred to Adam as a boy before his Fall, and notes provocatively that "it was by sinning that Adam became a man." Anderson also notes that the patriarch, Theophilus of Antioch, described Adam and Eve as "infants." St. Irenaeus, Bishop of Lyons, the ecclesiastical doctor and father of the church, viewed them as devoid of sexual feeling and called them "innocent and infantile."[5]

> Adam and Eve "were naked and were not ashamed," for there was in them an innocent and infantile mind, and they thought or understood nothing whatsoever of those things that are wickedly born in the soul through lust and shameful desires. (Irenaeus, Bishop of Lyons—ca. 190 AD)[6]

St. Augustine and other early theologians concurred with Irenaeus's opinion that Adam and Eve were innocent of sexual awareness before their Fall. Tertullian posited that Adam and Eve were physically pre-adolescent before the Fall and attained puberty at some point after eating the fruit. George Boas and Brian Murdoch have shown that Christian theologians of late antiquity and throughout the Middle Ages speculated broadly regarding the nature of Adam and Eve's sexuality before and after eating of the Tree of Knowledge. Hildegard von Bingen declared that when Adam sinned, "the holy and chaste nature of begetting children was changed into a mode of carnal delight." Imaginations ran wild with little regard for the biblical text, and linguistic analysis has never resolved the mystery of what Genesis actually means. Even if the authentic, original, archaic proto-Hebraic Urtext—if such ever existed—were suddenly to be discovered, miraculously preserved on baked clay tablets, the discovery would simply engender new controversy.[7]

It may be, as Irenaeus maintained, that Adam and Eve were like infants before eating the forbidden fruit, but their behavior was demonstrably childish thereafter. Their feeble attempt to cover their nakedness with fig leaves, and their infantile scrambling at the approach of their Father, could serve only to confirm their guilt. God's response was exactly what Saint Paul, Tertullian, and Augustine would have expected of any responsible father—scolding them and having them more properly cover their nakedness. A good father in ancient times would almost certainly have imposed punishments, both mental and corporal. This fable, with its ingredients of nakedness, terror, humiliation, punishment, and exile, has terrified children through the ages.

The moral of the story is that the Father must be obeyed because he is omnipotent; he has the power to punish. The second lesson is that He cannot be deceived. He can detect guilt even before his foolish children betray themselves, for Adam and Eve merely confirmed their guilt by their secretive behavior, proving to themselves what the Father already knew. This leads to the ancillary truth of the story, that nakedness is self-evidently shameful. When Adam and Eve's disobedience opened their eyes and uncovered the "knowledge of good and evil," they recognized the incontestable axiom that to be caught naked is horrifying. We must address the fact that every society has some sort of nakedness anxiety, although definitions of nakedness differ across cultures.

FORBIDDEN FRUIT AND NAKEDNESS ANXIETY

Small siblings, if caught by a parent in a game of "show-and-tell," will experience unease, which suggests an augury of *Inzestscheu*, Sigmund Freud's word often translated as "horror of incest." Around the age of seven, many children—while studying their catechism and reading their Bible history in preparation for their first visit to the confessional—have been perplexed by this fable's seemingly gratuitous ingredient of nakedness, which places in the mind of a child, however amorphous, something sexy. The adults who transmitted this story to me sometimes compressed or entirely elided any such suggestions. The Dominican Sisters did not have us reading the Bible at Nativity of our Lord Parochial School in the Catholic Archdiocese of Detroit, where I made my first communion and was confirmed. In the bookcase at the back of our sixth-grade classroom, conducted by Sister Grace Bernard, I found a copy of the Benziger Brothers' *Bible History, Containing the Most Remarkable Events of the Old and New Testaments* by the Right Rev. Richard Gilmore, with a letter of approval by Pope Leo XIII. I quote here from my late father-in-law's copy of the 1904 edition, with its idiosyncratic tense form, and its exceedingly oblique reference to nakedness:[8]

> 3. One day while Eve was looking at the forbidden tree, the serpent, coming near, asked her why she did not eat of the fruit. Eve answered, God had forbidden them to touch it, lest they die. But the serpent artfully replied, they would not die; on the contrary, their eyes would be opened and they would be as gods, knowing good and evil. Eve looked again upon the tree; her curiosity was excited: the more she looked, the more the forbidden fruit appeared enticing. At length she stretched forth her hand, plucked the fruit, ate and gave to Adam, who also ate. This was their first sin.
>
> 4. Immediately their eyes were opened, but far from otherwise than they had expected. Covered with shame, they sewed together and made garments for themselves, and, trembling, hid among the trees.

One might argue that the element of nakedness is merely subsidiary to the fable and entirely unnecessary to its main purpose of instruction;

the moral is, in John Milton's words, that "Man's first disobedience . . . brought death into the world." When the fable of Eden is related to young children, its ingredients of nakedness and shame may sometimes be omitted, but other "bare essentials" are preserved. These are the elements of horror at the imbalance of power and the imposition of the parent's will over the helpless will of the child. In the background broods the serpentine presence who initiates the nightmare of exile. But if the story terrifies, it also titillates. Children long to be free of parental domination while also fearing separation from their parents. The dread of being lost or abandoned haunts children's nightmares; thus, the motif occurs in biblical and classical mythology, fairy tales, medieval literature, Renaissance paintings, and Wagnerian opera. Analogies are, by definition, imperfect, but Adam and Eve, like Hansel and Gretel, are exiled by their Father due to the influence of a malign presence and His own negligence. Thus, the biblical myth and the fairy-tale legend overshadow infancy, when the imagination is terrorized by tales of children exiled or abandoned by their parents. The main point of the fable is that God's absolute power warrants absolute obedience—or, putting it bluntly, His might makes right.

The Almighty offered no explanation or justification for issuing a death threat at the beginning of his unequal relationship with Adam. He pronounced His will but not His reasoning when he said in Genesis 2:16, "Thou shalt not eat of it: for in the day that thou eatest thereof thou shalt surely die." The threat turned out to be ambiguous, if not lacking in candor, because Eve did not die "in that day." Tertullian attempted to justify this incongruity with a hyperbolic reference to "Eve, expelled from Paradise, already dead," and an additional swipe at "woman in her condemned and dead state." True enough, Eve gained knowledge of her destined punishment and eventual death, but Tertullian knew quite well that at that moment she was neither dead nor dying. She was hale and hardy enough to give birth to several children.[9]

As for Adam, the one to whom the Lord actually delivered the death threat, Holy Scripture attests to the fact that he endured long enough to generate Cain as well as other sons and daughters. In fact, Genesis 5:4 says, "Adam lived an hundred and thirty years, and begat *a son* in his own likeness, after his image; and called his name Seth." Moses writes that after he begat Seth, presumably with Eve, he lived "eight hundred years and begat sons and daughters," also presumably with the assistance of Eve. Obviously, neither Adam nor Eve died "in that day," and obviously the serpent was telling at least a half-truth when he said, "Ye shall not surely die: For God doth know that in the day ye eat thereof, then your eyes shall be opened, and ye shall be as gods, knowing good and evil." Speaking, indeed, with a forked tongue the serpent nonetheless revealed a biting reality, as the Lord himself later admitted when He remarked with infinite sarcasm, "Behold, the man has become like one of Us, knowing good and evil."

Eve and her consort, Adam, could not appreciate the irony and deceptive wordplay in which the Lord and his serpent were engaged. They could not question the justice of their Father testing them as He did; they could only wonder at the reasons for His doing so or the consequences of failing the test. They had no precognition of Abraham's passing the test of Isaac's sacrifice. They had no premonition of the test of Job, whose sons and daughters were massacred. If the serpent and Satan were one and the same, they were simply God's advocates, his servants, his instruments for a divine plan that was deliberately hidden. Long-suffering Job complained, "Thou art become cruel to me." (Job 32). But Elihu's "wrath was kindled because Job justified himself rather than God." John Milton felt it his duty to "justify the ways of God to Man," but William Blake presented the God of Genesis with the following question:

> Why darkness & obscurity
> In all thy works & laws,
> That none dare eat the fruit but from
> Thy wily serpent's jaws?[10]

The God of both the Old and New Testament governs not by reason but by power and authority. He does not rule according to the childish reasoning of his flawed creatures who perceive the world "as through a glass darkly." If indeed Adam and Eve were like little children, it's all the more reason they should have obeyed their Father unquestioningly and placed their faith in His "knowledge of good and evil." But according to the ancient rabbis, He consulted with the angels in the shaping of the world, and in the book of Job, we see him taking counsel with Satan, who is His instrument.[11] Elsewhere, He makes an instrument of Nebuchadnezzar, "king of Babylon, my servant," by planting a serpent in his garden. For those who ask why this deliberate exposure of naive children to a clear and present danger, St. Augustine's justification is echoed by a multitude of sages. We are told that the Father's purpose was to bring good out of evil, to exalt mankind, and to work a cosmic Providence by means of Adam's "fortunate fall," or his *felix culpa*, his "happy fault." An anonymous poet famously summed up the entire event in Medieval English:

> Ne hadde the appil take ben,
> Ne hadde never our lady, a ben hevene quen.[12]

Thomas Traherne, a seventeenth-century Puritan divine, offered the consolation that "God made man greater when He made him less." In a consequence of their first parents' weakness, all "children" come into the world predisposed to sin, not "trailing clouds of glory," but wayward, willful, and rebellious.[13] Adam and Eve were "sufficient to have stood, but free to fall," and thus their failings cannot be attributed entirely to immaturity. The book of Jubilees saw them as ripe adults who spent seven years in Paradise.[14] Others went so far as to claim the prelapsarian pair had dwelt in Eden for centuries before the Fall, but such assertions were uncommon. We deal here with a venerable Christian tradition that compared Adam and Eve to small, sexually immature children. This view accords with Irenaeus's assertion that Eve, although "having a husband, Adam, nevertheless was still a virgin," as proven by the fact that she and Adam, although created naked in Paradise, were at first not ashamed.

To Irenaeus, it was self-evident that "they had been created only a short time before and possessed no understanding of the procreation of children. For it was necessary for them first to grow, and only thereafter to multiply." It required no intellectual contortion for contemporary scholar Christopher R. Smith to arrive at the reasonable surmise that "for Irenaeus, Eve in the garden was actually prepubescent."[15] But this leads to the recognition of a contradiction in the two Genesis accounts of creation. In Genesis 1:27, the man and woman are expected from their beginning to "be fruitful and multiply," but in Genesis 3, they discover their sexuality belatedly as a consequence of eating the fruit of knowledge. Not until Genesis 4 does Adam know Eve.

Prepubescent youngsters are regarded by most contemporary societies as vulnerable and needing legal protection from parental abuse, but parental abuse is a modern idea. In the traditional cultures of the eastern Mediterranean and the Levant, parental authority was not to be questioned. The abandonment of a child, like Ishmael, or the sacrifice of a child, like Isaac, did not seem so horrific as it does to the mind of a modern Quaker or Unitarian. In "pre-modern" societies, stories correlative to that of Adam and Eve's exile are abundant. Children are often abandoned or driven into exile in classical literature and folktales.[16] Greek mythology gives epic examples of unwanted children left to die of exposure (discussed in due course), as do several fairy tales in this tradition, such as the Grimm brothers' *Hänsel und Gretel,* and Charles Perrault's *Le Petit Poucet.*

Eve's Promethean defiance, followed by Adam's acquiescence, was a threat to the authority of the Father as Lord of the cosmos. His banishment of his children—if we are to take the words of Genesis literally—was less a punishment than a defensive and preventive measure.

> . . . the LORD God said, Behold, the man is become as one of us, to know good and evil: and now, lest he put forth his hand, and take also of the tree of life, and eat, and live for ever: Therefore the LORD God sent him forth from the garden of Eden.

Although the words above focus on "the man," it was not "the man" but the *woman* who first "put forth her hand" in defiance. Eve first desired the forbidden fruit of knowledge, and Adam merely followed. Eve's initiative forced the Father to recognize that this initial act of disobedience was a harbinger of things to come. No different than the titans and gods of Greek mythology, He feared usurpers. Jealous of His power and anticipating rebellion, He takes steps reminiscent of those taken by Kronos, Uranos, and Zeus to stifle the ambition of progeny who present a threat to the established order. Like Uranos, who confined his children in the depths of the earth; like Kronos, who swallowed his children; and like Zeus, who swallowed Metis lest she give birth to a child greater than himself, God the Father fears a challenge to his power. Zeus's exile of Prometheus is analogous to God's exile of Satan. Adam and Eve are exiled with similar dispatch because Yahweh perceives them as having the potential to become immortal and more godlike.

BROTHERS AND SISTERS IN GENESIS: EXILE AND WANDERING

The forced exile of Adam and Eve from the Garden of Eden is the first brother-sister exile narrative in Genesis, followed by the exile of Cain and his wife, presumably his sister, for the land of Nod east of Eden. Subsequently come the meanderings of Abram and his wife, Sarai, whom he claims as his sister. The account of Adam's expulsion says only that "the LORD God sent him forth from the garden of Eden," without mentioning Eve, the "flesh of my flesh," whose seduction of Adam supposedly occasioned his exile. Even the most exacting textualist would have to assume that both "the man" and the woman were expelled. After all, the ensuing chapter, Genesis 4:1, has them together when it begins, "And Adam knew Eve his wife and she conceived and bare Cain."

Since Cain's conception, birth, and further adventures occurred after the exile, it must be deduced from the context that Eve was expelled from Eden along with Adam. While this and other details in the Genesis narrative are left to the imagination, no intuition or deduction is necessary to know why the exile was decreed. It is stated explicitly that the expulsion from Paradise was not merely a punishment but a preventive measure, "lest he put forth his hand, and take also of the Tree of Life, and eat, and live for ever." Despite the curious fact that scripture mentions only the threat of Adam's usurping the properties of the Tree of Life, Eve was obviously banished along with him, and with good reason. After all, it was she who showed the greater propensity to put forth her hand and grasp the godlike powers of knowledge and immortality.[17]

The second exile narrative in Genesis describes Cain's departure from the presence of the Lord and dwelling east of Eden. The reader must imagine that, as in the case of his father, Cain was either accompanied by or followed by a woman, because Genesis 4:12 states that

"Cain knew his wife." I shall follow after Saints Augustine and Thomas Aquinas and accept the tradition inherited from ancient rabbis that Cain's wife was one of his sisters. Her name was Awan according to the non-canonical book of Jubilees, but other ancient commentators have given her additional names: Aclima, Kalmana, Lusia, Cainan, and Luluwa. Medieval author John Gower, who receives considerable attention in the present work, accepted a tradition in which the sisters of Cain and Abel were named Calmana and Delbora. In the interests of simplicity, convenience, and consistency, one is tempted to abide by tradition and call her Calmana.[18]

There is no biblical support for the opinion that Cain's wife was his sister. In fact, a literal reading of Genesis might support a supposition that Cain could have found a spouse elsewhere than among his siblings. Genesis 4:14-15 implies the existence of other human beings contemporary to Cain and Abel and might seem to indicate that the canonical narrative was patched together from more than one preexisting narrative. Furthermore, the conversations between Cain and God refer to unspecified persons who might seek to kill Cain, and God resultingly promises "whosoever slayeth Cain, vengeance shall be taken on him sevenfold." Immediately thereafter, we see Cain removing to the land of Nod, which is populous enough to build a city. Up to this point, Genesis makes no mention of Adam and Eve's additional children, but this does not necessarily negate the possibility that the additional sons and daughters, later attributed to Adam in Genesis 5:3 (with no mention of Eve), could have been born before the death of Abel. There is, however, a venerable tradition that Eve was the mother of Cain's wife. The opinion has been handed down with the powerful authority in the Talmud, stated in the book of Jubilees, and substantiated in the writings of Saints Augustine and Thomas Aquinas.

A third biblical narrative that focuses on the wanderings of a brother and sister is the story of Abram and Sarai, or Abraham and Sarah, as they are later called. Sarai is first described as Terah's daughter-in-law. She leaves the city of Ur with the family of Terah, Abram's father. Although Abram will later claim, in Genesis 20:12, that Sarai is Terah's daughter, there is no mention of this supposedly important relationship in Genesis 11:31.

> And Terah took Abram his son, and Lot the son of Haran his son's son, and Sarai his daughter-in-law, his son Abram's wife; and they went forth with them from Ur of the Chaldees, to go into the land of Canaan; and they came unto Haran, and dwelt there.

At God's command, Abram and Sarai, accompanied by his nephew Lot "and the souls they had gotten in Haran," depart for Canaan, where God has promised them land. It is at this point in Genesis 12:1-3 that the Covenant of God with Abraham is first mentioned. But there is a famine in the land, so Abram and Sarai continue south into Egypt, apparently accompanied by Lot, because he is still with them in the following chapter, at the point of their departure. On entering Egypt, Abram, aware of Sarai's beauty and desirability, advertises that she is his sister.

> And it came to pass, when he was come near to enter into Egypt, that he said unto Sarai his wife, Behold now, I know that thou *art* a fair woman to look upon:
>
> Therefore it shall come to pass, when the Egyptians shall see thee, that they shall say, This *is* his wife: and they will kill me, but they will save thee alive. Say, I pray thee, thou *art* my sister: that it may be well with me for thy sake; and my soul shall live because of thee.[19]

There is no record of how Sarai felt about this, but things could not have worked out better for Abram. As anticipated, the Egyptians recognized Sarai's beauty and commended her to Pharaoh, and she was "taken into Pharaoh's house. And entreated Abram well for her sake: and he had sheep, and oxen, and he asses, and menservants, and maidservants, and she asses, and camels." The scripture leaves to the imagination how far things went between Sarai and Pharaoh, but regardless of how happy Abram was with the arrangement, the Lord was displeased, so accordingly, He "plagued Pharaoh and his house with great plagues because of Sarai Abram's wife." There is imprecision here as to whether the plagues were instilled at Pharaoh's having sexual relations with Sarai, or were activated merely as a preventive measure. Scripture does not reveal how Pharaoh deduced that Sarai was the source of his difficulties, but he somehow became aware of Abram's deception and "commanded *his* men concerning him: and they sent him away, and his wife, and all that he had."

Abram and Sarai, although exiled, were allowed to retain all the benefits derived from this bargain, from which apparently Abram learned his lesson well. He made a second profitable use of Sarai's beauty, traveling under his new name, Abraham, and arriving in the land of Gerar. Once again he led the people to believe that Sarai, whose name was changed to Sarah, was his sister, and she was taken into the house of King Abimelech, but this king was prevented from adulterous contact by divine intervention, as God came to him in a dream with the warning that Sarah was another man's wife. Abimelech claimed innocence, reminding God that both Abraham and Sarah represented themselves to him as brother and sister.

> And God said unto him in a dream, Yea, I know that thou didst this in the integrity of thy heart; for I also withheld thee from sinning against me: therefore suffered I thee not to touch her. Now therefore restore the man *his* wife; for he *is* a prophet, and he shall pray for thee, and thou shalt live: and if thou restore *her* not, know thou that thou shalt surely die, thou, and all that *are* thine.[20]

Immediately the following morning, Abimelech confronted Abraham, who explained, "indeed *she is* my sister; she *is* the daughter of my father, but not the daughter of my mother; and she became my wife." A possible explanation for the earlier identification of Sarah merely as Terah's daughter-in-law in Genesis 11 is that she may have been an extra-marital daughter by a servant or a slave, in which case the patriarch may not have acknowledged any relationship until she became his daughter-in-law. Abraham must have been telling the truth, because God himself set great store in his words and said to Abimelech, "he *is* a prophet, and he shall pray for thee, and thou shalt live." But in spite of God's character reference, some Bible scholars have questioned the honesty of Abraham's testimony to Abimelech that Sarah was his sister.

The entirety of Abraham and Sarah's story occurs before the Law of Moses forbidding marriage to a sister or a half-sister. There is a similar episode in Genesis 26:1-33 when Abraham's son Isaac brings his wife Rebekah into the land of Abimelech to avoid a famine and states that she is his sister. But one day, Abimelech "looked out at a window, and saw, and, behold, Isaac was sporting with Rebekah his wife." Isaac, when confronted by Abimelech, admitted Rebekah was his wife, making no claim that she was his sister, but her origins and the events leading up to her marriage with Isaac are carefully described in Genesis 24. By contrast, Abraham claiming Sarah is his sister is unequivocal, and in his dealings with Abimelech, as in his prior dealings with Pharaoh, he profits from the ruse, for "Abimelech took sheep, and oxen, and menservants, and womenservants, and gave *them* unto Abraham, and restored him Sarah his wife."[21]

The three sibling exile narratives of Genesis, the exile of Adam and Eve, the emigration of Cain and his sister, and the peregrinations of Abraham and Sarah exemplify the brother-sister marriages that St. Augustine justified as "dictated by necessity" and "quite allowable in the earliest ages of the human race." Thomas Aquinas justified the sexual intercourse between brothers and sisters in Genesis on the same grounds, employing the axiom that the natural purpose of sex is reproduction, and since it was potentially fruitful, it could not be called unnatural. By contrast, he condemned as unnatural any employment of the genitalia in ways that precluded conception, such as homosexual activity, masturbation, bestialism, or *coitus interruptus*. To engage in sex or sex-related activity that inhibited reproduction, as Onan did when he spilled his seed on the ground, was unnatural, "And the thing which he did displeased the LORD: wherefore He slew him."[22] In his *Summa Theologiae,* on "The Parts of Lust," Aquinas presented without challenge or contradiction the proposition that "intercourse between those who are related by consanguinity or affinity does not, of itself, contain any deformity, else it would never have been lawful."[23]

Nonetheless, Aquinas firmly insisted that consanguineous intercourse was forbidden by the Law of Moses and, "wherefore, as Augustine says (De Civ. Dei xv, 16), whereas the union of brothers and sisters goes back to olden times, it became all the more worthy of condemnation when religion forbade it." Neither Aquinas nor Augustine disputed the rabbinical presupposition that the children of Adam and Eve became sexual partners, and the early Christian authorities took it for granted that Adam and Eve's children had practiced consanguineous procreation.[24]

CLONING AND THE PARTHENOGENETIC ORIGINS OF ADAM AND EVE

Eve was Adam's clone, pure and simple. She was his genetic duplicate. Although she was fashioned as a full-grown woman, she was analogous to a twin sister, although obviously closer. She was not Adam's mother, despite the single-minded imagination of Otto Rank, which I shall discuss in due course. Eve was not Adam's daughter, despite the assertion of Milton, whose obsession with father-daughter incest I shall later address. Adam and Eve were parthenogenetic siblings in the rabbinical and ancient Christian traditions I discuss in the coming pages. Eve was not "conceived," nor was she any man's daughter; she did not spring from human loins but was fashioned from Adam's "rib," according to some Bibles, or, according to others, from his side. Some erudites have seen them as analogous to so-called "Siamese twins," taking the second account of creation in Genesis 5:2, "male and female created he them," to mean that Adam was originally hermaphroditic. They fancied that the first human beings were created as conjoined twins, male and female joined back to back until God divided them.[25]

Numerous students of scripture have argued that there are no irreconcilable contradictions between the first Genesis account of creation, which says, "God created man in His own image, in the image of God created He him; male and female created He them," and the second account, which declares that Eve was created from Adam's rib. The first account does not exclude the second since both aver that they were *ab initio* of one identical physical body. The creation of a fully formed adult human being from the substance of another was a one-time performance by God, and the only contemporary experiential cognate of such a unique supernatural cloning is in the rare instance of semi-identical (sesquizygotic) twins, as discussed below. Adam and Eve are cognates of monozygotic twins, and their relationship is consanguineous, as Adam recognizes in Genesis 2:23, when he calls Eve "bone of my bones and flesh of my flesh."

Cloning is neither a modern concept nor is "clone" a modern word. The English words "clone" and "scion" have common roots in old French and archaic Greek, as well as in Proto-Indo European. Even Aristotle recognized cloning. Asexual reproduction through cuttings was the most common mode of ancient grape cultivation because it duplicated the original stock. The primal pair was analogous to rare instances of genetically identical twins originating in a single zygote but later diverging sexually. Since Eve was a "cutting" from Adam's body, she was nothing other than Adam's clone or scion. Cloning, as a horticultural process, was known and widely utilized in the ancient Near East for cultivating the "fruits of the earth." In the context of vegetative reproduction, some readers will recall the venerable studies of George Smith's *The Chaldean Account of Genesis* (1876) and Sir James G. Frazer's *The Golden Bough* (1890), both of which draw analogies between biblical and other vegetation myths in their relationships to mortality and regeneration.[26]

Adam and Eve were obviously unique but just as obviously related, although outside of any recognizable biogenetic kinship category. If there is a need to locate them in the scientific terminology of today, they might be thought of as "sexually discordant monozygotic twins," except for the discordant fact that neither of them was ever a zygote; neither of them progressed through the phases from gamete, to zygote, to embryo, to fetus, to birth and infancy.[27] While it remains a matter of speculation whether they had navels, there is no doubt of their consanguinity. They were biogenetically much closer than any fraternal twins, and this being so, I am handling their story as the model narrative, if not the first, of siblings in exile.[28]

ADAM AND EVE, OF ONE FLESH AND CLOSER THAN BROTHER AND SISTER

While greviously dated, Otto Rank's Freudian interpretation of *Das Inzest-Motiv in Dichtung und Sage* (1912) is still respected for its erudition. In comparative literature, Rank is frequently cited in scholarly bibliographies despite Freud's declining popularity. Rank exercised extreme poetic license in declaring that Adam was Eve's son, an idea that is bizarre but no more fanciful than John Milton's pontification that Adam was Eve's father. Obviously Eve did not spring from anyone's loins and, just as obviously, Adam is not the fruit of anyone's womb. Neither Eve nor Adam is the product of natural gestation. Eve is cloned from Adam's body, much as an ancient Hebrew might have taken a cutting from a plant in his vineyard. She may be described as the product of asexual vegetative propagation, the product of a unique generation. If we can find a reference to any such relationship in modern medical jargon, Eve might be called Adam's "sexually discordant identical twin."[29]

Otto Rank's bold assertion that "Adam is created from Eve, the mother" is a remarkable and seemingly unjustifiable departure from the text, but it is necessary in order for Rank to force Adam's sexual "knowing" of Eve into Sigmund Freud's Oedipus paradigm. This contortion is remarkable, for if Eve is to function symbolically as Adam's mother, should not Adam have been created from her rib? John A. Phillips, in his scholarly and useful study *Eve: The History of an Idea,* accurately portrays the biblical meiosis of Eve emerging from Adam's side, or, alternately, as she is molded from his rib. Religiously devout scholar Peter Enns treats the biblical account of Eve's creation as a metaphor, in tacit agreement with Stephen Greenblatt's dry comment, "It was Darwin's position that ultimately prevailed in the modern science." Without stating the obvious, Greenblatt takes note using a painful allusion to Genesis in the *Confessions of St. Augustine,* when the saint, under maternal pressure, divests himself of his beloved concubine, "torn out of my side."[30]

ORIGINAL TWINS AND PARTHENOGENETIC CREATION MYTHS

Hans Holbein, Michelangelo, and other painters and sculptors have portrayed the emergence of Eve as a fully formed woman from Adam's sleeping body, although in Genesis 2:22, she is fashioned from his previously extracted rib. The artistic tradition reconciles the first account of creation, in which man and woman are created simultaneously—possibly sharing the same body, or perhaps as conjoined twins—with the second account in which Eve is fashioned later from Adam's side, but in either instance, they are of one flesh in their origin. The human species is generated by primeval sibling pairs in the creation myths of several ancient peoples, and this holds true in several myths of regeneration after a great flood. In the *Journal of the American Psychoanalytic Association,*

Jules Glenn, a clinical psychologist, observed the frequent occurrence of sibling pairings in sundry ancient and modern creation myths:

> In a sense Adam and Eve are opposite sex twins too. For they were one organism that was evenly split in two. . . . A Balinese legend describes the origin of the first Raja, a twin. Batara Indra killed a fierce demon, Maya Danawa, by dividing him in two. The spirit of the demon was transformed into male-female twins called Mesula-Mesuli, who ruled the land as the first Raja and his wife. These twins married and gave birth to opposite-sex twins who again married. Seven generations of twins succeeded each other in marriage to rule Bali.[31]

In that same journal, Glenn reported a belief persistent in Bali as late as 1966 that "male-female twins are thought to engage in incestuous union in the womb" and, after ritual purification, were free to marry. We find a recent report in the Bangkok press in 2015 that "Superstitious parents in Nakhonsawan province hosted a big traditional wedding for their 3-year-old twins in attempt to fix their bad karma." The *London Daily Mail* reported as late as 2018 that six-year-old brother and sister twins were married in a Buddhist ceremony in Thailand, "because their parents believe 'they were lovers in past lives' and 'karma' meant they were born together."[32]

The Babylonian creation epic, *Enūma Eliš,* features the primal pair Tiamat and Abzu, who produce three generations of brother-sister gods. Their children are Lahamu and her brother consort Lahmu, who produce Kishar and her husband-brother Anshar. In Zoroastrian mythology, Mashya and Mashyana, the first man and woman, grew out of a rhubarb plant; their mating produced fifteen sets of twins whose sibling pairings produced the various races of mankind. In some traditions, stories of the world-flood tell of sibling pairings that regenerate the human species. In Greek mythology, the problem of regeneration by incest was avoided since after the deluge, the surviving couple, Deucalion and Phyrra, were not siblings but first cousins who revived humanity by throwing "their grandmother's bones" over their shoulders. In the Genesis account of the deluge, the problem of sibling inbreeding was avoided through first-cousin marriage. Noah's three sons and their wives produced an adequate number of first cousins to allow for regeneration in accordance with the prohibitions yet to be mandated in Leviticus and Deuteronomy.

Creation myths involving brother-sister progenitors have arisen far removed from ancient Egypt, Mesopotamia, or Greece. Such legends exist among the Bantus, Hindus, and Hawaiians, and there are also intimations of such pairings in Chinese and Japanese creation myths. A myth of the West African Mande people relates how the human species was generated by the progeny of a single ancestor, four pairs of male and four pairs of female twins. While similar stories were preserved among other African ethnic groups, almost no remnants of these mythologies survived among African Americans. Their cultural divestation was poignantly illustrated in Harriet Beecher Stowe's *Uncle Tom's Cabin* through the voice of little Topsy, an American slave-child with no knowledge of her parentage, ancestral myths and legends, or Christian concepts of human generation.

> "Have you ever heard anything about God, Topsy?"
> The child looked bewildered, but grinned as usual.
> "Do you know who made you?"
> "Nobody, as I knows on," said the child, with a short laugh.
> The idea appeared to amuse her considerably; for her eyes twinkled, and she added,
> "I spect I grow'd. Don't think nobody never made me."

Topsy's response to the mystery of human origin differed little from the response of modern scientists searching for the origins of life. Without implementing creation myths like those of the ancient Near East or other civilizations, science's only response at present is to "feign no hypothesis" other than life just "grow'd." The ancient Hebrews embellished the Genesis account of creation with numerous elaborations. Louis Ginzberg, who compiled his erudite *Legends of the Jews* from ancient scrolls, oral traditions, and rabbinical commentaries, noted a tradition in which Adam was first provided with Lilith, an unsuitable wife who fled from him. When Adam complained, God furnished him Eve, his second wife.

> The woman destined to become the true companion of man was taken from Adam's body, for "only when like is joined unto like the union is indissoluble." The creation of woman from man was possible because Adam originally had two faces, which were separated at the birth of Eve.[33]

In accord with this ancient hermaphroditic tradition, Rabbi David Cooper, a student of ancient texts, stirs the pot with his statement that "Adam and Eve were Siamese twins," an opinion he derives from the first account of Creation (Genesis 1:27) and the *Midrash Rabbah*:

> When the Holy One created Adam [Ha-Rishon], it was androgynous. God created Adam Ha-Rishon double faced, and split him/her so there were two backs, one on this side and one on the other.[34]

Rabbi Henry Abramovitch, founding president of the Israel Institute of Jungian Psychology and a professor in the department of medical education at the Sackler School of Medicine in Tel Aviv University, offered a substantively similar, if not precisely identical, interpretation based on the second account of Creation (Genesis 2:22):

> Adam is created before Eve, who then is constructed from his *tzela.* The Hebrew word tezla, usually translated as "rib," may equally mean "side." In fact the word appears thirty-nine times in the Hebrew Bible and most often it clearly means "side." If we follow this Hebrew tradition, reading Adam's tzela as "side," then Adam was not male. Rather he was an androgenous Siamese twin, in which male and female halves were joined side by side.

In his Jungian study *Brothers & Sisters: Myth and Reality*, Abramovitch posits that "Adam and Eve were the very first brother-sister pair." He touches briefly but substantially on the "archetypal image of brother/sister-lover" and the tradition of "poignant poems" that "express symbolic yearning for an 'inner marriage' with the ideal sibling." Abramovitch writes with passion, and his text "explores in depth, the myth and reality of brothers and sisters in a variety of religions and cultures." We rely on non-identical source materials, however, and his humanitarian goal, while admirable, is not identical to my own. His purpose, to which I can hardly object, is the promotion of world sisterhood and brotherhood. I fear I am less ambitious, but I must applaud his insightful readings on the literature and mythology of brother-sister marriage and his recognition that "This powerful tradition clearly implies that the natural state of humankind is one of brother and sister becoming husband and wife."

Unlike Abramovitch, Cooper devalues the second account of creation in which Eve is made after Adam and fashioned from his removed rib. Cooper privileges the first account, asserting that "Adam and Eve were born simultaneously side-by-side, or back-to-back, attached like Siamese twins." He justifies this with the assertion that "it was known two thousand years ago the idea that Eve came from Adam's rib was a common misunderstanding." Nonetheless, the second account of creation is given primacy by scholar Joe Allotta, although he, too, is a modern proponent of the twins doctrine. Allota is a trained Protestant theologian, preaching pastor of Essential Church in Hudson, Florida, and professor and chair of the Ministry Department at Trinity College. He says, "God made a genetic clone of Adam, except instead of being a guy, she's a lady. Doesn't that make them twins?" In fact, either of these exegesis would make the primal pair analogous to clones or to monozygotic twins.

Under the "Adam" entry in *Dictionaire Philosophique,* Voltaire cited the opinion of Antoinette Bourignon de la Porte, a seventeenth-century Flemish mystic, "who was sure that Adam was a hermaphrodite, like the first men of the divine Plato." God had revealed this secret to her, but since Voltaire had not experienced the same revelation, he chose not to venture an opinion. In *Eve: The History of an Idea,* John A. Phillips acknowledges the hermaphrodite thesis of the first account of Creation and, in due course, criticizes the preference of the rabbinical and Christian traditions for the misogynistic second account of Creation to the neglect of the first. There have been notable exceptions to this rule, as I have observed. In an attempt to reconcile Genesis with Darwinian evolution, Roman Catholic biologist J. Paquier proposed in 1932 that Adam and Eve were the twin offspring of an anthropomorphic progenitor into whom God breathed human souls. Two Catholic apologists for the biblical accounts of creation, Robert Sungenis and Brian Harrison, have acknowledged Paquier's hypothesis without specifically endorsing it.[35]

Sorbonne evolutionist Jérôme Lejeune (1927–1994), while conducting research on monozygotic twins, fancifully employed twinning "to explain the occurrence, during the evolution of species, of an ancestral male/female couple where the individuals bore the same modification: the translocation of chromosome 2, reducing the chromosomic number from N=48 in Pongidae to N=46 in man. This couple could only be Adam and Eve."[36] Lejeune noted the extremely rare cases in which "a male zygote, carrier of forty-six chromosomes, including one X and one Y, splits into twins. One of the twins continues its male identity. The other, not having received the Y chromosome, becomes an imperfect female with forty-five chromosomes, including only one X."

The National Genome Research Institute, part of the National Institutes of Health, refers to identical twins as "natural clones."[37] Professor Lejeune theorized fancifully, but nonetheless appropriately, that Adam and Eve were closer even than their rare and remarkable equivalents that were later described in the scientific terminology of academic journals as "sexually discordant monozygotic twins."[38]

"In one sense, Adam and Eve—prior to being husband and wife—are brother and sister, siblings in their common descent," Marcia Landy observes, repeating for emphasis that "the children of God, Adam and Eve, are brother and sister." True enough, but Adam and Eve's sibling affinity is much closer than the ordinary kinship between all children of God, and the medieval imagination noted this. Landy appropriately drives home her point that Adam and Eve's brother-sister relationship derives from common parenthood, and she recognizes that "In noting the sibling role of Adam and Eve, we must also recognize the relationship of sibling to parent. . . . God is the father, certainly the father of Adam, and nature is the mother." More strikingly, however, some scholars have focused not only on their shared parentage but on the fact that Adam and Eve were, like monozygotic twins, literally of one flesh.[39]

Adam and Eve's original shying away from one another's nakedness was history's first recorded evidence of incest aversion. Elizabeth Archibald notes that "Medieval writers sometimes interpreted incest as representing original sin."[40] William Arens's study, *The Original Sin: Incest*

And Its Meaning, is well conceived and well researched, but nowhere does the author imply that the original sin committed by Adam and Eve was incest. In fact, he demonstrates no interest in the biblical legend from which he derives his intriguing title. Neither Archibald nor the other scholars who comment on the tradition that Adam and Eve were siblings claim that their original sin was incest. Their sudden awakening to their nakedness was not marked by sexual arousal but by grasping at fig leaves. Their initial behavior was indicative of incest aversion, *Inzestscheu*, which some modern social psychologists exhibit as the final proof that they were siblings.[41]

Philologist Brian Murdoch states that in the literary heritage of medieval Europe, Adam and Eve are "of one flesh, [and] must be even closer than brother and sister." He observes that in some medieval texts, Adam refers to Eve as his sister, citing an example fromn Arnoul Gréban's *Mystère de la Passion*, where Adam addresses Eve as "*ma sœur.*"[42] Margarita Stocker, a Milton scholar, considers that "Adam and Eve were equal siblings, both children of God," to which she adds, "Satan and Christ are also siblings under God."[43] This advances our case only slightly, since all creatures great and small may be called children of God, including the "sons of God" in Genesis 6 who consorted with the "daughters of men," presumably the same "sons of God," including Satan, who are acknowledged in Job 1:6 and again in Job 38:8.

We repeat our prior observation that Adam himself calls Eve "flesh of my flesh" and Heidi Hunter's assertion that Adam and Eve were brother and sister. Ellen Pollak observes that Adam and Eve's sibling relationship has frequently been assumed since ancient times. Annette Volfing has discovered a text anticipating the most imaginative reflections of Rabbi Cooper, Reverend Alloto, and the above-cited Roman Catholic geneticists. She presents a medieval source that not only made Adam and Eve twins but gave them a mutual birth date:

> *In dem czeichen des czwillings wart geborn Adam und Eua.*
> In the sign of Gemini were Adam and Eve born.[44]

Thus it seems that some commentators have considered it a trifling technicality that Adam and Eve were never actually "born," never cohabited a womb, and may possibly have lacked navels. They were, in effect, Gemini, closer than any of the famous twins of classical mythology: Phrixus and Helle, Apollo and Diana, or Isis and Osiris. But what renders the declaration that Adam and Eve were "born" under any sign at all so mind-boggling is that it deviates from the etiological goal of Genesis, which is to trace not only the origin of woman but of marriage, and the beginning of the nakedness taboo. We observe, for the nonce, the unequivocal annunciation in Genesis that Adam was not born, but fashioned by the hand of God, who then created Eve from his "rib;" and that Adam recognizes her as "bone of my bones and flesh of my flesh." Thus the following line is perplexing:

> Therefore shall a man leave his father and his mother, and shall cleave unto his wife: and they shall be one flesh.[45]

In traditional societies, it is the woman, not the man, who separates from her parents at the time of marriage, so the use of the word "therefore" is mystifying. The "cleaving" refers to marriage, as Jesus Christ so famously observed, and not to mere sexual union.[46] In the vocabulary of King James, the word "cleave" is an contranym—a word that can signify its opposite; it can mean either to seal together or to put asunder. The archaic language aids modern understanding, but the play on words is lost if the translation replaces the word "cleave" with "cling." Eve was "cloven from" Adam before he ever "cleaved to" her. She was his protoplasmic duplicate, and their flesh was as integral as if they had developed in the same womb. Neither had parents to leave, and they required neither marriage nor sexual coupling to become one flesh. Conservative Christians and Jews have employed the text to demonstrate the "normalcy" of heterosexual copulation, and Jesus used it in his declamation against divorce. Adam and Eve constituted a family from the beginning and did not require copulation to become "one flesh;" for, as Adam recognized and proclaimed, they were from the start literally "of one flesh."[47]

Before their original sin, the original twins were like those unembarrassed in childhood by the presence of naked opposite-sex siblings but terrified in adulthood by the sight of a normally attired brother or sister accidentally encountered upon the road.[48] The innocence of Eden, or

Oceania, may have survived in some western European countries until very recently, but even there, and in most other "civilized" societies, children are conditioned from the earliest age to feel shock and shame at even a fleeting glimpse of an opposite sex sibling's nudity.

Alternative interpretations may be affixed to Adam and Eve's acquisition of "knowledge," and they are not mutually exclusive. The lesser possibility is that they have engaged in sex; the more likely is that they have attained knowledge of a cultural bias ancient storytellers held to be self-evident, that nakedness is shameful in itself. The latter interpretation does not automatically preclude a bourgeois nineteenth-century Viennese analysis of their reaction as *Inzestscheu*, or "horror of incest." In James Strachey's English translation of Freud's work, the reaction is amplified from "shyness" to "horror," and it is fully expected, and "only normal" for pubescent brothers and sisters to experience discomfort with one another, and to engage in gratuitous displays of feigned mutual repugnance. And it is expected that opposite-sex siblings past the age of four will shriek and scramble at any possibility of inadvertent indecent exposure. Even persons who grow up without brothers or sisters express horror at the idea of sibling incest, and social scientists occasionally express the same "third-party" reactions in the course of academic papers.[49]

ETIOLOGICAL MYTH AND MORAL FABLE

As a moral fable, the sibling exile narrative of Hansel and Gretel is similar to Adam and Eve and the legend of Pandora. These fables combine in children's minds to warn against the enticements of strangers and the temptations of sweets, and they contain the threats of betrayal, abandonment, and exile. These fables contribute to collective consciousness and subliminal fears of abandonment, advise submission to power and authority, caution against venturesome curiosity, and warn of the penalties of disobedience. They remind children of their dependency on their parents for shelter and nourishment. In various combinations, these reminders are repeated to children in homes, Sunday schools, and catechism classes.

But here it is worth invoking Jack Zipes's observation: "You cannot predict whether a child will really understand the moral or the message of a particular tale." To this point, one might add that the meanings of a fairy tale can be as baffling to adults, especially when that tale has been repeatedly told and filtered through numerous languages, cultures, and civilizations over millennia. Not every tale conveys a moral or message, but if it does, that message may not be universally accessible or understood. Many fairy tales portray siblings attempting to outwit parental or other adult authority figures, and this may well be justified as in Hansel and Gretel's futile attempt to overcome their parents' attempts to abandon them, and in their later successful deception of the witch. The witch is a cruel, arbitrary adult, and she possesses supernatural powers. Hansel and Gretel, unlike Adam and Eve, successfully defy parental power, usurp authority, and strike back at the witch who, in several versions of the Grimm fable, is identical to the stepmother. But what moral lesson should we draw from their story? Certainly not that a little girl ought to shove a surrogate stepmother into an oven.

The story of Adam and Eve has both a moral and etiological function. It teaches children the moral obligation of submission to authority. God is almighty, and His might is the justification of His right. The story offers, incidentally, several etiologies, or explanations. It explains the loathsomeness of serpents, the pains of childbirth, and the existence of evil in the cosmos. But more than incidentally, it explains the origins of the nakedness taboo and alludes, however indirectly, to its unstated erotic implications. While the story was meant to teach obedience, it also suggested something much more, albeit the word "naked" does not appear in every version a child might encounter. As noted, it was not present in the Benziger Brothers' *Bible History* of 1904: "Covered with shame, they sewed together fig leaves and made garments for themselves, and trembling hid among the trees."[50]

The association of nakedness with sexuality is firmly implanted in children's minds by the age of six, when Sunday School classes instruct them in the mysterious commandments of "thou shalt not commit adultery" or "thou shalt not covet thy neighbor's wife." Freud echoed Thomas Aquinas and Aristotle, although perhaps inadvertently, in observing the necessary and proper restraints society places on children's sexual impulses, stating, "A cultural community is perfectly justified, psychologically, in starting by proscribing manifestations of the sexual life of children, for there would be no prospect of curbing the sexual life of adults if the ground had not been prepared for it in childhood."[51] Freud believed the story of Adam and Eve exacerbates sexual anxiety as it simultaneously enhances and suppresses sexual curiosity long before the child has any idea of the mechanics or the social and biological consequences of sexual activity.

"The Bible is not suitable for children," declares Dr. Christine Hayes, a distinguished professor of Old Testament at Yale University, who says, presumably with tongue in cheek, "I have a twelve-year-old and an eight-year-old. I won't let them read it." She knows, of course, that her children don't need to read the Bible to be aware that much of it is sexy and scary. It is impossible for anyone, especially the clever child of a Yale professor, to reach the age of eight without some exposure to the story of Adam and Eve and their "apple tree," just as they are exposed to the story of George Washington and his "cherry tree." Every school child knows about the young couple who partake of a forbidden fruit, an act associated with sexual awareness and shame, and are caught naked when they scramble to hide at the approach of their Father.[52]

Some version of the legend of Adam and Eve's guilt, shame, and horror must be as ancient as language itself. Infantile eroticism and the nakedness taboo existed long before the fifth century BCE, when scholarship suggests the fiction of Eden took its present form. Primeval storytellers created this fable at prehistoric firesides ages before it was written down, and the fable's basis is as ancient as the sexual anxiety of childhood, with its ingredients of shame, concealment, and the threat of banishment. Children fear rejection, and from the earliest prehistoric times, children have been intentionally lost, exiled, exposed to the elements, abandoned to savage beasts, or allowed to die of hunger. The "collective consciousness" of such horrors was preserved in old wives's tales and mothers' warnings—"You just wait until your father gets home!" Biblical, rabbinical, and early Christian traditions accentuated the tacit suggestion that Adam and Eve's original sin had something to do with sex.

ETIOLOGICAL MYTH, NAKEDNESS, AND UNEASE

It is not far-fetched to view the story of Eden as an "etiological myth" that explains the sexual unease between brothers and sisters that develops in childhood. The myth also explains the origin of the nakedness taboo, why serpents don't have legs, and why childbirth is painful. When biblical scribes announce in Genesis 2:24 that the man and his wife were naked and yet unashamed, they reveal an *a priori* notion that nakedness is shameful. Etiological myths offer explanations for elements in the universe that are obvious and taken for granted: obviously snakes don't have legs, obviously married couples are ashamed to see one another naked.

Abraham ben Meir ibn Ezra, a medieval Jewish commentator, is credited by Kyle Greenwood with first proposing the view that eating from the Tree of Knowledge represents the beginning of sexual desire.[53] Greenwood, a professor of Old Testament and Hebrew Language, notes that after eating the fruit, Adam covered his nakedness and "knew [Hebrew, yada]" his wife, Eve, "and she conceived and bare Cain." The words "knew" and "knowledge" are ambiguous in English, and they may have been so in the archaic language from which biblical Hebrew is derived. The meaning of "knowledge" is unclear in the Greek of the Septuagint, the Latin of St. Jerome, the English of King James, and the German of Martin Luther. Deployed in such proximity to the word "naked," the word "knowledge" easily lends itself to such an interpretation. The story is easily associated with the naive sexual curiosity of children, who also know that "curiosity kills the cat." It matters not that the nakedness taboo is mysterious to young siblings and their playmates—they become aware when quite young that ignoring the taboo can have dire consequences, and their awareness is reinforced by the story of Adam and Eve.

"Naked came I into the world," says Job. Clearly his employment of the word "naked" in this emblematic passage has nothing to do with sex. Likewise, the story of Noah's nakedness need not carry any sexual implications. What it does show is that nakedness was considered shameful and intolerable even for a man who is unconscious and alone. There is nothing either stated or implied of a sexual nature in the story of Ham's ridicule of Noah's nakedness. Ham does not see his father's drunken stupor as an opportunity for sexual exploitation; on the contrary, he exposes his father to contempt. Although Noah's nakedness is absolutely private, Ham finds it disgusting, and he cannot resist making his father an object of ridicule.

Noah's other sons' reactions are even more reprehensible, for they find it necessary to intrude upon Noah's privacy a second time. Rather than leaving their father alone to sleep off his drunkenness, they endorse Ham's condemnation of Noah's private nakedness as shameful and must bear witness to his shame by covering it. Thus they walked backward "and covered the nakedness of their father; and their faces *were* backward, and they saw not their father's nakedness."[54] The scripture makes axiomatic the equivalency of nakedness with shame, but there is no implication in this instance that nakedness has anything to do with "carnal knowledge."

Perhaps it was the original intent of whatever committee cobbled together the fables of Genesis to employ the terms "nakedness" and "knowledge" as figurative representations of sexual intercourse. The terms are ambiguous in their narrative context, and Milton did not invent but simply improved upon a traditional view that saw these terms as analogies for sexual activity. He did, of course, exercise considerable license in describing Adam and Eve's prelapsarian connubial activity even in making it a public ritual.[55]

> Espoused Eve deckt first her Nuptial Bed
> And heavenly Choirs the Hymenaean sung

Milton tells us that before the Fall, Adam and Eve enjoyed the marital bliss that Pius X would later approve of as *casti connubii*. It was only after they acquired the "knowledge" of good and evil that their coupling was reduced to the level of lust as the fallen couple vainly sought solace from their shame through carnal activity.[56]

> The Parts of each from other, that seem most
> To shame obnoxious, and unseemliest seen,
> Some Tree whose broad smooth Leaves together sowd,
> And girded on our loyns, may cover round
> Those middle parts, that this new commer, Shame,
> There sit not, and reproach us as unclean.

Genesis seeks to explain the existence of a nakedness taboo but does not specifically employ the word "nakedness" as a synonym for sex. "Thou shalt not uncover thy sister's nakedness" is employed as a euphemism for sex in Leviticus 18:7–16 and Leviticus 20:11–21. In many traditional societies, nudity did not carry the same sexual implications as it did for the first Western interlopers. According to Freud and a famous Bronisław Malinowski study, brothers and sisters in some oceanic societies avoided all social contact and even avoided catching sight of one another.[57] Malinowski asserted that Pacific Islanders had an extreme horror of incest, echoing one of Freud's pontifications in *Totem and Taboo*, relying on Robert Henry Codrington's report that if brother and sister meet by accident on the road, "she flees into the bush, and he passes by without turning his head toward her." Paradoxically, Pacific Islanders could be amazingly tolerant of sibling incest under one specific circumstance. Hawaiians were ostensibly devoid of "incest horror, so long as it was confined to royal siblings.[58]

Malinowski and Freud were convinced that while *Inzestscheu* was universal, the lure of incest was just as universal; therefore, it was constantly present in the subliminal consciousness. Malinowski found its manifestation in dreams as wish fulfillment, and his musing included a biblical allusion to forbidden fruit:

> the *incestuous* dream, especially as between brother and *sister*, occurs frequently and disturbs the mind. . . . The lure of forbidden fruit, which everywhere haunts men in dreams, and day dreams . . . and folk-tales.[59]

Malinowski relates incest to the"forbidden fruit" of Adam and Eve's transgression and its association with nudity and sexual taboos. Lure and loathing are first encountered through interactions with siblings for those who have them. Incest aversion arises as they are provided with reasons to abstain from erotic pastimes, which may include corporal punishment or the threat of it.

In contemporary society, parents are expected and legally required to impede "erotic play," and not only between siblings. Most persons first become aware of the existence of sexuality through contact with neighbors or siblings unless they have been subjected to criminal abuse by adults. In most instances, this is not the case, but spontaneous sexual interest, when it occurs, and if detected by parents, is discouraged, and any association of infantile sex awareness with eroticism is disapproved.

Eventually most persons outgrow the fear implanted in their infantile consciousness that sex is sinful, shameful, and dirty and may engage in sexual activity by the age of twenty. The horror of sex inculcated within the family is overcome by locating acceptable sexual partners outside the family. The earliest awareness that sexuality exists usually occurs within a domestic context, and there it is disapproved and discouraged. In young adults, the generalized horror of sex, inculcated in childhood, is eventually displaced, while the horror of incest intensifies.

"The Heavenly Hosts," illustration to Paradise Lost *by Gustave Doré (c. 1866)*

– CHAPTER TWO –

ADAM AND EVE: THE URTEXT, AND MILTON'S *PARADISE LOST*

FEW SCHOLARS are sufficiently erudite to participate in the perpetual impassioned discussion among Bible specialists over the "original meanings" of the story of Eden. What, for example, does Genesis 2:21-22's description of Eve's creation from Adam's "rib" actually mean?

> And the LORD God caused a deep sleep to fall upon Adam, and he slept: and he took one of his ribs, and closed up the flesh instead

> thereof; And the rib, which the LORD God had taken from man, made he a woman, and brought her unto the man.

The biblical Hebrew word translated as "rib" in the King James Bible, Jewish Study Bible, Douay-Rheims Bible, and as *Rippe* in Luther's German, has been read metaphorically by many scholars as a symbol for "life." Others have reasonably assumed that when the prophet Ezra authenticated the text of the Torah to the Jewish people in the fifth century BCE, he referred literally to Adam's rib. The problem of whether the term should be taken literally cannot be solved simply as a matter of translation, since there is no extant copy of the text as Ezra read it to the assembled population of Jerusalem. Some scholars, Christian and Jewish, believe the original Torah was burned by the Babylonian emperor Nebuchadnezzar when he destroyed the First Temple, but faithfully reconstructed by Ezra under divine inspiration.[1]

If there ever was an Urtext (original text) of Adam and Eve's story, it is not the version of the Tanakh known as the Masoretic text, which is the definitive Hebrew version of the Torah as established in the seventh through tenth centuries CE. The source text was not written in biblical Hebrew, and the original wording cannot be found in any such existing artifact as the Aleppo Codex, the Leningrad Codex, the Bologna University Torah, or the Dead Sea Scrolls. Any existing text of the Tanakh derives from Ezra's time, and the Hebrew Masoretic text is based on irrecoverable writings from the Second Temple period, commonly assumed to reflect Babylonian and Persian influences.[2] Modern Bibles, whether Jewish or Christian, ostensibly transmit the story of Adam and Eve as it was fixed by the sixth century BCE, before the destruction of the First Temple, but no one knows for certain.

I most frequently cite the King James Bible Version (KJV) for this study despite my Roman Catholic background due to the KJV's impact on Anglo-American literary heritage. The KJV is the Bible cited by Matthew Arnold, T. S. Eliot, C. S. Lewis, Aldous Huxley, and W. E. B. Du Bois. It probably influenced John Milton as well, although he knew Greek and Hebrew and did not require translations.[3] I have frequently consulted Martin Luther's German translation since the German literary tradition is central to this study. My smattering of Greek is less than rudimentary, and my high school Latin is vestigial, so I feign no access to the Greek Septuagint or the Latin Vulgate. I have augmented my readings with the Jewish Study Bible and the Catholic Study Bible, both published by Oxford University Press.[4]

The "original meaning" of Adam and Eve's story cannot be determined since we lack the original text. The text we have has passed through the kaleidoscope of changing times and the prisms of several languages. Its "authorship," whatever that means, cannot be established, and the same must be said of myths and legends from Egypt, Mesopotamia, Greece, and medieval Christendom. The Torah—the first five books of the Jewish Bible—have traditionally been ascribed to Moses, and other portions of the Tanakh—which Christians call the Old Testament—are attributed to numerous omniscient narrators. Some passages in Genesis are purported to be words spoken verbatim by God. Some of its words are supposed to penetrate His private thoughts, His emotional frustrations, or His changes of heart. Talmudic scholars since ancient times, and Christian commentators, both ancient and modern, have attempted to reconcile apparent inconsistencies in Moses's writings or to fill presumable *lacunae*. By the same token, classical scholars, from Plato to Plutarch to Robert Graves, have tried to explain discrepancies in classical mythology. Some may recall Pausanius's commentary in Plato's *Symposium* on the contradictions and inconsistencies in the mythological presentation of Aphrodite, who makes occasional appearances in the present study.[5]

In recent times, liberal and reform students of the Bible have expressed discontent with its gender designations, whether in the KJV or more recent translations. Some scholars have focused on what they perceive as its ethnic and/or gender biases; others have attempted to explain them away. The Union For Reform Judaism website calls for a rendering of the words of creation with maximum gender neutrality. Accordingly, for example, in feminist and progressive Judaism, it is argued that the name "Adam" in Genesis 1:26-27 must be translated as "human" rather than as "man," and the verse, "male and female God created them" translated as indicating the simultaneous creation of male and female.[6]

"So God created man in his *own* image, in the image of God created he him; male and female God created he them."[7] This introduces the observation that "The sages explain the unusual language as meaning that God created the first human being as an androgynous person, containing both male and female characteristics simultaneously."[8] This is sometimes reconciled with the second account of creation in Genesis 2:21-22 by a translation in which Eve is taken from the side rather than the rib of the androgynous Adam with whom she previously co-existed. Academic scholars, among them Jacob Neusner, recognize the significance of the semantical problem of what is meant by "Adam" without subscribing to any radical feminist implications or impassioned gender discourses, and he cautions that the interpretation of Genesis can be complicated and problematic even for masters of biblical Hebrew.[9]

Modern scholarship on the fable of Adam and Eve, including the diverse disciplinary perspectives of Stephen Greenblatt, Christine Hayes, and Brian Murdoch, acknowledges that Genesis is a concatenation of inconsistencies compiled from myriad irretrievable sources. These sources include lost Paleo-Hebraic texts, and written and oral legends with sources and cognates in Mesopotamian, Egyptian, and Greek mythologies. There can be no means of discovering how ancient the story may be, or of establishing its "original" content, authorship, or textual history. The "original version" of the fable of Adam and Eve is an anonymous legend like the folktales discovered and recorded by the Grimm brothers.[10]

The story of Adam and Eve was cobbled together from a hodgepodge of sources, written and oral, before 700 BCE and known in its present form since 500 BCE. Like the story of Hansel and Gretel, it is the product of numerous contradictory retellings transmitted by word of mouth long before they were ever recorded. For this reason, among others, it expresses broad patterns of experience that were familiar but not identical to several cultures and civilizations, albeit some of its mythologies are closely identified with the peculiar experiences of specific tribes of Semitic peoples under specific historical circumstances. Its Masoretic reconstruction in Hebrew was concocted from Paleo-Hebraic, Aramaic, Samaritan, and Greek sources. Christians have a tradition of reading the New Testament's Revelation as a prequel to Genesis. For example, Milton's *Paradise Lost* borrows from Revelation in its account of Satan's fall and identifies him with the serpent of Eden, although Revelation was not written as a preface to the creation story of Genesis.[11]

Most scholars consider Genesis to be a collection of discrete stories told under various circumstances, bearing no relationship to Revelation, which was written centuries later, and whose authenticity was questioned even by some early church Fathers. Ancient rabbis and modern theologians have sought to reconcile anomalies in Genesis, such as the apparent discrepancies in the two accounts of creation. Devout religionists have attempted to justify God's apparently inconsistent dealings with mankind through trial and error. The portrayals of a God who could soften His judgment on Cain, "repent" that he had made mankind, or reveal uncertainty regarding the future seem to suggest that the original authors of Genesis did not conceive of an omnipotent or omniscient Creator. One early Christian commentator, Marcion of Sinope, went so far as to assert that the God of Genesis was an Evil Genius and not the God of Love revealed in the teachings of Jesus. For this, Marcion was denounced as a heretic.

The authors of Genesis created a God who was neither omnipotent, nor omnipresent, nor omniscient, but frustrated, changeable, and given to "repentance." The word "repent," as used in the King James Bible, was intentional and reflects the Hebrew version, expressing sorrow or regret. In every language and in every version, this word signifies God's having second thoughts when reviewing his past actions. Many modern evangelicals deny the King James translation of what the ancient scribes wrote in Genesis 6:6, to wit: "the LORD repented that he had made mankind" and therefore ordained the Deluge. These same evangelicals abandon textual literalism in reading Exodus 32:14: "the LORD repented of the evil which he thought to do unto His people." Although modern Christianity insists on divine omniscience, the Torah does not reveal a God who knows the future, or an inevitable teleology or a fixed divine plan.

But erudite lay readers, even during the Age of Enlightenment, clung to the idea of a "Divine Plan." Thomas Jefferson, for example, saw a divine purpose and affixed it to his God of nature, whom he conceived as a God of Reason. Isaac Newton and Benjamin Franklin believed that God intervened in history and occasionally adjusted the cosmic order. The authors of the Talmud attributed a divine plan to the Torah's God of Law. The early Christians adopted Revelation, which they interpreted as a prelude to Genesis and a prophecy of things to come. The four gospels deliver contradictory guides along the pathways to salvation, and the epistles of Saint Paul express an incoherent theology as to the meaning of Adam's fall and Christ's redemption. Some Christians believe that charity is the greatest virtue and charitable deeds justify salvation; other Christians deny this and maintain that salvation is by faith alone.

The medieval play *Everyman* implied that good works could save a human soul, an idea preserved in the benevolent deism of Benjamin Franklin, who thought "the most acceptable service of God is doing good to man." No doubt he recalled Jesus's parable about feeding the hungry, clothing the naked, and performing such other works of charity as outlined in St. Matthew 25:40, "Verily I say unto you, Inasmuch as ye have done *it* unto one of the least of these my brethren, ye have done *it* unto me." This was the religion of Jefferson, Adams, and Franklin. This was the transcendental religious philosophy expressed by Leigh Hunt in his deeply moving poem, "Abou Ben Adhem," the eponymous Muslim who, despite his indifference to Jesus, was "justified" by his love for his fellow man.

Such ideas are not appalling to evangelical Christians, who condemn the *Everyman* as heretical. They cite John 2:5. "Except a man be born of water and *of* the Spirit, he cannot enter into the kingdom of God." Such words were the basis of Luther's and Calvin's assertions that we are not redeemed by charitable deeds but solely by grace, and they are the basis of the Christian dogma that "there is no salvation outside of the church." Catholics moderated this dogma during Vatican II, but it remains an article of faith for evangelical Protestants. Many American Christians find these doctrines narrow-minded and suggestive of anti-Semitism; for that reason, if for no other, they must be rejected. So, too, are many Christians troubled by the exclusionism of John 14:6, "I am the way, the truth, and the life: no man cometh unto the Father, but by me." Genesis does not reveal any such doctrine, although Milton's *Paradise Lost* projects the coming of "one greater Man."[12]

MILTON, GENESIS, PANDORA, AND CLASSICAL PAGAN MYTHS

In addition inventing a prelapsarian sexual episode, Milton took many liberties in his epic poem, *Paradise Lost.* He started with a prologue in heaven, loosely patterned on the New Testament's Revelation, where

Satan foolishly leads a host of angels "durst defy th'Omnipotent to arms." Obviously a revolt against Omnipotence could have but one result—abject failure. Satan and his angels are "Hurled headlong flaming from the ethereal sky. With hideous ruin and combustion / down To bottomless perdition; there to dwell In Adamantine chains and penal fire." Milton then places in Satan's mouth a soliloquy of defiance "vaunting aloud, but racked with deep despair." This Satan came to be admired by Thomas Jefferson, William Blake, and many others. Satan sets about founding the city of Pandaemonium and plotting revenge, then assuming the guise of a serpent—something that does not happen in Genesis. He entices Eve into tasting the fruit of knowledge with words of flattery. Thus, Milton departs from Genesis in describing Eve's behavior. In the biblical narrative, she is motivated by her senses, her curiosity, and her desire for knowledge; not so in Milton's retelling.

Milton's relocation of Revelation, from the end of the New Testament to the beginning of the Old, was not original to him, but he added details such as equipping the armies of Satan with seventeenth-century artillery, including apocryphal angels, adding new ones, and providing them with blushing homoerotic interactions. Not surprisingly, some readers have suggested that Milton's tampering with scriptural narrative and theology approaches heresy. While making a general reference to Milton's "unwholesome influence," T. S. Eliot avoided the specific accusation of heresy with the disingenuous disclaimer, "On these questions I hold no opinion." Far more forthright was C. S. Lewis, who came to Milton's defense with his assertion that any "heretical elements" in *Paradise Lost* were "only discoverable by search."[13]

In Milton's version, Eve is subjected to several lines of Satanic flattery, and this insertion can distract the reader from the more precise Scriptural description of her temptation. It is not Scripture but Milton who suggests she is motivated by feminine vanity rather than a desire for knowledge. But Genesis says "the woman saw that the tree *was* good for food, and that it *was* pleasant to the eyes, and a tree to be desired to make *one* wise, she took of the fruit thereof."[14] Her principal motivation is clearly stated at the end of the sentence. Adam, however, is motivated simply by her handing him the fruit. It has been said that Eve is not only a temptress but the embodiment of temptation. Tamar Kadari notes that one ancient text even has Eve giving Adam wine she pressed from the fruit of the tree. Genesis offers no suggestion that it was an intoxicant or that, as Milton states, it stimulated anyone to take "their fill of love and love's disport."[15]

APHRODISIAC? INCEST REPRESSANT?: CIVILIZATION AND DISCONTENT

If we are to take Genesis literally, the "fruit of that forbidden tree" was anything but a stimulus to "amorous play" and the opposite of aphrodisiac.[16] Nonetheless, Milton, a man of rich learning and creative genius in the ripe maturity of his fifties, familiar with traditional interpretations of Genesis, stirred his poetic imagination to transform the forbidden fruit into an aphrodisiac. But in Genesis, that Fruit had just the opposite effect; it evoked the shock of recognition, and Adam and Eve's hastening to cover their genitalia was remarkably like the *Inzestscheu* that adolescent siblings might experience.[17] Milton described their prelapsarian sexual activity as marital bliss and their postlapsarian sexual activity in association with their burden of guilt. But the Genesis account attributed to Moses is vastly more ambiguous than Milton or the church fathers regarding sexuality.

Eve was the mother of civilization; her disobedience was a titanic act of the will that made her as godlike and ungodly as Prometheus or Satan. Satan and Prometheus were rightly perceived as mythic analogs by scholar R. J. Zwi Werblowsky, with Carl Jung's endorsement, but they missed the opportunity to state that, in questioning the order of Eden, Eve was like Prometheus who challenged the order of Olympus.[18] She was thus no mere victim of Satan but a heroic figure similar to Hesiod's patricidal Zeus, Wagner's Siegfried, and Milton's Satan, all of whom defied the mandates of heaven. In some versions of his myth, Prometheus is portrayed as the creator of mankind and in others as humanity's benefactor, but in all versions, he endows mortals with knowledge and civilization. For this defiance, Prometheus and his Germanic counterpart, Loki, are condemned to excruciating punishments. Milton's Satan is cast into a hell the authors of the Pentateuch never mentioned.

Whoever wrote Genesis credited Eve with a desire for knowledge but also accused her of intellectual dishonesty in her attempt to shift the blame for her disobedience. Rather than boldly justifying her quest for knowledge and wisdom, she says, "The serpent beguiled me, and I did eat."[19] While the role of the serpent cannot be ignored, the words of Genesis 3:6 state that Eve was attracted to "a tree to be desired to make *one* wise." Plato might have noticed, and Jung actually did observe, that Eve took action to lead herself and Adam out of the cave of ignorance: "[she] gave also unto her husband with her." Most Bibles, including the King James, include the words "with her." This calls into question John Milton's presentation of Eve as capriciously separating herself from her husband through childish whimsy and feminine stubbornness, thereby providing Satan with the opportunity to seduce her.

Milton recognized, as many children do, that Eve's fateful grasp at knowledge resembles the catastrophic curiosity of Pandora. While resemblances between the fable of Eden and the Sumerian *Epic of Gilgamesh* have attracted the attention of modern scholars, previous generations of scholars, unaware of the Sumerian cognate, alluded to the story of Pandora, which is more closely analogous.[20] Of course, there are significant differences; for example, Pandora's myth contains no references to nudity; Hesiod's Pandora arrives in the world splendidly "girded and clothed" by the "bright eyed Athena and the divine graces."[21] Milton may possibly have been recalling Tertullian's analogy, which is recycled in the epigraph to this section when he wrote the following:

> What day the genial Angel to our Sire
> Brought her in naked beauty more adorn'd,
> More lovely than Pandora, whom the Gods
> Endow'd with all their gifts, and O too like[22]

Milton recalled, as Tertullian had, the attention Hesiod paid to Pandora's "silvery raiment," her "embroidered veil," and her "crown of gold" in contrast to Eve's original nakedness. Tertullian spoke metaphorically of Eve's burden of iniquity, the "penitential garb that which woman derives from Eve—the ignominy, I mean, of original sin and the odium of being the cause of the fall of the human race."[23] Thus he frets not only about the nakedness of women but equally about the decoration of her body "with a lot of frilly and foolish pomps and luxuries." Thus, Pandora's adornment is more problematic than Eve's nudity at the moment of her creation, at which time Genesis associates nakedness with shame and revulsion, not allure. Eve perceived "a tree to be desired to make *one* wise" and anticipated nothing related to sexual awareness. While it is obvious that, in Genesis and elsewhere, "knowledge" and "nakedness" may be employed as euphemisms for coitus, in most instances, these words have nothing to do with sex.

Throughout the Bible, "knowledge" and "nakedness" are employed as tropes for misfortune, famine, destitution, vulnerability, shame, and ridicule. "Nakedness" is obviously a euphemism for the prohibited varieties of sex enumerated in Leviticus and Deuteronomy. The linkage of the forbidden fruit, nakedness, and sexuality are present in Eden, but Milton and other commentators endowed the Tree of Knowledge and its forbidden fruit with an explicit sexuality that was not present in scripture. It is easily forgotten that Adam and Eve's nakedness symbolized their vulnerability and the futility of their attempts to conceal it. While Milton recognized correctly that there are sexual nuances in Genesis's attention to nakedness and shame, and while he focuses on both, the meaning of original sin, even in his reframing of the story, has less to do with sex than with "man's first disobedience."[24]

Milton blended Christian and pagan elements into his poetry, as did many Christian authors before and after him. Protestants have been critical of such admixture, disparaging Catholics for preserving the "pagan mysteries of the Renaissance," but Milton contributed to the same practice and so did others of his persuasion.

The roots of the brother-sister exile myth are buried in prehistory; its roots are tangled, and over the millennia, its flowers have cross-pollinated one another. If there ever was a pure or "original" version of the story of Adam and Eve or Homer's *Iliad* or Hesiod's *Theogony* or the sagas of Gilgamesh and Isis and Osiris, we cannot find them, but some of their ideas are as ancient as language itself, and insofar as any of them have a ring of truth, it is because they contain experiences that are understandable to most people. The communal process of fabricating folklore and fairy tales has been an essential element in human evolution, and the artifacts of language are like stone-age spear points, carefully honed and crafted. Their utilitarian purposes could never have evolved independent of imaginative instinct. And language is inseparable from the mimetic impulses of baby primates and kittens at play.[25] It required fancy for *homo ludens*, the first tribe of liars, the prehistoric forerunners of Odysseus, to create, amplify, and distort the story of the fish that got away, the athlete who died young, the serpent that swallowed the flower of life—or its own tail—and the goddess who bestowed the fruit of good and evil.

As described in the King James Bible, Adam and Eve's transgression and exile were familiar to Jefferson and Adams, as was John Milton's reconstruction in *Paradise Lost*. The founders were aware that Milton followed a tradition of inserting elements from Revelation into the Genesis account. Most Christians, even the multitude who ignore *Paradise Lost*, accept the Miltonic account, but the Age of Enlightenment's reactions to Milton's synthesis were not uniformly admiring, and there has been considerable controversy concerning his presumption to improve the Genesis account. Furthermore, by adhering to the conventions of epic poetry, Milton inadvertently endowed Satan with a sympathetic character of heroic defiance. Two recent scholars have noted that "Adams unfailingly regards Milton's Satan as evil; Jefferson consistently regards him as admirable." And here we see a paradox. Jefferson, a slaveholding patrician, admired the libertarian spirit of democratic revolution he perceived in Milton's characterization of Satan. Adams, who never owned a slave, believed that democracy would "infallibly destroy all Civilization," and was no admirer of Satan's revolutionary rhetoric.[26] Willam Blake's reactions to *Paradise Lost* are well known; his most often quoted observation is, "Milton wrote in fetters when he wrote of Angels & God, and at liberty when of Devils & Hell."

The only morality unveiled in Genesis is the doctrine of absolute and unquestioning submission to absolute power and authority. The paradox of John Milton's life and work is the internal contradiction of his revolutionary liberalism with his Puritanical authoritarianism. The author of *Areopagitica*, the champion of free speech, also penned *Paradise Lost*, a story that represents the quest for knowledge as a mortal sin. Milton's party challenged the divine right of kings, only to establish the intellectually repressive theocratic dictatorships of Oliver Cromwell and Cotton Mather. Milton's Christian fanaticism allowed him to assign no heroic qualities to Adam and Eve's disobedience, and yet, paradoxically, he used traditional heroic/epic conventions in his depiction of Satan.

It was obviously not Milton's intention to make Satan admirable, but his memorable readers—Thomas Jefferson, William Blake, and Mary Wollstonecraft Shelley—seized upon the heroic defiance of Satan's "vaunting aloud" and recognized how fatally Milton's aesthetic triumph made a shambles of his moral and theological goals.

Despite its celebration of *casti connubii* in the prelapsarian bower of bliss, *Paradise Lost* reinforced the nakedness taboo and the Puritanical shame and fear associated with sexuality. Genesis specifically identifies the forbidden fruit with "knowledge" but only implicitly with "carnal knowledge." Magic fruit and talking serpents are beyond the experience of most people, but fear of parental authority is not, and the memory of that fear is what gives *Paradise Lost* its universality. Milton misrepresented Eve's disobedience and desire for knowledge as the idle whim of a foolish woman who defied God's commandment and the authority of her husband. He misrepresented Adam's grasping at knowledge as the folly of listening to a woman and ignoring God. The moral legacy of Milton's myth-making, *Areopagitica* notwithstanding, is that knowledge is dangerous, and the only lesson of *Paradise Lost* is that might makes right.

In this fashion, Milton deprives Eve of independence of intellect and reasonableness of motivation. Eve's culpability consists in her disobedience, not only to God but to Adam, and fault consists ultimately in separating herself from Adam's guidance. This is true in Milton's rendition. He has decided to take a step beyond that provided in the Genesis account, which makes her the victim of seduction rather than persuasion. Milton's is the pejorative construction accepted by most Christians and Jews, but Louis Ginzberg presents us with a more pernicious tradition, in which it is claimed that Satan was the father of Cain, thereby accusing Eve of fickleness and infidelity and directly contradicting scripture.[27]

According to the Bible, Eve defiantly "put forth her hand" after knowledge, and Adam was "with her."[28] In *Paradise Lost*, Milton fabricated the story that Satan rejoiced to discover Eve out of Adam's presence and devoid of his moral guidance, but Scripture clearly says Adam was with her. This differs from the misogynistic message Milton wanted to transmit—that women are morally and intellectually helpless without the guidance of men. But elsewhere in Genesis and in other Bible narratives, women take commanding roles. Eve first shows signs of lawless ambition, and Adam merely follows where she decides to lead. It is Eve, in a reckless exercise of free will, who first assumes the risk of stealing heaven's fire.[29]

Like her Olympian counterparts, Eve presented God with a challenge and a threat, although He acknowledged only Adam when He said, "Behold, the man is become as one of us."[30] Nonetheless, His bitter sarcasm and divine wrath were directed at both "the man" and the woman, and Eve's punishment is actually more severe than Adam's. If, on one level, they are pathetic babes in the woods, they are also reminiscent of Satan cast out of heaven and Prometheus exiled to his rock. Their banishment recalls the barbaric practice of infant exposure, which students of mythology have noted as an archetypal ingredient of fairy tales and heroic sagas.

Milton created Adam and Eve's sexual activity before the Fall in accordance with rabbinical tradition and the opinion of St. Augustine, as supported by the second account of creation in Genesis 1:28, where the man and woman are commanded to "Be fruitful and multiply." It is in conflict with St. Irenaeus's hypothesis, based on Genesis 3, that Adam and Eve were virginal before the Fall, and it undercuts any interpretation of the forbidden fruit and the word "knowledge" as symbolizing sexual awakening.[31]

That ambiguous "knowledge" may encourage such an assumption, although the word "know" does not specifically denote sexual activity until after Adam and Eve have left the Garden where it is written that "Adam knew Eve his wife, and she conceived, and bare Cain." For the first time in Genesis 4:1, the word "know" is employed to unequivocally and one-dimensionally denote conjugal activity. Obviously Adam and Eve eventually surmounted the shame they had experienced after eating from the Tree of Knowledge, but there are no biblical grounds for Milton's suggestion that the fruit of the tree was a sexual stimulant. References to Eve as Adam's wife did not prevent some church fathers from insisting on her prelapsarian virginity, nor do references to man and wife obviate the fact that this man and wife are like siblings, because Eve is cloven from Adam's flesh.

Heidi Hunter's assertion that "most commentators" have regarded Adam and Eve as siblings may be somewhat hyperbolic, but many commentators have described them as a brother and sister, not merely because of their mutual status as God's children but because they are of the same flesh.[32] Lynda Boose sees Adam and Eve as siblings, and God's giving her to Adam as authorizing the primeval necessity of brother-sister marriage.[33] Eve is not the only mythical female to be born without a mother. Aphrodite, according to Hesiod's account, arose from the foam generated when her father's severed genitals were cast into the sea. In the dream world of magic, myth, and poetry, female figures are easily conjured up as the emanations of masculine archetypes. Thus, in Book II of *Paradise Lost*, Milton conceives of Sin as Satan's daughter, sprung from his head, as Athena springs from the head of Zeus.

The underlying similarity between their predicament and that of Adam and Eve is that they are thrust into the woods by implacable parents whose commands are beyond their understanding and whose decisions are seemingly beyond appeal. But as we shall see in the case of Cain's expostulation, protest is not always fruitless, and it may even be rewarded.

"Cain" by Fernand Cormon (1880)

– CHAPTER THREE –

EVE'S PROMETHEAN DEFIANCE

WE HAVE no idea how many sleepless nights the primal couple spent contemplating the meaning of knowledge, but Eve's fateful grasp of it appealed to the irony of at least one Enlightenment intellectual, Abigail Adams, who wrote: "Well, knowledge is a fine thing, and mother Eve thought so; but she smarted so severely for hers, that most of her daughters have been afraid of it since."[1]

Genesis does not mention Eve receiving any commandment directly from God regarding the Tree of Knowledge, so perhaps the prohibition was conveyed to her solely through Adam. Her conversation with the serpent indicates a prohibition stricter than God's direct commandment. Adam was simply told not to eat the fruit, but Eve told the serpent an altered version: "God hath said, Ye shall not eat of it, neither shall ye touch it, lest ye die."[2] Regardless of how Eve received the message, Scripture says her disobedience was kindled by something more than concupiscence and a serpent's deception. The words of Genesis 3:6 make clear that "the woman saw that tree *was* good for food, and that it *was* pleasant to the eyes, and a tree to be desired to make *one* wise." For better or worse, she chose wisdom over faithful obedience. Paul would have denied the legitimacy of her choice, for she saw "through a glass darkly." John the Evangelist would have counseled her against reliance on her senses instead of faith, "for blessed *are* they that have not seen, and *yet* have believed."

"Sight, taste, and touch are fallible, but I believe everything I hear," Thomas Aquinas famously wrote, perhaps with more irony than he intended. Eve had heard, if only secondhand through Adam, the word of the Lord: "in the day that thou eatest thereof thou shalt surely die."[3] Perhaps God changed his mind, as He sometimes did in Genesis, or His words were not literally true. The words spoken by the serpent were true, if only in a diabolically ironic sense, for the forbidden fruit certainly did not kill Adam and Eve "in that day," and if it did not give them godlike powers, it did fatefully endow them with the knowledge of good and evil.

Both God and His serpent spoke with hidden sarcasm and ambiguity. Adam and Eve were created in a state of ignorance and subjected to the cruel test of unquestioning obedience. Their Creator endowed them with curiosity and a desire for godlike status without any corresponding right to pursue knowledge or godlike wisdom.

But "there is no respect of persons with God."[4] The aphorism is replete with ambiguity and irony, as are most biblical maxims. God makes no judgments based on merit, and persons never "deserve" anything from God. Eve could never have "merited" the comforts and joys of Paradise or the fruits of wisdom. Her only proper relationship with God was one of submission and unquestioning obedience. She had no rights God was bound to respect. They were placed in the garden "to dress it and keep it," and when they refused to submit to the workplace rules, they were fired.

Eve was obviously discontented in her primordial state; she was restless in Paradise and curious by nature. From the moment she looked at the fruit and lusted after wisdom, she had already sinned in her heart. Inclined to adventure, she infected her counterpart with her unruly spirit. According to the ancient rabbis and early doctors of Christianity, the Mother of All endowed her children with the stain of original sin and infected Cain, her firstborn son, with an inclination to depravity. His brooding discontent was the necessary antecedent to "civilization," for he abandoned the thankless cultivation of the earth, and established history's first city *(civitas),* ergo civilization.[5] Cain and his family were not the Neanderthaloid ruffians lurching across a barren landscape as portrayed in Fernand Cormon's *Caïn*, housed in the Musée d'Orsay.[6] Cain was the first civilized man and, according to Scripture, his progeny invented architecture, metallurgy, and the musical arts. The family of Cain was thriving at the time of Genesis's composition; they did not devolve into savagery and were not exterminated in the Deluge.

Competition over sisters was the cause of rivalry between Cain and Abel according to the Book of Jubilees retrieved among the Dead Sea Scrolls. Louis Ginzberg, in his *Legends of the Jews*, forwards the extra-canonical legend that Cain and Abel competed for the approval of God in their competition for a mate by means of a burnt offering. Biblical and legendary accounts generally agree that Cain's anger resulted from the Lord's displeasure with his sacrifice. The ancient interpolation in Genesis avers that Abel selected the best of his flocks for his sacrifice, but Cain ate his meal first, and after he had satisfied his appetite, he offered unto God what was left over, a few grains of flax seed. The smoke from Abel's sacrifice rose to heaven, but "unto Cain and his offering he had not respect."[7]

> But this was not the only cause of Cain's hatred toward Abel. Partly love for a woman brought about the crime. To ensure the propagation of the human race, a girl, destined to be his wife, was born together with each of the sons of Adam. Abel's twin sister was of exquisite beauty, and Cain desired her.[8]

Genesis does not declare that Cain's wife was his sister, although most theologians—ancient, medieval, and modern—have assumed she must have been a daughter of Adam and Eve. A rabbinical tradition states that Cain and Abel were each born with sisters. Cain, it is said, felt entitled to the more beautiful of the sisters as his wife, and Adam decreed that the matter would be settled by a sacrifice. When the smoke from their sacrifice favored Abel's having the first choice, Cain murdered him.

God immediately placed a curse on Cain: "When thou tillest the ground, it shall not henceforth yield unto thee her strength," "cursed from the earth," and he seemed fated to be "a fugitive and a vagabond."[9] Cain expressed no remorse, only the following expostulation:

> And Cain said unto the LORD, My punishment *is* greater than I can bear.
>
> Behold, thou hast driven me out this day from the face of the earth; and from thy face shall I be hid; and I shall be a fugitive and a vagabond in the earth; and it shall come to pass, *that* every one that findeth me shall slay me.[10]

But God gave Cain a protective mark, effectively a blessing, saying, "whosoever slayeth Cain, vengeance shall be taken on him sevenfold." While not revoking his penalties, God converted them into a blessing.[11] Cain, forced to abandon agricultural pursuits, established himself and the city of Enoch. Cain's direct descendants through his son Enoch were Jabal "the father of such as dwell in tents, and *of such as have* cattle," and Jubal, "the father of all such as handle the harp and organ." Thus, according to scripture, Cain was the progenitor of David, the shepherd, who dispelled evil spirits by playing on the harp. According to legend, Cain murdered a man to get his wife and, according to scripture, so did David, but their line of shepherds and harp players became the House of David that brought forth Joseph, Mary, and Jesus Christ.

CIVILIZATION AND DISCONTENT: EVE AND CARL JUNG

Culture and civilization, in Carl Jung's reading of Genesis, were the results of Eve's "happy fault." Eve is the anima, "the living thing in man," who drags Adam out of the "inertness of matter," and his primeval "nakedness and timidity." Eve represents the longings of the Soul:

> She makes us believe incredible things, that life may be lived. She is full of snares and traps, in order that man should fall, should reach the earth, entangle himself there and stay caught, so that life should

> be lived; as Eve in the garden of Eden could not rest content until she had convinced Adam of the goodness of the forbidden apple. Were it not for the leaping and twinkling of the soul, man would rot away in his passion, idleness.[12]

But the message of Genesis is not "Dare to be wise!"[13] The message is that Eve foolishly allowed herself to be deceived by the serpent and that Adam departed from the natural order of things by heeding a woman's counsel. While there is no evidence that God ever directly told Eve not to eat the fruit, it is presumed Adam so instructed her. While no passage in her creation narrative subordinates her to the authority of Adam, this was imposed on the text by Milton and other readers, ancient and modern. Eve is easily seduced because, unwisely separated from Adam and deficient in faith in his moral authority, she manifests her intrinsic female character, a "naive, childish, daring, playful, sinful curiosity."[14]

Ginzberg's *Legends of the Jews* reports a bizarre and even more misogynistic tradition that directly contradicts the standard text of the Hebrew Bible.

> But after the fall of Eve, Satan, in the guise of the serpent, approached her, and the fruit of their union was Cain, the ancestor of all the impious generations that were rebellious toward God, and rose up against Him. Cain's descent from Satan, who is the angel Samael, was revealed in his seraphic appearance. At his birth, the exclamation was wrung from Eve, "I have gotten a man through an angel of the Lord."[15]

Freudian interpretations, namely those of Carl Jung and Otto Rank, missed the opportunity to explore the sibling relationship of Adam and Eve, although Jung came closer than Rank. Jung established the active agency of Eve's discontent in the *Archetypes of the Collective Consciousness* and endowed her with semi-divine attributes. In his very late theological tract, *Antwort auf Hiob* (*Answer to Job*), he tentatively associates Eve with Sophia, the goddess of wisdom, and other divine apparitions and archetypes. He then proceeds to describe her apparition as the "second Eve," as the Virgin Mary, and her role in Christian mysticism as "Queen of Heaven and Mother of God," and as "bride of God." In a later chapter of *Archetypes of the Collective Consciousness,* "The Phenomenology of the Spirit in Fairytales" makes the following observation to establish the linkage of royal and divine incest in mythical and fairy-tale archetypes: ". . . in accordance with the archaic prerogative of kings which takes the form of incest, which, though somewhat repellent, must be regarded as more or less habitual in semi-divine circles."[16]

Otto Rank's exploration of sibling incest in his stupefyingly erudite study *Das Inzest-Motiv in Dichtung und Sage* was limited by the author's fulsome deference to Freud. Rank explored the presentation of incest in classical and biblical mythologies and traced its development in modern literature but almost invariably placed his subjects on the procrustean couch of Freud's Oedipal hypothesis. His commentary on the Midrash tradition that attributes the rivalry of Cain and Abel to competition over their sisters is warped by his supposition that male siblings never compete for anything other than maternal attention. In the Genesis narrative, Cain and Abel make their offerings in competition for the attention of God, their Supreme Father, but Rank substitutes the undemonstrable assertion that the brothers were actually competing for the attention of Eve, their mother. An arbitrary and unprovable assumption leads him to superimpose a Freudian interpretation of the Midrash, which asserts that the brothers were competing over their sisters.

> In the Midrash it is written: "Rabi Huna teaches that they fought over the twin sister who had been born together with Abel. Abel made claim to her because she had come into the world with him, but Cain believed he had the right to her as firstborn." From psychoanalysis of neurotics we realize that rivalry over the (incestuous) love object is only a renewal of early childhood rivalry, ultimately dealing with possession of the mother.[17]

Thus, Rank forcefully yokes his analysis's framework to Freud's Oedipal hypothesis, supported by a vague reference to "psychoanalysis of neurotics." It allows him to ignore the seldom-discussed subject of sibling incest on the basis of a spurious assumption. Although he acknowledges and documents the perfectly reasonable rabbinical postulation that two brothers might compete for a woman, Rank leaps compulsively to an Oedipal hypothesis, displacing their mother with their sister as the object of their competition. Henry Abramovitch has observed a tendency among Freudians to "the neglect of sisters and brothers in depth psychology." Similarly, George Woodcock finds Rank's study at times enlightening but "marred" by its Freudian denial that sibling rivalry might have other motivations besides sexual competition for the mother.[18]

In the Genesis account of Cain's slaying of Abel, neither their parents nor their other siblings play even a minor or incidental role. Genesis does not specifically state Cain's motive for killing his brother, but the text implies it was jealousy when Abel's offering found greater favor with God than Cain's. In the words of the *Jewish Study Bible*,

> In the course of time, Cain brought an offering from the fruit of the soil; and Abel, for his part, brought the choicest of the firstlings of his flock. The LORD paid heed to Abel and his offering, But to Cain and his offering, He paid no heed. Cain was much distressed and his face fell.[19]

The Torah offers no indication that Cain offered the Lord anything less than his prime virgin olive oil and the best wines of his cellar. It does not explain why "the Lord paid heed" to Abel's offering and not to Cain's. Nor is there is any indication in the Torah that Cain ever spoke a word of regret or repentance for slaying his brother. On the contrary it shows him complaining about the severity of God's threats in words that sound almost reproachful. His protest is rewarded with a mark of blessing and a removal of the curse. He is not condemned to become a fugitive but allowed to settle down and build a city. Otto Rank rejected, and with complete justification, the Talmudic interpretation, which invents the competition over a sister, for there is no indication of any such rivalry in Genesis. There is equally no justification for Rank's displacing what was obviously a competition for the Father's approval with an invented competition for sexual possession of the mother.[20] Rank's magnificent knowledge and Herculean labors are to be admired, but not his filiopietistic compulsion as a precocious twenty-eight-year-old to propitiate his intellectual father by binding up this extraordinary work of erudition on the Freudian altar.[21]

DARWIN, SUMNER, WESTERMARCK, AND FREUD

It is lamentable that the rich nuances of the Edenic myth received little if any attention from the famous William Graham Sumner, who is commonly viewed as an emblematic "Social Darwinist" and is rivaled in that respect only by Herbert Spencer. Convinced by the available evidence, Darwin posited that the offspring of unrelated persons have a survival advantage because they "are more vigorous and fertile than those from parents which are closely related." Therefore, incest aversion became an inbred instinct in most mammalian species. Sumner's theory challenged Darwin's biological absolutism and approximated cultural relativism. In emphasizing philosophical stoicism and religious asceticism, Sumner not only departed from the view previously maintained by E.B. Tylor that the universality of incest aversion derives from the social and economic advantages of exogamy. He deviated from Darwin's evolutionary biology, which disputed cultural relativism and economic determinism, and posited that the abhorrence of sibling incest was so universal that it must exist independently of particular societal influences.

Sumner squandered an opportunity to beatify his comments on the sibling incest taboo in his classic study, *Folkways* (1906), when he ignored the legend of Adam and Eve and its relation to the revulsion of Eurasian civilizations at nakedness and incest.[22] Nonetheless, Sumner was hardy misguided in attributing these taboos to three cultural elements: Greco-Roman stoicism, Jewish "hostility to sensuality," and the asceticism of early Christian authors. Sumner, although an ordained minister himself, was critical of the Christian influence, and wrote, "Our missionaries have unintentionally and unwittingly done great harm to nature people by inducing them to wear clothes as one of the first details of civilized influence." He pontificated that incest had been widespread among prehistoric populations and that it persisted in ancient "civilized states," notably those of Egypt, Peru, Persia, the Biblical Hebrews, and some modern primitives. He attributed sibling incest taboos to societal and economic pressures, a direct challenge to Charles Darwin's prior opinion that incest aversion is predetermined by biology: "the former rather than the latter unions, would be augmented through natural selection, and thus might become instinctive; for those individuals which had an innate preference of this kind would increase in number."[23]

Edvard A. Westermarck, a Finnish sociologist, augmented Darwin's theorem in his *Human Marriage* (London, 1891) with the observation that siblings who grow up in close proximity from early childhood are indifferent to, or repulsed by, the idea of incest due to a congenital reaction as normal and as beneficial as the gag-reflex. His work was challenged by Sigmund Freud, Emile Durkheim, and numerous others. Generations of evolutionary biologists, social scientists, moralists, and criminologists have attributed the so-called "Westermarck effect" to a hereditary genetic trait that carries the survival value of discouraging deleterious inbreeding. Westermarckeans attribute the universal incest taboo to natural selection in that the hominid species is endowed with an "incest avoidance instinct," providing an evolutionary advantage that minimized inbreeding and the concentration of deleterious genes. Westermarck's biological determinism has attained the status of a natural law, a dogma proclaiming that the phenomenon of sibling incest aversion has little to do with social conditioning, cultural tradition, or economic exigencies, but is predetermined by instinct.[24]

Support for the Westermarck hypothesis is frequently discovered by comparing human behaviors to that of closely related primate species, since chimpanzees and bonobos share 99% of their DNA with humans, and gorillas share 98.3%. While gorillas are slightly less closely related to humans than chimpanzees and bonobos, they share with humans the trait of opposable thumbs, which neither chimps nor bonobos possess. The four species under discussion share a common ancestor that possessed opposable thumbs, but chimps and bonobos lost this advantageous trait through evolution, while gorillas and humans retained it.

To varying degrees, all hominid species demonstrate promiscuity, which carries with it uncertainty of paternity and, therefore, accidental incest. Humans are more inclined than apes to place a strong emotional value on paternity, and the human institutions of marriage and family presumably facilitate the identification of fathers, paternal siblings, and half-siblings. Promiscuity and marital infidelity undermine kinship recognition and increase the possibility of incest between fathers and daughters as well as half-siblings. Before the invention of DNA tests, the means of ascertaining paternal and half-sibling relationships were indefinite and unreliable despite all moral constraints and legal devices. Knowledge of the degree to which paternal incest occurs among chimpanzees is limited, but a study by Walker, Rudicell, Li, Hahn, Wroblewski, and Pusey indicates that the "mating frequency between father-daughter dyads was surprisingly high. A study of gorillas by Harcourt and Kelly raises a suspicion that genetic mechanisms for kinship recognition and incest avoidance may not be highly evolved."[25]

"Ambiguity of offspring," as one commentator delicately phrased it, is one reason for skepticism regarding incest aversion as an evolutionary "strategy" for discouraging inbreeding. For this and other reasons, the Darwinian hypothesis for incest avoidance was unsatisfactory to E. B. Tylor and other social theorists who asserted that incest aversion is the product of culture and civilization, which beneficially stifle innate incestuous impulses. Freud famously surmised that the conflict between *kultur* and the lure of incest is therefore a source of "*unbehagen*," or unease.[26] Supporters of the Westermarck hypothesis often cite primatology in support of their position, noting that, to some indeterminate degree, incest aversion is observable in wild chimpanzees. Westermarck, having no opportunity to benefit from data on primate studies, resorted to Plato's authority to strengthen his Darwinian premise.[27]

> An unwritten law, says Plato, defends "as sufficiently as possible," parents from incestuous intercourse with their children, brothers from intercourse with their sisters: "ἀλλ' οὐδ' ἐπιθυμία ταύτης τῆς συνουσίας τὸ παρ 'παν εἰσέρχεται τοὺς πολλοὺς"—"nor does even the desire for this intercourse come at all upon the masses."

Aristotle was inconsistent on the point, and Aquinas cited his observations both on the natural attraction between close kin and the natural repugnance of incest. Freud made no appeal to ancient authority but joined Sumner in maintaining that the sibling incest taboo is socially induced. All authorites are in agreement with Plato that, whatever its origin, sibling incest aversion is universal. Given the undeniable ubiquity of the taboo and the fact that even biologically unrelated persons who have been raised together may find one another sexually uninteresting or repulsive, Westermarck's biological determinism argument has carried the day with most social scientists. Those who have examined the question and supported the Westermarck thesis include such convincing scholars as Arthur P. Wolf, Carl Degler, and Robin Fox, who is credited with inventing the term "Westermarck effect."[28] Cultural and biological determinists agree that sibling incest aversion, whether as a spontaneous reflex or the product of social conditioning, is both universal and essential to civilization.

FOBIDDEN GAMES: WESTERMARCK, FREUD, AND GATES

The Tree of Knowledge introduced Adam and Eve to the idea that nakedness alone is shameful. Elsewhere in the Bible, notably in the book of Job, nakedness symbolizes weakness and poverty, and God's disfavor inflicts sources of shame to those so unfortunate as to be naked. Although the words "knowledge" and "nakedness" happen to be associated with sex in other scripture, we need not assume the terms represent Adam and Eve's discovery of sex. They would certainly have observed the mating behavior of animals. In days of yore, children gained what little knowledge they had of sex from ignorant peers, but never from their parents, who were horrified by the thought of discussing the topic with their children. Adam and Eve lived in isolation from the adult world, isolated from the childhood experience of innocent sexual misinformation.

In the middle-class culture of the twenty-first century United States, young children are seldom beyond the watch and guard of parents or other adult authorities and seldom "go out to play" without supervision. Nonetheless, in the "information age," and despite "parental controls" on electronic media, young persons are prematurely exposed to explicit enactments of adult sexuality—much of it unhealthy—and often before puberty. The harmless infantile culture of show-and-tell has been supplanted by pornography that seeps into the immature consciousness courtesy of older siblings and acquaintances. Furthermore, children have always been perversely creative in evading parental controls. In days of old, children found opportunities for *jeux interdits* away from grownups in barns, haylofts, basements, attics, and abandoned cars.

The tolerance for sibling and half-sibling incest in Athens, Sparta, Persia, and Ptolemaic Egypt was undermined by Roman law and completely repudiated when the Roman Empire was Christianized. The subsequent rise of Islam contributed mightily to its decline.[29] There are few persons today whose emotions are untouched by the sexual taboos rooted in the "Abrahamic religions," with their ancient folklore, myths, and legends. Eastern Asian cultures are obviously influenced both by Abrahamic morality and by Western secularism and modernity, as evidenced by the abandonment of the embarrassingly old-fashioned practice of *Shim-pua* marriage in China since the early twentieth century.[30] Paradoxically, both Christianity and modern cosmopolitanism have guaranteed the universal encounter—verbatim or subliminally—with the legend of Adam and Eve, the forbidden fruit, the loathsome serpent, and the shame of nakedness.

The persistence of the myth of Adam and Eve, naked and ashamed, is an illustration of how culture and civilization inculcate sexual attitudes that extend beyond Sunday school lessons and catechism classes. Popular culture, religious mythology, folklore, legends, and other means, both subtle and direct, have reinforced the myth of Adam Eve rather than obscuring it. Future studies of sibling incest aversion should not ignore the fact that myths and legends can effectively transmit behavioral values, nor should future studies ignore the Pavlovian reinforcement provided over millennia by the Father's chastening rod and staff that were anything but a comfort to young siblings if caught in shameful *jeux interdits.*

The story of Adam and Eve is widely diffused today on the Greater Eurasian continent, and it inculcates and/or reinforces a nakedness taboo that prevails from Japan to Ireland, and from Iceland to the Cape of Good Hope. Throughout the "civilized" world, there is an *a priori* assumption that nakedness is a shameful thing in itself. When Christian missionaries first came bearing their gifts of civilization and progress to "primitives," they conflated barbarism with nakedness and "carnal knowledge." Thanks to the superior enlightenment of our present age, we now realize that neither primitives nor children "instinctively" see any relationship between nakedness and sex. While civilizing missionaries may have possessed some sense of Wordsworth's romantic belief that every child is born "not in utter nakedness, but trailing clouds of glory," they simultaneously bore Kipling's image of the "half devil and half child." There is a contradictory notion that innocent children, even though they are "noble savages," must be brought up to civilized behavior. The story of Eden teaches children from earliest childhood that nakedness is shameful, and this lesson is learned long before the sexual or reproductive implications of Adam and Eve's nakedness are understood. Only gradually, subtly, and indirectly does the child become aware of any implicit link between nakedness and carnal "knowledge."

NEGATIVE IMPRINTING AND SEXUAL AVERSION

Melford E. Spiro, in his classic study of children brought up in the Israeli kibbutz, observed small children showering together who did not deny the spontaneous impulse to engage in erotic play. This behavior was terminated at the onset of puberty, usually at the insistence of the girls. Some scholars have noted the possibility that adult influence and Jewish religious tradition contributed to the fact that the boys and girls eventually became squeamish about this mutual exposure to the opposite sex. Spiro's study indicated that children who mingled in the kibbutz showers never married, and most social scientists accept this as adequate proof for the theory of childhood negative imprinting and sexual aversion. This conclusion was challenged, however, on the basis of subsequent research and Spiro's own finding that "children of the same peer group engaged in intense sexual play with one another until the age of 9 or 10." There have been additional studies of the kibbutz which have led to the cautions expressed by Eran Shor and Dalit Simchai in the *American Journal of Sociology* that "growing up together does not by itself produce sexual aversion, and in many cases, not even sexual indifference."[31]

The kibbutz showers were supervised by adults who, even if only inadvertently, would certainly have transmitted traditional attitudes toward infantile eroticism. The caretakers, while obviously disinclined to associate nakedness with shame and unlikely to overreact to erotic play, were nonetheless influenced, if only subliminally, by millennia of Jewish tradition.

Thus, it seems worth considering whether the kibbutz shower experiences may have induced or even reinforced tendencies of avoidance or indifference among those who underwent the experience. There are, of course, no reports of the caretakers encouraging erotic play. Nonetheless, such play did occur, and interviews with adult alums of the kibbutz kindergarten showers conducted by Shor and Simchai revealed instances of sexual contact in later life, even though the participants chose not to marry.[32]

Among the most influential studies of incest aversion in relation to early childhood association are those conducted by Arthur P. Wolf, who amassed "a vast archive of information on early twentieth-century Taiwanese households" and the practice of *Shim-pua,* in which families adopt a female child and raise her alongside a son, with the expectation that the two will eventually marry.[33] His and subsequent studies have cited low birth rates and high divorce rates as evidence that even quasi-siblings, raised in proximity from an early age, may demonstrate incest aversion or the "Westermarck effect." Challenges to Wolf's conclusions are rare and seldom note that his studies were conducted amid the "American Century," at a time when Asian cultures were undergoing "westernization," and the practice of *Shim-pua* was considered embarrassing, old-fashioned, and morally questionable. Wolf's goal did not include tracing the practice's history or its evolution over the centuries concerning class. His studies and those of others linked *Shim-pua* with poverty and patterns of forced labor or servanthood, as in cases where the adoptive daughter was much older than her intended husband and brought into the household as his caretaker when he was a child.

Wolf's and other studies of *Shim-pua*, along with the Kibbutz studies, have tended to conflate the related but non-identical factors of marriage, sexual activity, and fertility rates. In addition, these were investigations of a custom in decline and held in low esteem. Further research is needed to discover whether the patterns observed by Wolf were present in centuries or millennia prior to his investigations. In the spatial and temporal setting where Wolf observed the phenomenon, *Shim-pua* was perceived by both interviewers and the interviewed as symbolizing "racial retardation." The Taiwanese who were interviewed were often under the influence of or striving toward "modern" Western, urban-industrial societal values. It would obviously be embarrassing to endure the questions of a Caucasian male intruding into their society and asking questions regarding sexual behavior. It is hardly surprising that many of those interviewed were inclined to express shock, horror, and contempt for the practice when speaking to their white American interlocutor.[34]

Scholarly biographers and literary critics have shown a perennial interest in the relationships of the British Romantics with their siblings, and using the sibling incest theme in their writings. In the course of this study, I take note of the attention devoted to sibling incest by such literary scholars as Eric Murdoch, Elizabeth Archibald, Ellen Pollak, and Stefani Engelstein. These authorities have noted the irrepressibility of the theme in Western literature and tacitly acknowledged the difficulty of discussing the topic with readers.

In classical literature, sibling consanguinity may be described unequivocally as it is in the marriage of Zeus and Hera in Homer's *Odyssey* or merely suggested as in the bond of Apollo and Artemis in the *Homeric Hymns*. It may involve the immortal gods and pharaohs of ancient Egypt or the Ptolemaic royals, who emulated the ancients. The literary tradition of antiquity, which dealt repeatedly, and sometimes even sympathetically, with the tragic consequences of love between sister and brother, was recycled in the Middle Ages, most notably by John Gower and Hartmann von Aue. In the Romantic Movement of Western literature, the love between a brother and sister may be consummated happily, as in the instance of Montesquieu's Apheridon and Astarte in the *Lettres Persanes*, or it may run less smoothly as in François-René de Chateaubriand's novel *René*.

Literary historian Alan Richardson has noted the presupposition of Samuel Coleridge and other nineteenth-century authors that a sister and brother raised together from infancy might naturally view one another as ideal soulmates were it not for opposing social pressures. A similar assumption pervades the works of Montesquieu, Shelley, and others.[35] Recent literary treatments of the theme seem consecrated to the Westermarck hypothesis that sibling incest is so unnatural as to occur only in rare circumstances and usually within the context of abuse, as when an older brother exploits a vulnerable younger sister.

Every fiction is effectively a thought experiment, and most novelists are interested in their readers' emotions and/or moral stimulation. As a similar thought experiment, but one lacking the elements of violence, drunkenness, and other glaring pathologies, psychologist Jonathan Haidt constructed a hypothetical narrative and surveyed the reactions of college students to it.

> Julie and Mark are brother and sister. They are traveling together in France on summer vacation from college. One night they are staying alone in a cabin near the beach. They decide that it would be interesting and fun if they tried making love. At the very least, it would be a new experience for each of them. Julie was already taking birth control pills, but Mark uses a condom too, just to be safe. They both enjoy making love, but they decide never to do it again. They keep that night as a special secret, which makes them feel even closer to each other.[36]

While both characters in the fiction were of college age, their sexual activity was mutually consensual, and they took multiple precautions against the risk of pregnancy, students expressed moral disapproval of Julie and Mark's behavior. Notably, most respondents found it impossible to entertain the premise that such an experience could be without damaging consequences. Several scholarly analyses of this experiment have faulted Haidt's methodology, but one of his conclusions has gone unchallenged. Even a fictional portrayal of consensual sibling incest can evoke the moral outrage of third-party non-participants. Expressions of disgust bear little correspondence to whether or not the commentator ever had siblings, which suggests that moral revulsion regarding sibling incest can and does occur independently of the preconditions of negative sexual imprinting outlined by Westermarck.

NATURAL LAW: ARISTOTLE, AUGUSTINE, AND AQUINAS

The Church broadened and extended the definition of incest beyond the prohibitions of Leviticus during the Middle Ages. The law of Moses did not prohibit marriages between first cousins or between uncles and nieces, but medieval Christian authorities went so far as to forbid marital unions of fourth cousins. One must be suspicious of the motives; such prohibitions were useful and convenient since they empowered the Church to grant dispensations for political and economic considerations. The legal arguments could be recondite and imaginative, but there seem to be no cases in which the Church granted a dispensation to siblings. Thomas Aquinas, in *Summa Theologiae*, condemned parental incest and incest between siblings. While both were wrong, parental incest was as "contrary to natural reason" as homosexuality, bestiality, and masturbation.

Modern adherents to the Abrahamic religions and inheritors of the law of Moses view sibling incest as abhorrent, but parental incest as even more abominable, because it implies the abuse of authority and the violation of trust. Aquinas likewise viewed incest between parents and their offspring as fundamentally abominable and furthermore as unnatural.[37]

Elizabeth Archibald argues that "Sibling incest seems to have been regarded in medieval writing as less heinous than parent-child incest."[38] Aquinas draws a fundamental distinction between sibling and parental incest in citing the Oedipal shock of recognition that drove a horse to suicide, for even an animal realized, when it "covered its own mother," even by mistake, that it had violated the law of nature. Sibling incest, although unequivocally sinful and unequivocally condemned by Augustine and Aquinas, was seen by neither of them as "naturally" repugnant, and Aquinas could not pronounce it "unnatural," for he believed that the marriage of siblings had been necessary and divinely ordained for the initial propagation of the species. Elizabeth Archibald has observed "that horses are the most lascivious of creatures (after men), and that stallions even cover their mothers and daughters, a match which is considered particularly desirable by breeders."[39]

Unlike Plato, Aquinas never suggested that siblings naturally find one another uninteresting or repulsive. Quite the contrary, he cited Aristotle and foreshadowed Freud's dismissal of Westermarck when he asserted that brothers and sisters can be naturally attracted to one another. Nonetheless, although Aquinas viewed kinship attraction as intrinsically natural, he viewed acting on it as immoral, because the act of incest "is contrary to the natural respect which we owe persons related to us." Hence the reasonableness and necessity of the incest taboo, which not only originates in the law of Moses, but must be reinforced by justifiable societal restraints.

> Because blood relations must needs live in close touch with one another. Wherefore if they were not debarred from venereal union, opportunities of venereal intercourse would be very frequent and thus men's minds would be enervated by lust. . . . Aristotle adds another reason (2 Polit. ii): for since it is natural that a man should have a liking for a woman of his kindred, if to this be added the love that has its origin in venereal intercourse, his love would be too ardent and would become a very great incentive to lust.[40]

"In other words, incest is so bad because the sex is so good!" writes scholar Gerald T. Massey, who sees Aquinas as "disturbingly close to positing a natural or quasi-natural inclination to incest." In fact, *New Advent,* the Catholic encyclopedia, observes that some Catholic authorities find it "difficult to accept the opinion of some theologians that the marriage of brother and sister is against the law of nature; otherwise, the propagation of the human race would have begun by violation of the natural law."[41] This is a restatement of Aquinas's position, for while Aquinas invokes the law of nature in condemning parental incest, he condemns "venereal intercourse" between siblings on alternative grounds by appealing to the law of Leviticus and the reasoning of Aristotle, and he deploys the rational argument that incestuous marriages would undermine the formation of exogamous social bonds. Incest is not only a manifestation of lust; it carries with it the potential to generate even more lust, which would have harmful social effects. By implication, if brothers and sisters growing up in the same household were to become sexually involved, culture, society, and civilization would be swept away in a deluge of adolescent hormones.[42]

WESTERMARCK AND THE UNFASHIONABLE DR. FREUD: A CASE HISTORY

The views expressed in Aquinas's *Summa* were recycled, perhaps fortuitously, by Sigmund Freud, who never acknowledged any such debt. He never translated Aquinas's references to the "natural liking" of siblings for their kindred into German, but Freud did assert that "the first objects of sexual desire are within the family." One of Freud's concerns in *Die Inzestcheu* is to explain what he later develops in *Totem und Tabu*

(1913), the "prohibition against an incestuous choice of object," and in *Das Unbehagen in der Kultur* (1929), a title James Strachey famously translated as *Civilization and its Discontents*, but I offer the more literal translation, *Culture and Unease,* in order to emphasize the tension Freud sees between libidinal drives and the demands of social institutions. Freud's opinions on incest are remembered today almost overwhelmingly in connection with the so-called Oedipus complex, but that is not a central concern of the present discussion, which is focused on the Edenic myth and siblings close in age.

Freud's patient, Sergei Pankejeff, the subject of his famous study of the "Wolf Man," alluded directly to the story of Adam and Eve when the patient described a memory of infantile sex play between himself and his sister, Anna, and his attempt to renew the activity when he reached puberty. Freud's observations and most subsequent commentaries have focused on Pankejeff's accidental observation of his father mounting his mother during sex, the putative cause of his nightmares and drawings of wolves perched in trees, which inspired a classic Hollywood horror film of 1941. Less frequently remembered is Freud's description of Pankejeff's "seduction" of his sister when she was seven and Sergei was five.

> It was in spring, at a time when his father was away; the children were playing on the floor, while their mother was working in the next. His sister had taken hold of his penis and played with it, at the same time telling him incomprehensible stories about his Nanya, as though by way of explanation. His Nanya, she said, used to do the same thing to all kinds of people—for instance with the gardener. She used to stand him on his head and take hold of his genitals.

Westermarckians ignore the childish experiment initiated by Pankejeff's sister accompanied by "incomprehensible stories," a source of anxiety and guilt in the mind of the adult Pankejeff, and Freud bundled this "seduction" scene together with apparently unrelated childhood experiences in describing the neurosis of his patient. This so-called "seduction" indicated nothing more than curiosity on the part of a seven-year-old and almost nothing of childish eroticism, and therefore it can hardly be categorized as a "seduction." Freud never wrote a treatise on the sexual symbolism of Adam and Eve, but he did record Pankejeff's reactions to the fable.

> When he was told the story of the first of mankind he was struck by the similarity of his lot to Adam's. In conversation with his Nanya he professed hypocritical surprise that Adam should have allowed himself to be dragged into misfortune by a woman, and promised her that he would never marry. A hostility towards women, due to his seduction by his sister, found strong expression at this time.

It is the "Oedipus complex" that dominates discussions of Freud and of Pankejeff's neurosis, not sibling incest. Freud never suggested that the serpent in Eden was anything other than an ordinary, garden-variety talking snake. Unlike his patient, he imposed no allegorical interpretation on the myth of Eden, nor did he suggest that it was an allegory for the transition from infant sexuality to adolescent morality. What he did say was that the sexual anxieties of children can carry into adulthood. Civilization breeds discontent, but sexual repression within the family is a social necessity, since "there would be no prospect of curbing the sexual life of adults if the ground had not been prepared for it in childhood."[43]

As previously noted, Freud's theory of sibling *Inzestscheu* was not the first deviation from the Darwinian hypothesis founded in Plato and buttressed by Westermarck. Freud's assertion that the incest taboo was socially induced resonated with the opinions of Aristotle and Aquinas without invoking them, and cultural anthropologists, notably E. B. Tylor, W. G. Sumner, and Emile Durkheim, had maintained that the universality of the sibling incest taboo arose from universal sociocultural exigencies.[44] Nonetheless the Westermarck hypothesis is accepted overwhelmingly by social scientists who stress that biologically unrelated stepsiblings, if raised together from early childhood, seldom desire to marry, and, if forced to do so, show low fertility rates.

These studies can only conclude that sibling incest aversion is spontaneous and universal, at least on the sister's part. Understandably, researchers approach the subject with third-party aversion, which is understandable given the criminal pathologies under inspection. Some investigators have been known to declare "I don't have any siblings" as evidence of their objectivity.[45] Peter K. Jonason and Laura K. Dane opine that "beliefs get in the way" of evolutionary theory as the basis of incest avoidance. Behaviorists, they maintain, are predisposed to resist the Westermarck approach "because the motivation behind the denial stems from a (perceived) need to protect one's values and morals."[46] Fair enough, but the same might be said of the "motivation" of those who gravitate toward Westermarck's theory. No school of thought claims that *Inzestsheu* develops outside of the socialization process.

Socialization is an important determinant of primate sexual behavior. Some contemporary social scientists seem to disregard the effects of social conditioning during their own childhood as a source of distaste at the thought of sibling incest. It is only "natural" that social scientists, acculturated in a society permeated with myths, legends, fairy tales, and artistic and literary allusions to original sin, should think of the Westermarck effect as spontaneous, instinctive, and inherited.

The late Arthur P. Wolf, Stanford professor of anthropology and the foremost authority on sibling incest, argued vigorously that "innate moral emotions" are at the root of the universal sibling incest taboo. In his well-placed and influential article "Westermarck Redivivus," he pontificated in 1993 that the socialization approach to explaining the sibling incest taboo was unsustainable, and that its proponents were "trapped in an impossible position by their initial assumptions." He asserted that disinterested investigations, such as his own, had overwhelmingly demonstrated the biological basis of the sibling incest taboo.

> The view that innate moral emotions are the source of these judgments is not likely to appeal to most contemporary anthropologists, but they need to consider new evidence suggesting that as early as the third year of life children judge violations of moral rules more serious than violations of conventional rules (25:42-48). I think that having been proven right about the effects of both in-breeding and childhood association, Westermarck deserves more careful consideration than he has been given in the past. As a homosexual, he may very well have understood better than most the way society responds to sexual behavior that is disinterested but not general.[47]

Wolf's rhetoric hardly seems disinterested, however, and certainly he did not intend to imply that homosexuals as a category are more "disinterested" or more "understanding" than other social scientists. Nothing in Westermarck's autobiographical or academic writings lends support to such a conclusion. Nonetheless his conjecture concerning the implications of Westermarck's sexuality might lead to a wider discussion of moral disapproval as the source of sexual taboos. The erosion of the homosexual taboo in Euro-American society has not been accompanied by a corresponding erosion of the sibling incest taboo. Social scientists show considerable resistance to studies that might link homophobia to evolutionary biology. By contrast, studies that confirm the Westermarck hypothesis offer its challengers admonitions, such as the following: "Social science theories claiming that morality is free of biological regulation require revision. If the mind is not a blank slate, then theories of culture will have to accommodate this fact."[48]

The best research methodologies are not infallible; those of the Israeli kibbutzim studies and the Chinese *Shim-pua*, while persuasive, should not shut off the possibility of ongoing discussion. Infantile eroticism is always scrutinized by adults and invariably disapproved in the kibbutz as elsewhere. Being "caught" in what are putatively common instances of infantile eroticism, such as kissing or cuddling, are most likely to be detected and disapproved between close-in-age siblings (ages four to seven), and the consequent chastisement would have the lasting effect of Pavlovian conditioning. When detected, infantile curiosity and experimentation, even if non-erotic, may have uncomfortable consequences and permanently undermine the future "objectivity" of the detached social scientific investigator.

"Eve Tempted by the Serpent" by William Blake (1799)

– CHAPTER FOUR –

SERPENT OF EDEN AND INCEST AVOIDANCE

IN EGYPTIAN mythology, serpents are naturally associated with poison and death, but also mystically with healing. Moses is known to have made a bronze serpent with magical healing powers, although the first of his Ten Commandments forbade making graven images. As Barbara Walker notes, serpents are symbols of healing in classical mythology and medieval lore.[1] In modern times, various professional healthcare associations employ the rod of Asclepius as their symbol. In Catholic churches, statues of the Virgin with a serpent writhing sensuously between her toes are strongly suggestive of her paganistic associations with virginal Artemis and fruitful Isis, both of whom were associated with serpents. A cobra graces the crown of Isis, and a serpent guarded a sacred grove of Artemis in northeastern Mysia.[2]

The story of Isis and Osiris, conveniently preserved by Plutarch, is no less "epic" than the story of Gilgamesh, largely forgotten until the nineteenth century. Like the much simpler and homelier fable of Adam and Eve, the Egyptian and Mesopotamian legends originate in the remote past of human prehistory. They all began as fireside stories. The Urtexts for all of them vanished millennia before the construction of the pyramids or the ziggurat. Ancient mythologies are replete with stories of dragons and snakes, and there are legendary women, such as Eve, Artemis, Isis, and the Virgin Mary, who are positively or negatively associated with them. Sometimes, especially in Christian iconography, the serpent is presented as a serpent woman, or a Lamia, responsible for a sister and brother's exile from Eden.

The Lamia as serpent woman appears commonly in the iconographies of Western Art, including the works of many of Michelangelo's forerunners and contemporaries. In a sculpture over one of the portals of Notre Dame Cathedral, Eden's serpent is endowed with the upper body of a woman. In the history of Western art and literature, the serpent is often an allusion to the legend of Lilith, Adam's first wife, but alternatively—in Kabbalistic thinking—God's wife or harlot. As such, she is Adam and Eve's wicked stepmother and a cognate of the stepmother in fairytale lore.[3] Lilith (or Lamia) appears in rabbinical and Christian fables during the Middle Ages and persists in Renaissance iconography.[4] In Michelangelo's famous depiction of the temptation and exile, the serpent is reptilian from the thighs down but possesses the upper body and exposed breast of a woman. The serpent is more feminine than Eve, who, although she lacks a penis, has all the other characteristics of a mesomorphic male. Michelangelo's painting, like many others, is at variance with the Genesis story. His angel's sword is not flaming, and his exiles are divested of the animal hides with which the Father clothed them. The serpent-woman is a poetic and artistic derivative of the Lamia of Greek mythology.

ANCIENT, MEDIEVAL, AND MODERN BESTIARIES

Collections of animal fables, known as *bestiaries*, are examples of ancient and medieval stories that illustrate moral laws supposedly manifest in the natural world. The serpent fable of Genesis may be considered one of these, associated with etiological and didactic purposes. Etiological fables explain the origins of things, and didactic fables contain moral lessons. The story of Eden's serpent is etiological in that it explains why the snake crawls on its belly and moralizing in that it admonishes deceit. The animal fables attributed to Aesop are usually invested with moral lessons; so, too, are the pious animal bestiaries of the Christian Middle Ages and the irony-laden fables of La Fontaine in the seventeenth century. But while the medieval bestiaries have moralizing functions, they serve additionally as allegories to demonstrate the moral economy of the Universe and illustrate the splendor of Divine Providence. As such, they may present examples of real or imaginary characteristics attributed to various animals, as in Aristotle's previously mentioned horse fable cited by Aquinas.

Christian fabulists notably presented the presumably "natural" patterns of animal behavior as demonstrations of Providence. A splendid example of this practice is found in Henry More's 1660 treatise, *An Explanation of the Grand Mystery of Godliness*:

> I will only mention some few of the more refined Passions that are observable in some Brutes: such as are, The sense of Praise and glory, The strength of natural affection, The exercise of craft and subtlety for self-preservation, Their real and effectual Policy for common safety, and an obscure Imitation of some acts of Religion. . . . As for example, That there is the sense of praise, glory and victory in Brutes, is evident in the Peacock, Elephant, Horse, and in Cocks of the game. That there is natural affection in them to their young ones, almost all Creatures witness; but of reciprocal affection of their young to them that brought them forth the most eminent Example is in the Stork, whence is to do the duty of an affectionate childe to his aged Parent.

The tradition of referencing animal behavior in discussions of human nature persists in contemporary secular society, and I shall cite three examples: Environmental activists in the twenty-first century have been known to decry the human tendency toward environmental pollution with the spurious argument that animals do not defecate where they eat, ignoring the fact that pigs, a highly successful and intelligent species, do exactly that. The Dominican Sisters who were entrusted with my high school education illustrated the naturalness of marital fidelity by asserting that birds mate for life. This may hold true for some avian species, but recent studies have shown that infidelity is common even among those species that do mate for life, and that the results of infidelity can be beneficial rather than deleterious to a species. Another example of the contemporary invocation of animal behavior is that social scientists have been known to reference the behavior of bonobos and chimpanzees when dragged into discussions of "human nature." This tendency has sometimes been politicized in popular discussions of "human nature." The ripe scholar Raymond Williams has opined that "Nature is perhaps the most complex word in the language," but I suspect the concept of "human nature" may be even more complex.[5]

While Freud mentioned snakes, fear of snakes, and dreams of snakes in his writings, he cannot be accused of reducing Eden's serpent to a crude "phallic symbol."[6] In his stunning series of essays, *The Dragons of Eden*, Carl Sagan posited that a distrust of reptiles was embedded in the brains of our primate ancestors in bygone eons when dinosaurs stalked their prey. According to this eminently reasonable theory, an instinct of serpent avoidance aided the survival of our mammalian ancestors who possessed it, and the legend of Eden's serpent was the social expression of a biological legacy.[7] Sagan offered no discourse on the sexual implications of Genesis, other than a casual neo-Freudian allusion to the serpent as a phallic symbol. Neither Freud nor Sagan attempted a mytho-poetic interpretation of the "instinctive" dread of serpents, the "instinctive" horror of incest, or the naked children in the Garden of Eden.[8]

The snake avoidance instinct, supposedly common to chimpanzees and humans, has been introduced into discussions of the serpent of Eden. Sagan did not reference the work of Edward O. Wilson and others who weighed the scholarly evidence on the putatively innate dislike of snakes. A study by the National Academy of Sciences showed that the activity of neurons in the central nervous system responded more measurably to images of snakes than to other images. "These results identify a neurobiological substrate for rapid detection of threatening visual stimuli in primates" and provide "neuroscientific evidence in support of the Snake Detection Theory, which posits that the threat of snakes strongly influenced the evolution of the primate brain."[9] There is apparently no evidence that the mythic enmity between females and serpents, pronounced in Genesis 3, has an instinctive cognate among chimpanzees. Nor does there seem to be any evidence that chimpanzees are susceptible to "penis envy" or a fear of phallic symbols. It has been suggested that the putative instinct of human incest avoidance might bear a relationship to the feminine hostility to snakes preserved in Eden's myth of the serpent.[10]

STEPMOTHER IN SIBLING EXILE NARRATIVES

Martin Luther had no choice but to feminize the serpent in his translation of Genesis 3:1, "*die Schlange war listiger en alle Tiere auf dem Felde,*" since the word for snake or serpent in German is feminine, "*die Schlange.*"

The serpentine symbol can be a stepmother or a witch, a Lilith or a Lamia. Lilith is a Hebrew word, but in the Latin Vulgate Bible, Jerome substitutes "lamia," alluding to a figure in Greek folklore, a woman with the lower body of a snake. "The lilith" is mentioned only once in the Hebrew Bible (Isaiah 34:14), in a prophecy of evils destined to befall the land of Edom, but the modern reader will find no clue therein as to who or what is meant by "the lilith." The word appears without capitalization in the *Jewish Study Bible,* with a note explaining that the term refers to "a group of female demons" in "ancient Semitic belief," rabbinical writing, and kabbalistic folklore.[11] No lilith is mentioned in the Septuagint, the Latin Vulgate, the King James, the Douay-Rheims or the Luther Bible.

Lilith, like the witches of fairy-tale lore, is associated with threats to children, as in multiple versions of the Grimms' "Hansel and Gretel." While serpents are always phallic symbols in vulgar pseudo-Freudian mythology, they may possess a traditionally feminine character in Christian iconography. Thus, serpentine females appear frequently in Renaissance art and may be associated with the serpent of Eden or with Lilith, Adam's legendary first wife. There is another manifestation of Lilith in the Kabbalah that makes her the wife of God, hence the stepmother of Adam and Eve.

The wicked stepmother is the serpent in Hansel and Gretel's garden, and her spite triggers their exile. In the Grimms' narrative of "*Brüderchen und Schwesterchen*," the stepmother does not exile the brother and sister; they take flight into the forest to escape her cruelty. As the story progresses and she persists in her torments, we learn that she and the witch are identical. They are likewise identical in the Grimm brothers' narrative, "*Lämmchen und Fischchen.*" European folklore contains several sibling exile narratives of this type. Giambattista Basile's "Nennillo and Nennella" is echoed in the variants of the Grimms' sibling exile narratives. In all these tales, the malice of a serpentine personality—a stepmother, Lilith, or Lamia—sets the events in motion. "Hansel and Gretel" is reiterated in an eighteenth-century British novel, *The Adventures of David Simple* by Sarah Fielding, where a wicked stepmother turns a father against a brother and sister, leading to their banishment with accusations of incest.[12]

Myths and fables do not always convey a moral, and it is difficult to extract one from the several Greek myths that deal with stepmother archetypes. It is difficult to extract any lessons useful to mortals from any of them. The tragic legend of Phrixus and Helle, children of the half-nymph Nephele, tells of a brother and sister driven into exile by their stepmother, Ino, who bribed false witnesses to say that the oracle required the sacrifice of Phrixus.

A serpent is often linked to the stepmother in myth and folklore. Thus, in Greek mythology, Hera sends serpents to attack the children of her rivals. Insulted by her husband's affair with Alcmene and its product, the infant Heracles, she sends two serpents to strangle the baby in his cradle, but the mighty son of Zeus strangles them instead. Enraged when Leto gives birth to Artemis and Apollo, Hera employs the python, or serpent, to pursue and destroy the twins, but like Heracles, the other son of Zeus, Apollo is victorious over the python. Hera's serpents bear no obvious relation to the serpent of Eden, but it requires little imagination to see how elements in the primeval "collective conscience" can assign serpentine qualities to stepmothers.

"The Plague in the Reign of King David" by Guy-Louis Vernansal (1675-1700)

– CHAPTER FIVE –

DIVINE INCEST, ROYAL INCEST, AND BROTHER-SISTER GODS

ADAM AND Eve have counterparts who are divine siblings and progenitors of mankind in several creation myths from diverse ancient civilizations. Among gods and godlike beings, brother-sister marriages occur so frequently as to be unremarkable. In Japanese mythology, the progenitors of mankind are Izanagi and his sister-wife, Izanami. Their counterparts in ancient Chinese mythology are Nüwa and her brother, Fuxi, the first parents of humanity, sometimes called Nu wa and Fu xi. It is beyond dispute that divine siblings can be, or even must be, lovers in the classical theologies of various peoples, and this holds true both within and outside of Indo-European traditions.

The gods are allowed the privilege of sibling incest in those mythological traditions where the gods are divided into male and female. Thus, in the Hindu, Egyptian, and Shinto traditions, some gods and goddesses take their sisters and brothers as consorts. In the Judeo-Islamic tradition, there can be no "divine incest" since the God of both these monotheistic religions is defined as a spirit, and orthodoxy allows him neither a mother, nor a wife, nor a sister. But Trinitarian Christianity, with its invocation of Jesus Christ as "true God and true man," offers possibilities for contemplating divine incest, as we see in the sermons of Saint Bernard of Clairvaux and Thomas Mann's satirical treatment of the "mother of god" paradox in medieval mysticism.[1]

Divine incest and royal incest have been justified or promoted by various ruling classes. "A brother-sister union guaranteed the preservation of the parents' blood in the children's bodies," writes scholar Fuminobu Murakami. Thus, the Japanese divinities, "Izanagi and Izanami, like Amaterasu and Susa-no-o, committed incest to allow their parents' souls to be reborn in their children." Murukami's thesis can be applied to several Asian, African, and Native American myths where a brother and sister may engender or regenerate the human race after a great deluge.[2]

There are various accounts of the ancient Egyptian myth of Osiris, who was slain and dismembered by his brother, Seti, and how Isis, his wife and sister, reassembled and revitalized his corpse.

ROYAL INCEST AND THE ANCIENT WORLD

When Greco-Egyptian Emperor Ptolemy decided to assert his own divine status in the fourth century BCE, he resurrected the Pharaonic custom of divine incest by marrying his sister. In claiming the status of a god, he was not only entitled to an incestuous marriage; he actually validated his status. Full sibling incest was perfectly congruent with the behavior of the gods and "royal incest,"and it has occurred frequently enough in human history that some might call it a social convention. Marriages of commoners who were half-siblings had traditionally been tolerated but not actually encouraged in Athens and Sparta.[3] Full sibling incest did not become acceptable to the Greeks until it was combined with royal incest and the Pharaonic tradition of divine incest by the Ptolemaic dynasty in post-Alexandrian Egypt. The marriage of full siblings was traditional with the Incan and the Hawaiian royals, and William Graham Sumner's observation is valid, that the practice was not universally extirpated prior to the impact of Western colonialism and its civilizing missionaries.

Prior to the Ptolemies, half-sibling marriage of commoners was condoned in ancient Athens and Sparta. The marriage of full siblings was illegal in ancient Greece, although paternally consanguinous half-siblings could be married in ancient Athens, and marriages of uterine half-siblings were acceptable in Sparta. Scholarly discussions of the practice have not fully explored the question's legality or frequency and are usually limited to the reactions of Aristophanes, Philo, Ovid, and Plutarch. Anise K. Strong cites this testimony by observing that "such relationships were extremely uncommon and subject to public ridicule."[4]

When the Greco-Egyptian Emperor Ptolemy II married his full sister, Arsinoe, he did not cite any Greek or Macedonian precedents. Although he did refer to the brother-sister marriage of Hera and Zeus, he relied mainly on Egyptian tradition rather than Greek myth for justification. Katje Lembke implies that little justification was necessary since the Egyptians were happy to witness the revival of an ancient custom, symbolizing the overthrow of Persian dominance by its Alexandrian successors. Under the Ptolemies, the custom of sibling marriage seems to have spread among the common people, but this is likely unrelated to the rare occurrences in Athens and Sparta.[5]

Historians acknowledge that brother-sister unions persisted among the Ptolemies, particularly in the well-known cases of Cleopatra's marriages to at least one of her brothers. There is also evidence of sibling marriages in Roman Egypt. It is not uncommon for scholars to express their personal discomfort with the idea and to conjecture that these marriages were never consummated. Proponents of Westermarck's theory argue that these relationships were exceptional among the royalty and nonexistent in the remainder of the population. Keith Hopkins argues, however, that the practice was common among ordinary people and its existence "challenges several well-established theories about a universal incest taboo."[6] There is, at present, considerable debate among scholars concerning whether the practice of full-sibling marriage was normalized at any time among Egyptian commoners. Strong argues not only that it existed, but that despite a Roman ban on sibling marriages, there was "a gap between the absolute theoretical ban in Roman law and the reality of common incestuous unions in Egypt."[7]

Conclusions drawn by Walter Scheidel based on census reports and other evidence are consistent with the above contentions. While Scheidel issues the caveat that brother-sister marriages in Roman Egypt were "for all we can tell, truly unique in human history," he asserts that "the exceptional amount of this inbreeding load—or rather its very existence—has not only failed to catch the eye of the professional custodians of the history of Roman Egypt but has also remained completely unknown to specialists of genetics and medical anthropology."[8] Other scholars, including Jane Rowlandson and Ryosuke Takahashi, have argued in confirmation of such findings, and prior to Scheidel, Brent D. Shaw, on examining the evidence, concluded that the Ptolemaic practice of royal incest

> mimicked the Greek settlers in Egypt who, however rich or poor, weak or powerful they may have been, perceived themselves to be an integral part of the whole privileged Greek ruling "class" in Egypt (and therefore in very close proximity to the "top" people at the upper end of that same social order). Certain types of "incest" may well be seen as morally repellent, and might be "proved" to be "biologically disadvantagous." But the behavior is not part of an immutable "law of nature."[9]

While not predominant among commoners in Egypt, full-sibling marriage existed and persisted until the fourth century, when Roman law abolished it and Christianity and Islam's advances doomed any remants of it. Thus, Sumner attributed its decline to Roman stoicism and the sexual taboos of the Abrahamic religions. Nonetheless, some scholars reject the sociological hypothesis and the reports of full-sibling marriage among commoners in Egypt or Zoroastrian Persia. They note the relative scarcity of documentation of half-sibling marriage in Athens and Sparta vigorously defending the Westermarck thesis, disagree with Sumner that sibling incest was ever common anywhere, and counter that the taboo has its source in biology and merely was reinforced through custom and tradition. The taboo was certainly reinforced by the burgeoning of

Christian and Islamic influences between the third and seventh centuries, which permanently shaped the sexual mores of modern times.

SIBLING INCEST AND KING DAVID

Most students of the Hebrew Bible have recognized that its precepts of incest, adultery, and marital duties are not precisely stated until Leviticus and Deuteronomy, and even these books make no statement as to the necessity of a formal marriage ritual. Whoever originally cobbled together the discordant narratives that constitute Genesis did not describe the institution of marriage in any detail and, apparently, viewed sibling incest dispassionately

Genesis makes no mention of formal marriage ceremonies, but most commentators, whether Christian or Jewish, have agreed that the sons and daughters of Adam and Eve married one another and that sibling marriage was not forbidden prior to the Law of Moses because consanguinous marriage was necessary for the original propagation of the species. On the other hand, Genesis clearly indicates that at least some Mosaic laws related to marriage were retroactive. For example, Onan, whose older brother, Er, had died childless, was presumably bound by the commandment of Deuteronomy 25:5 to take Tamar, the wife of his deceased brother, "and perform the duty of an husband's brother unto her." Most Bible scholars interpret Onan's duty as an obligation to attempt the impregnation of Tamar. The "evil deed" of Onan was coitus interruptus, not masturbation, although the word "onanism" has become synonymous with masturbation in modern vocabularies.

Another instance of retroactive sexual prohibition is implied in the destruction of Sodom, presumably for the crime of "sodomy," one of the sexual abominations forbidden by the Law of Moses.[10] Most readers of Genesis 19 interpret it to mean that the men of Sodom intended to have sexual relations with the two angels who were Lot's house guests since they commanded of Lot: "Bring them out unto us, that we may know them." Lot's response was to offer his two virgin daughters as sexual substitutes, with the words, "Do ye to them as *is* good in your eyes: only unto these men do nothing." The mob is not satisfied with the offer and threatens to break down Lot's doors and, to protect his household, the angels "smote the men that *were* at the door of the house with blindness." Later, in Genesis 19:31-38, Lot has sexual relations with each of his daughters on consecutive nights, after each of these two wily virgins have got him so drunk "he perceived not when she lay down, nor when she arose."

I note in passing that the chroniclers of Genesis hint only vaguely at any moral issue in Lot's impregnation of two virginal daughters who could have been no more than thirteen or fourteen, if older. According to the customs of the ancient Hebrews, they would probably have been married. Scripture describes dispassionately and without condemnation their supposed seduction of their father, to which he presumably would not have acquiesced unless very drunk. The old man is supposed to have performed satisfactorily on two successive nights while unaware of his actions. Be that as it may, the chroniclers of Leviticus and Deuteronomy do not include father-daughter incest in their detailed prohibitions. The banning of sexual intercourse with a sister is specific in Leviticus 18:9, whether with "the daughter of thy father, or daughter of thy mother." The prohibition in Deuteronomy 27:22 applies equally to "he that lieth with his sister, the daughter of his father, or the daughter of his mother."

Even after the sexual restrictions and obligations of Leviticus and Deuteronomy were delivered, presumably at the time of Moses, there were conspicuous deviations from them at the height of Israel's glory under Kings David and Solomon. For example, there is a suggestion that royal incest was not impossible in the household of David, who was both a king and a prophet in Israel.[11] Scripture reveals that David and his children were lax in their observance of the Mosaic code, and there are intimations that David tolerated, perhaps even facilitated, royal incest in 2 Samuel 13:7-16. According to scripture, David's son Amnon fell in love with his agnate half-sister, Tamar, and, feigning illness, asked his father, "let Tamar my sister come, and make me a couple of cakes in my sight, that I may eat at her hand." This request was unusual but not necessarily aberrant; nonetheless, it suggests that the legendary king aided and abetted his lovesick son in his groping after forbidden fruit. Perhaps the chronicler intended to emphasize David's legendary laxity in adherence to Mosaic law, previously illustrated when he seduced a married woman and subsequently arranged her husband's death. A king notorious for one violation may not have balked at indulging another as a special favor to his favorite son.

When she came to his chambers, Amnon seized his sister and, after taking her by force, cruelly expelled her, then had his servants bar the door. Before the rape, Tamar is supposed to have said to her brother, "Speak unto the king, for he will not withhold me from thee." Perhaps she was ignorant of the law, which seems unlikely. Perhaps she was stalling for time, which seems possible. Either way, Amnon and Tamar both knew their father and understood such a request was not inconsistent with David's character, as came to be proven later by the fact that David never exacted a penalty for Amnon's dual offenses of rape combined with incest. Tamar is reported to have reproached Amnon after the rape, saying, "this evil in sending me away is greater than the other that thou didst unto me." The chronicler would have us believe that Tamar found her rejection and expulsion even more outrageous than the rape itself. In that case, she would have considered the law prohibiting sibling incest, Leviticus 18:9, to be less binding than the law of Deuteronomy 22:28-29, prescribing that the rapist of a virgin must marry her.[12]

How David might have responded to Tamar's suggestion that he give a daughter to a son as a wife or concubine can only be imagined. We know David did not always observe the Law of Moses with utmost punctilio. The *Jewish Encyclopedia* suggests that "Even in David's time, although it is represented as unusual for a royal prince to marry his sister (II Sam. xiii. 13), it was still regarded as neither objectionable nor forbidden."[13] Nonetheless, Tamar's rape and the intrafamilial bloodshed that ensued are commonly viewed as God's punishment for David's adultery with Bathsheba. The chronicler may have included this episode as a parable of warning against David's acknowledged sinfulness and his presumable toleration of "royal incest" as practiced in Egypt and elsewhere in the ancient Near East.

Royal families have practiced close-kin marriage or "royal incest" in regions as distanced from one another as Hawaii, Korea, and Peru. Social scientists acknowledge royal incest as the single exception to the "universal" sibling incest taboo. The chronicler of Amnon and Tamar's story suggests a neglect of the Mosaic ban on incest within the royal family and further suggests that the divine penalty ultimately exacted for sexual laxity was a civil war leading to the deaths of two of David's favorite sons.

Possibly Tamar was correct in her expectation that King David would have tolerated royal incest, but whether or not Tamar truly believed David would have encouraged Amnon to marry her, she asserted her claims under the code of Deuteronomy that the rapist of a virgin "shall give unto the damsel's father fifty shekels of silver, and she shall be his wife; because he hath humbled her, he may not put her away all his days." In the Hebrew Bible, Leviticus does not unequivocally prescribe a death penalty for sibling incest. Saint Jerome translates the text in this way, but the King James version does not. The Douay Bible follows after St. Jerome, but the Tanakh insists on no such translation. Whether or not Tamar actually believed royal incest acceptable, David was certainly complicit in exposing her to the danger.

The chronicler of this story knows the details of Tamar's protests, struggles, and rebuke of Amnon. The perspective is that of an omniscient narrator, but an author can be omniscient only when writing fiction or under divine inspiration. The chronicler knows of the conversation between Amnon and David, in which the king either willingly or unwittingly facilitated Amnon's deed. It is written that "when King David heard all these things he was very wroth," but it is not written that he imposed a legal penalty. The Law of Moses implicitly considered incest a crime against the father of the victim. The legal compensation for rape was stated in Deuteronomy 22:28–29, which is ascribed to Moses, although many Bible scholars think it was written several centuries after the deaths of Moses, David, Tamar and Amnon: "If a man find a damsel *that is* a virgin, which is not betrothed, and lay hold on her, and lie with her, and they be found; Then the man that lay with her shall give unto the damsel's father fifty *shekels* of silver, and she shall be his wife; because he hath humbled her, he may not put her away all his days."

According to Deuteronomy, David had no remedy other than to demand payment from his son and require his son to marry his daughter. We don't know whether David tolerated consensual incest in this case. We have only the chronicler's report, and in reading any narrative, including those in the Bible, it is reasonable to ask how the chronicler discovered the details. The chronicler of 2 Samuel 13 reports on conversations between Amnon and Tamar in Amnon's private chambers after he had dismissed his servants. The only evidence of the rape comes from Tamar's implicit testimony and her subsequent behavior: "And Tamar put ashes on her head, and rent her garment of diverse colours that *was* on her, and laid her hand on her head, and went on crying."[14]

Eventually Tamar revealed her violation to her uterine brother, Absolom, who took revenge on Amnon by having his own servants kill him. Afterward, there was a civil war in the kingdom, and Absolom was slain in battle.

There is no evidence in support of any of the stories concerning King David and his children other than the biblical narratives. While this lack of evidence presents many frustrations for historians who seek to recover historical facts, it provides a rich mythological treasury to the student of European and American systems of belief.

BROTHER-SISTER REFERENCES IN SONG OF SOLOMON

Song of Solomon in the King James Bible is called Song of Songs in the Jewish Study Bible, *Canticum Canticorum* in the Latin Vulgate, and Canticle of Canticles in the Douay translation. Many persons read it simply as a book of erotic poetry, while others see it as an allegory or mystical prophesy. A male speaker in the song speaks three times, "my sister, *my* spouse," and once the line, "my sister, my love," thus presenting the possibility that the lovers may have at least one parent in common. The female speaker eliminates the idea that the lovers could be uterine siblings when she says, "O that thou *wert* as my brother, that sucked the breasts of my mother!"[15]

Metaphorical or not, brother-sister references survive in examples of ancient Near Eastern love poetry and are usually interpreted as terms of endearment, not necessarily representing sibling relationships. Jewish and Christian commentators traditionally reject literal interpretations, citing the Law of Moses, which strictly forbids sexual union between siblings or half-siblings and provides punishments for transgressors; these, however may vary by translation. Nonetheless, extreme deviations from Mosaic law were tolerated under the successful kingships of David and Solomon.

There were several sexual transgressions and other violations of the law under the kingship of David, often averred by biblical commentators: the troubles of David's reign, particularly the deaths of his favored sons Amnon and Absolom, were divine chastisements for his disregard of the law. But David's transgressions did not lead to the kingdom's immediate decline, and ultimately, his adultery with Bathsheba was rewarded by the birth of his most magnificent son, "Solomon in all his glory."

Solomon's reign was even less free of pagan influence than David's due to his marriages to Egyptian and other pagan wives. While the brother-sister trope in Song of Solomon need not be interpreted as evidence of royal incest, it has been common to observe influences from Greece or Egypt, the Babylonian exile, or the Persian conquest.

The song attributed to Solomon may have been written by him or some unknown author between the twelfth and sixth centuries BCE. Some scholars maintain it was not canonized until the second century BCE. Ancient Hebrew scholars and early Christian fathers tended to explain away its erotic content as purely allegorical. Some rabbinical traditions came to interpret the brother-sister dialogue as representing the mutual love between God and Israel. Many Christians adopted and modified this allegorical tradition and saw it as a prophecy of Jesus's love for his church. I suggest in a later chapter that the allegorical usefulness of Song of Solomon was recalled, if not directly referenced, by Montesquieu in the eighteenth century and exploited by several of the nineteenth-century Romantic poets as a representation of the most sacred and transcendent expression of human passion.[16]

Most college students today have not perused Song of Solomon, but some are aware that royal incest was once practiced in the land of the Pharaohs. Some college students may argue forcefully that Song of Solomon was inspired by the "black but comely" queen of Sheba, who could have been Solomon's lover but not his uterine sister. Whether metaphorical or not, the brother-sister references in Song of Solomon, if such language were to appear in a modern love song, it would occasion embarrassed titters. Textbook editors must explain to "readers less familiar with Egyptian literature that the terms 'brother' and 'sister' were used by Egyptian lovers to indicate intimacy and affection":[17]

My one, the sister without peer,
The handsomest of all!
She looks like the rising morning star
At the start of a happy year.

Shining bright, fair of skin,
Lovely the look of her eyes,
Sweet the speech of her lips,
She has not a word too much.

Upright neck, shining breast,
Hair true lapis lazuli;
Arms surpassing gold,
Fingers like lotus buds.[18]

It is certainly reasonable to regard the terms brother and sister merely as terms of endearment. This is the commonly accepted explanation for modern readers, regardless of Ancient Egypt's high tolerance for sibling incest among gods, royals, and sometimes even commoners. It requires some straining to disassociate the ancient Near Eastern celebration of divine incest from the poetic references to brothers and sisters in what are regarded as the world's oldest love poems.

Most commentators reassure us that there is no cause for discomfort or alarm at the well-known lines in Song of Solomon that refer to a sister as "my bride" or "my spouse" in the King James and Douay translations. The Luther Bible uses the words, "*Meine Schwester, liebe Braut* [my sister, dear bride]." These words are explained and most commonly accompanied by assiduous clarifications that they carry no implications of royal or divine incest. The translation in the Jewish Study Bible is "My own, my bride," with the following editorial comment on the vocabulary: "'My own,' literally 'My sister.' Brother and sister are also used as terms of endearment in Egyptian love poetry. They symbolized closeness here, and are not to be taken literally as biological siblings."

But most modern readers are aware, to their horror, that several Egyptian pharaohs married their sisters, and since it is acknowledged that the Persian Empire had some influence on biblical canon, it should not be inconceivable that echoes of Zoroastrianian, Pharaonic, and other forms of sibling marriage could have informed the brother-sister trope in Song of Solomon.[19]

> Thou hast ravished my heart, my sister, *my* spouse; thou hast ravished my heart with one of thine eyes, with one chain of thy neck.
>
> How fair is thy love, my sister, *my* spouse! how much better is thy love than wine! and the smell of thine ointments than all spices! . . .[20]
>
> I am come into my garden, my sister, *my* spouse: I have gathered my myrrh with my spice; I have eaten my honeycomb with my honey; I have drunk my wine with my milk: eat, O friends; drink, yea, drink abundantly, O beloved.[21]

The *Jewish Encyclopedia* refers to some debate over the canonical authority of Song of Solomon in the early years of the Common Era, saying that "Probably the ground of opposition was its non-religious character: it does not contain the Divine Name (except 'Yah' in viii. 6, Hebr., as an expression of intensity); its love is sensuous; and its only ethical element is the devotion of one man to one woman in marriage." Solomon Frehof observes that "Many books were kept out of the biblical canon and there is a tradition that even this book was considered as one to be excluded." Benjamin Edidin Scolnic notes that some authorities even dismissed it as nothing more than "secular love poetry, a collection of love songs."[22]

In his encyclical *Ad caeli reginam*, Pope Pius XII "legitimately concluded" that Christ was the new Adam and Mary was the new Eve.[23] In his *Ineffabilis Deus,* on the immaculate conception, Pius IX invoked "the words of the prophets," regarding that queen "abounding in delights and leaning on her Spouse." J. A. Phillips pays scholarly tribute to the importance of the Virgin Mary as the "Second Eve," with solid documentation.[24] Marina Warner likewise recognizes the tradition with her admirable chapter on Mary as the "Second Eve" and bride of Christ.[25] There is a living Roman Catholic tradition that views Adam and Eve as precursors of Jesus and Mary. I view the sister-bride in Song of Solomon as an archetype in her own right. Sisters are not merely substitutes for mothers; in fact, within the complexities and contradictions of mythology, the sister may usurp the role of the nurturing mother or destroy the witch-mother, and she does both in the tale of Hansel and Gretel.

Maria Warner devotes a chapter to the tradition of Mary as "Second Eve," and Barbara Walker makes similar observations. But this mythology did not disappear in the Middle Ages. As of this writing, it can be found online, and not merely in some twittering blather but in a public statement by a Catholic scholar who possesses some of the highest credentials obtainable in Rome. Peter Howard, who earned his doctorate in Sacred Theology from the Pontifical University of St. Thomas Aquinas [Angelicum] in Rome, Italy, and is a member of the International Marian Association, speaks unequivocally of the Blessed Virgin as "the New Eve, acting as both Spouse of the New Adam (Jesus Christ) and His Mother."[26]

A striking and provocative development of the Second Eve image is in a painting by Cranach the Elder in which the Blessed Mother is seated beneath an apple tree, holding the baby Jesus, who holds an apple. This reverses the male-female roles in most portrayals of Eden, where it is customarily the woman who holds the apple. Cranach famously painted Aphrodite standing beneath an apple tree with the infant Cupid, and with a stag partially hidden in the background. Susan Foster has alluded to the painting's mixture of the imagery of Aphrodite, Artemis, and Eve.[27] Given Cranach's delight in clashing symbols and the orchestrating pagan and Christian iconography, it was almost inevitable that Prince Albert would perceive the painter's Artemis and Apollo as Adam and Eve.

SEXUALIZING THE VIRGIN AS BRIDE OF CHRIST IN SONG OF SONGS

As the New Adam and the New Eve, Jesus and Mary were envsioned as the bride and bridegroom of Song of Solomon by several of the early Christian fathers and medieval commentators with pronounced implications of divine incest.[28] Especially in medieval iconography, the Blessed Virgin reconciled the complicated theological symbolism of Mary as the New Eve, the mother, sister, and bride of Christ, combined in the notion of the queen of heaven. *Sermons on the Song of Songs*, by St. Bernard of Clairvaux Bernard of Clairvaux, blends these several iconic identities of the Blessed Virgin Mary and comes close to a celebration of divine incest.

Sister and bride of Song of Solomon, and appropriating the title queen of heaven from the book of Jeremiah, virtually make her the sister-wife of God and sister-wife of Song of Solomon. This was self-evident to the *Doctor ecstaticus*, Denis the Carthusian, when he commented:

> *For your breasts are more delightful than wine, more fragrant than finest oils.* . . . These could be the words of the special Bride addressed to her own Bridegroom and Son. . . . But they could also be the words of the Bridegroom addressed to his most beloved mother and so may be read: "You, O special Bride, mother and virgin, have asked for the kiss of my mouth, and I gladly consent to your request; *for your breasts are more delightful than wine*. . . . It may be said of those bodily breasts of the most divine Virgin that they, most blessed as they are, are made almost divine by the continual contact of the adorable, incarnate Bridegroom who sucked them; they are *more fragrant than the finest ointments,* more fragrant, that is to say, than the most delicious virginal milk which the Lord of all things took and sucked from them.[29]

Her coronation as queen of heaven is celebrated as the Fifth Glorious Mystery of the Holy Rosary, prayed daily by the Dominican Order, and declared in the Papal Encyclical of 1954 by Pius XII, *Ad caeli reginam*: "The Office of the Blessed Virgin applies to Mary many passages concerning the spouse in the Canticle of Canticles and also concerning Wisdom in the Book of Proverbs 8:22-31. The application to Mary of a 'garden enclosed, a fountain sealed up' mentioned in Canticles 4:12."

The erotic brother-sister pairing of Song of Solomon undergoes numerous transmogrifications in the writings of medieval mystics; these may involve transforming the identities of the speakers and assigning them unusual or "queer" sexual roles, as Shawn Krahmer and Stephen Moore have painstakingly demonstrated. Kramer, in particular, has demonstrated how intimations of divine incest crop up in Alan of Lille's twelfth-century *Cantica Canticorum ad laudem Deiparae Virginis Mariae*, which identifies the Virgin Mary with the sister-bride, and in Rupert of Deutz's *Commentaria in Canticum Canticorum (de Incarnatione Domine)* ca. 1125. The sister-bride, the beloved of Song of Solomon, has been viewed as a prophetic appearance of Mary's coronation as the queen of heaven. The following lines by twelfth-century mystic St. Bernard of Clairvaux are taken from *Sermons on the Song of Songs,* No. 8, and should be read in the sincerely devotional spirit in which they were written. Whether Bernard intended to advance a doctrine that the Blessed Virgin had become the wife of God invites speculation. What is definite here is that medieval mystics interpreted Song of Solomon as a prophesy of the role Mary would eventually be assigned by some spokespersons of the Roman Catholic Church.[30]

> Know yourself to be the Father's daughter in the Spirit of the Son. Know yourself to be the Bride, or sister of the Son, for you will find both these names given to her who loves the Son. Here is a text to prove it—I need not labor the point. The Bridegroom says to her, "Come into my garden, my sister, my Bride" (Sg 5:1). She is a sister because she is of the one Father, a Bride because she is in one spirit with him. For if carnal marriage makes two one flesh (Gn 2:24), why should not spiritual union make two one spirit (1 Cor 6:17).

Lines written by Father Victor Feltes, an ordained a Roman Catholic priest in the Diocese of La Crosse in 2009, demonstrate the spirit of St. Bernard of Clairvaux in *Sermons on the Song of Songs* and ring down through the ages:

> Mary and Jesus were mother and Son. They were never married in the way we think of marriage, so how can they be role models for your marriage? In Jesus and Mary, we see the perfect man with the perfect woman, we see the New Adam together with the New Eve, we see the King and Queen of Heaven and Earth. Jesus is the Bridegroom and Mary is the flawless image of the Church, which is His Bride. By seeing how Jesus loves her and how Mary loves Him we can learn much about how men and women are to serve and love each other.

I have invoked the encyclical Pius XII and Roman Catholic theologian Peter Howard with respect to the veneration of Jesus and Mary as the New Adam and New Eve. Again I invoke Peter Howard to frame their spousal relationship: "From the moment of her *fiat* to the Angel, Mary was inseparably bound up in God's work of Redemption, both in its accomplishment and in the distribution of its merits. And she exercises these roles as the New Eve, acting as both Spouse of the New Adam (Jesus Christ) and His Mother."[31]

As I write these words, the online edition *New Advent: The Catholic Encyclopedia,* dedicated to the Immaculate Heart of Mary, attests to the complex metaphor,

> to *the most holy Mother of God* as the most beautiful flower of the Church of God. (In regard to a twofold sense of this kind in the Scriptures, cf. "Zeitschrift fur katholische Theologie", 1903, 381.) The soul that has been purified by grace is also in a more remote yet real sense a worthy bride of Lord. The actual meaning of Canticles is not, however, to be limited to any one of these applications, but is to be appropriated to the elected "*bride of God* in her relation of devotion to God."

Mary's title, queen of heaven, was Latinized as *Regina Coeli* in the Latin Vulgate translation of Jeremiah's admonitions. Plucked from paganistic origins, these roles were attributed to the Virgin Mary in thirteenth-century Catholic hymnals and sung at Easter to commemorate her divine queenship and the resurrection of Jesus.

> *Regina caeli, laetare, alleluia;*
> *Quia quem meruisti portare, alleluia,*
> *Resurrexit, sicut dixit, alleluia:*
>
> Queen of heaven, rejoice, alleluia.
> For he whom you deserved to bear, alleluia,
> Has risen as he said, alleluia.

Queen of Heaven was mentioned in Jeremiah 44:18 when the prophet laments "burning incense to the Queen of Heaven and pouring out drink offerings to her." Raphael Jospe writes perceptively on the Roman Catholic veneration of the queen of heaven in his article, "Regina

Coeli: A Jewish Source," tracing its sources to the books of Jeremiah and Revelation: "And there appeared a great wonder in heaven; a woman clothed with the sun, and the moon under her feed, and upon her head a crown of twelve stars."[32] Mary is often depicted in statuary, paintings, and holy cards standing on a crescent moon. The queen of heaven, with starry crown standing upon the moon with a serpent beneath her foot, blends the prophesy of Genesis with the prophesy of Revelation, which endows the Second Eve with the attributes of royalty. Frequently in these icons, the serpent holds fruit in its mouth.

The woman herself will crush the serpent in some interpretations of scripture, while in others, it is "the hero born of woman."[33] Caravaggio famously painted Mary supporting the Christ Child as He places His foot on the serpent's head.[34] Attributes of the pagan goddesses were subsumed under her position as Theotokos (Mother of God); that position merited her assumption and she became queen of heaven and the sister and bride of Christ, signified in Song of Solomon.

DIVINE INCEST: ZEUS, HERA, AND MIXED REPORTS

Zeus and his sister, Hera, were lovers as well as siblings, although there are discrepancies as to the progress of their union. They were never exiles or fugitives, although the *Iliad* describes their sexual relationship as covert in Book 14: 290-95. Here Homer describes their lovemaking in terms suggesting secretiveness, as if they were an ordinary mortal brother and sister, employing terms that remind us of the almost universal human taboo: "and when he saw her desire was as a mist about his close heart / as much as on the time they first went to bed together / and lay in love, and their dear parents knew nothing of it."[35]

This casual suggestion of furtiveness is translated elsewhere as "they went to the couch and had dalliance together in love, their dear parents knowing naught thereof."[36] Homer, who is notably irreverential toward the gods, adds this mischievous innuendo to the legend, for Titans and Olympians were never bound by the incest taboos of mortals. Homer humanizes and domesticates the relationship between Zeus and Hera as if their parents, Cronos and Rhea, had brought them up in a normal household. Cronus made it a practice to devour all his children until Rhea gave him a stone to devour in place of Zeus, who grew rapidly to adulthood, overthrew Cronus, and banished him to Tartarus. Homer discarded various other accounts of the Zeus-Hera consortship, such as the legend that Zeus changed himself into a cuckoo and either raped or seduced his sister in this form, although this legend is not present in Hesiod's *Theogony*.

Homer wrote with lesser reverence about the sexual proclivities of Zeus, although he presumably wrote in same archaic period as Hesiod. His handling of the Olympians was less reverential, for throughout the *Iliad,* their faults, foibles, tyrannies, and deceits are frequently laid bare. While Hesiod's *Theogony* and the *Homeric Hymns* approach the gods with reverence and dread, Zeus consorts incestuously with several goddesses and adulterously with mortal women, "unknown to Hera, his sister and his wife." Zeus is not obliged to be circumspect when it comes to incest, but things are different for humans. The mortal brother or sister who imitate the consortship of Hera and Zeus suffer dire consequences, as in Ovid's treatments of the tragic moral fables of Biblis and Caunus, and of Canace and Macareus.

As far as mortals are concerned, the Greek and Hebraic revulsion and horror at sibling incest seem to coincide, and they have another overriding element in common—the depiction of a divine will that is arbitrary, capricious, cruel, and fearful of being challenged. The gods of the *Homeric Hymns,* like the God of Genesis, can do no wrong; they are right because of their might, and their virtue is identical to their omnipotence. Mortals must give all gods the respect they demand; it is the fate of humanity to submit to the will of the gods, to give evidence of their devotion, and to address the gods with the most obsequious reverence. Zeus, the king of the gods, like the Old Testament Yahweh, is a jealous God—jealous of other gods' powers and terrified of any challenge to his might.

ARTEMIS AND APOLLO AS ADAM AND EVE

The identification of Artemis and Apollo with Adam and Eve has not dominated the history of Western art and literature, nor has it been absent. There is vast literature on Artemis and Apollo, both individually and taken together. As brother and sister, they are perpetually intertwined in Hesiod's *Theogony*, and *Homeric Hymns* declares that they were fostered together and, therefore, twins. Both of them appear in the *Iliad,* where Apollo's arrows inspire dread, but where Artemis, "the virgin who delights in arrows," is humiliated by Hera with a physical beating. In terms of ancient shrines and religious veneration, both siblings received tremendous homage.

Physically beautiful and capable of great benevolence, Artemis and Apollo could be as wrathful and vengeful as any god and as whimsically cruel as wayward teenagers. Artemis transformed the unlucky Actaeon into a stag, who was ultimately ripped to shreds by his own hounds, simply because he inadvertently stumbled upon the woodland pool where she and her nymphs were skinny-dipping. Apollo revealed his jealous and vindictive nature when he flayed Marsyas alive after cheating in a musical competition. Marsyas played the flute, holding his own against Apollo, who played the lyre, until Apollo began to sing—a feat impossible for even the best of flautists.

Although incestuous pairings were hardly unusual among the Greek gods and titans—the marriage of Zeus and Hera, who were brother and sister as well as man and wife is frequently mentioned—Artemis and Apollo were never wedded. Although they sometimes worked as a team, were intimately linked in *Homeric Hymns,* and were venerated together at some shrines, they were never regarded as husband and wife and never portrayed as lovers, although many authors, both ancient and modern, focused on their perpetual closeness.[37]

Artemis was associated with the moon's supposed influence on the feminine cycle, and her lunar aspect contributed to her later identification with Rome's virginal moon goddess, the chaste Diana.[38] In Roman religion, however, Diana was incongruously identified with several other Greek and Roman women—whether virginal or not. She was, according to C. M. C. Green, practically a triune goddess, a splendid insight, and over the centuries, she was confused with numerous other figures, even the Greek moon goddess, Selene, who was said to have fifty children. In her Roman manifestation as Diana, Cicero noted she had numerous avatars, but she was not always virginal. Cicero simply noted that Diana's various appearances were as conflicting as the manifestations of Aphrodite, once noted by Plato.[39]

By and large, however, the ancient Greeks did not question the virginity of Artemis, an attribute, which, if we are to believe Robert Graves, may have been an innovation of the Greeks, who imported her from Asia Minor. Even Homer, who was not invariably respectful of the gods and slyly regarded the divine incest of Zeus and Hera as adventurous and spicy, offered no coy suggestions regarding Artemis and Apollo. Plutarch recognized that Apollo and Artemis were syncretized or melded with Egypt's amorous and fecund brother and sister gods Isis and Osiris, but resisted any impulse to follow up with a suggestion that Apollo and Artemis, like their Egyptian counterparts, were lovers in the womb.[40]

Given the complexity of and the contradictions inherent in all mythologies, it should not seem peculiar that Artemis was portrayed both as a goddess of childbirth and as a perpetual virgin. Nonetheless, her virginal character was important in Greco-Roman mythology and possibly influenced the Christian cult of the virgin. A body of scholarship and speculation has grown related to the merger of Artemis-Diana with Isis and the traditions in Christian art and iconography that preserved the symbolism of pagan goddesses in representations of Eve and the Virgin Mary, whom Christians viewed as the redemptive counterpart of Eve. Second-century Roman author Apuleius exemplified the ancient tradition of syncretization with his episodic novel, *The Golden Ass*, and his conflation of all the ancient goddesses into one.

> the Phrygians, first-born of men, call me Cybele, Mother of the Gods; in Attica, a people sprung from their own soil name me Cecropian Minerva; in sea-girt Cyprus I am Paphian Venus; Dictynna-Diana to the Cretan archers; Stygian Proserpine to the three-tongued Sicilians; at Eleusis, ancient Ceres; Juno to some, to others Bellona, Hecate, Rhamnusia; while the races of both Ethiopias, first to be lit at dawn by the risen Sun's divine rays, and the Egyptians too, deep in arcane lore, worship me with my own rites, and call me by my true name, royal Isis.[41]

Artemis's personality embodied Amazonian and Lesbian attributes, and she chose a train of nymphs as her closest companions to attend her at the hunt. She expected her companions to resist, as successfully as she did, all attempts on their virginity, regardless of how powerful the aggressor. She was the female cognate of her twin brother, the idealized athlete and forester; her emblematic portrayals are somewhat, although by no means entirely, masculinized, as in the statue *Diana of Versailles*, supposedly a fourth-century copy of an earlier Hellenistic original. Due to her ineluctable proximity to Apollo, there have been centuries of speculation concerning the closeness of their relationship, accentuated by an awareness of Apollo's jealousy of her friendship with her male hunting companion, Orion.

Apollo never had a wife, although his sexual escapades are notorious—both with males and with females. His emblematic heterosexual encounter is his attempted rape of the nymph Daphne, who was transformed into the laurel tree in her flight to escape him. The laurel crown, a wreath made from the bay leaf, the traditional crown of champion athletes and poets, is the symbol of Apollo's benevolence to mortals, but the flight of Daphne remains forever a reminder of his failure as a lover. This was not his only humiliating rejection; his approach to Cassandra, the princess of Troy, was another source of frustration. Enraged when she refused to grant him her favors in exchange for the gift of prophecy he bestowed on her, he made certain her prophesies would never be believed. Hyacinthus, a young Spartan athlete beloved by Apollo, was accidentally killed by Apollo's own discus, and from the tears of the god mingled with the blood of the fallen athlete, a flower grew that bears the name Hyacinth.

Artemis resonates, symbolically and on the lower frequencies, as both the mother and bride of Apollo. According to some accounts, she was born first, then assisted her mother in his delivery, which could be either the source of her position as the patroness of childbirth or its legacy. The Greek mythographers perpetually guarded her virginity and never made her the actual mother of anyone. Of course a virgin birth would have been possible within the Greek tradition of parthenogenesis.[42] Gods and goddesses alike begat children without the sweaty inconvenience of copulation, as in the case of Zeus, who brought forth Athena out of his own head and, according to *Homeric Hymns* and other sources, Hera gave birth to Hephaestus alone. Thus, Mary, the mother of Jesus, was not the first goddess to bring forth a god without engaging in sex. In this, as in other respects, she is alien to Jewish culture but in conformity with pagan tradition.[43]

The prenatal marriage of divine twins is often assumed in ancient mythologies, but if Artemis and Apollo were lovers in the womb, the archaic literature is not obsessed with the idea, although the ancient *Homeric Hymns* contain hints of a lover's relationship between them. The ninth of these hymns captures the perpetual affinity of the two, as if one cannot be mentioned without the other, for Artemis is not only fostered with Apollo but regularly returns to her brother, and he regularly anticipates her arrival.

> Muse, sing of Artemis, sister of the Far-shooter, the virgin who delights in arrows, who was fostered with Apollo. She waters her horses from Meles deep in reeds, and swiftly drives her all-golden chariot through Smyrna to vine-clad Claros where Apollo, god of the silver bow, sits waiting for the far-shooting goddess who delights in arrows.

The ninth hymn preserves them forever in a tableau of mutual expectation, and this is supplemented in the twenty-seventh hymn, which again shows Artemis as regularly drawn to her brother's dwelling, where she abandons the attributes of her accustomed hoydenism and presents herself in a more alluring costume and character: "this huntress who delights in arrows slackens her supple bow and goes to the great house of her dear brother Phoebus Apollo, to the rich land of Delphi, there to order the lovely dance of the Muses and Graces. There she hangs up her curved bow and her arrows, and heads and leads the dances, gracefully arrayed."[44]

Their eternal bonding resembles a marriage, for the two seem to be perfectly matched, and neither can form an enduring relationship with anyone else. Apollo exercises his masculine privileges with a series of escapades that produce several offspring; the faithful Artemis never engages in procreation. While the idea of their consortship is suggested in *Homeric Hymns,* it is never fully pronounced. The personalities of gods are not logical or consistent; they are the agglomerations of various contradictory oral legends arising from both the peasantry and the warrior-caste but not the property of the scribes and commentators who preserve them in written form. A myth comprises a hodgepodge of contradictory ideals, an *olla podrida* of folk and literary traditions. In Plato's *Symposium*, when Pausanias speaks of the two Aphrodites to represent the higher and the baser expressions of love, he reveals the inconsistency of mythology. The ambiguities that were true concerning Aphrodite were equally true for Artemis, especially when her identity became entangled with the mythologies of other goddesses.

Therefore, we may recognize the contradictory impressions of the relationship existing between Artemis and Apollo. Alberta Randall observes, "In their own way Apollo and Artemis were married. Unable to separate from each other, they found it difficult to form other relationships outside their own."[45] Randall is not an academically credentialed mythographer with an academic position, but the scholarly H. J. Rose says of Artemis, "with some certainty that originally she was a mother-deity and that she is not Greek." Her matronly functions as goddess of childbirth lead him to the assertion, reasonably enough, that "Artemis' virginity is not original."[46]

Robert Graves is impishly imaginative in his treatment of Artemis and Apollo in a passage revealing the influences of James G. Frazer, where he suggests a link between Apollo and Jesus, who die and are revived, and places Apollo in Adam's garden. Artemis, in Graves's interpretation, is traced to her Asiatic origins as a lovebird: "Apollo was also the ghost of the sacred king who had eaten the apple—the word Apollo may be derived from the root abol, 'apple', rather than from apollunai, 'destroy', which is the usual view. Artemis, originally an orgiastic goddess, had the lascivious quail as her sacred bird."[47]

With respect to her Mid-Eastern origins, her subsequent Romanization, and her survival as a venerated cult figure, classical authors have abided faithfully by the logic of Frazer in the twelve-volume third edition of *The Golden Bough.*

> Artemis was originally a great goddess of fertility, and, on the principles of early religion, she who fertilises nature must herself be fertile, and to be that she must necessarily have a male consort. On this view, Hippolytus was the consort of Artemis at Troezen, and the shorn tresses offered to him by the Troezenian youths and maidens before marriage were designed to strengthen his union

> with the goddess, and so to promote the fruitfulness of the earth, of cattle, and of mankind.[48]

The merging of contradictory attributes and the blending of all Greek goddesses into one is characteristic of Roman religion, but the tendency to fusion was already present in Greek religious mythology. The Romans came to link Artemis with Selene, goddess of the moon, who was not virginal, and whose consort was her brother, the sun god Helios. The Greeks, despite their consistent respect for Artemis's virginity, preserved her identity as a fertility goddess from earliest times. The contradictory and shifting attributes of the antique goddesses were retained in medieval allegories and symbolism that employed pagan mythology to reinforce the Christian concept of female chastity, as Jean Seznek has noted. Thus, we observe the merging of Aphrodite and Athena in the Britomart of Edmund Spenser's *The Faerie Queene,* and the merging of Artemis with Aphrodite, a tradition Edgar Wind has perceived as originating in Virgil's *Aeneid,* where "Venus appears disguised as a nymph of Diana, the goddess of love as a devotee of chastity."[49]

First the Greeks and then the Romans blended the Isis-Artemis imagery promiscuously with various goddesses in the Greek and pantheons, and Artemis played a role in later European iconography during the Renaissance. Christians copied and assigned some of her attributes to Mary, the Mother of Jesus. Plutarch alluded to her syncretization with Isis but avoided implying that Apollo and Artemis replicated the divine incest of Isis and Osiris. Greeks and Romans alike had a strong need for virgin goddesses, and to that end, they preserved the chastity of Athena, Hestia, and Artemis. Even Hera, the mother of numerous progeny, may call herself virginal due to her annual restorative bath. There are no virgin goddesses in Jewish tradition, but the Christian doctrine of Mary's perpetual virginity is strongly pre-echoed in Greco-Roman mythology.[50]

The paradox of Artemis's dual role as patroness of virginity and motherhood did not seem to bother the ancient Greeks, but by the late Renaissance, Artemis's virginity was somewhat compromised, and by the eighteenth century, it disintegrated entirely in the hands of the erudite, if erratic, John Lempriere. His *Classical Dictionary* subsumed her under her Roman counterpart, Diana, "supposed to be the same as Luna,

Proserpina, and Hecate," along with Isis and numerous other goddesses. In these manifestations, Lempriere endowed her with several lovers and at least one child, but he never married her to Apollo or blessed them with children.[51] At her shrine at Ephesus, Artemis was represented by a bizarre statue, its upper torso covered with the oval objects that led to her cognomen "multimamia," or many-breasted, representing her associations with fecundity, motherhood, and nursing.

The archetypal marriage of Artemis and Apollo was self-evident to Carl Jung, who related their pairing to numerous brother-sister consortships he found in Tarot cards, medieval alchemy, and the mythologies of various Western and non-Western peoples. This was a significant departure from his erstwhile subordination to the Freudian paradigm, which reflexively invoked the Oedipal longing as the source of eroticism.

> King and Queen, bridegroom and bride, approach one another for the purpose of betrothal or marriage. The incest element appears in the brother-sister relationship of Apollo and Diana. The pair of them stand respectively on sun and moon, thus indicating their solar and lunar nature in accordance with the astrological assumption of the importance of the sun's position for man and the moon's for woman.[52]

Plutarch and his contemporaries were conscious of the resemblance of Artemis and Apollo to Isis and Osiris but never entirely conflated these two sets of divine twins. The mythopoetic imagination suggests that Artemis should have lost her maidenhood to Apollo during the months when the two were embraced within Leto's womb. The problem of Artemis's virginity within the context of her syncretization with the Egyptian Isis was difficult for Plutarch to solve. He drops a hint but frustrates our curiosity with his suggestive placement of Artemis and Apollo so closely to their counterparts Isis and Osiris. Thus, Plutarch describes their syncretization:

> For my part, I think also that their naming unity Apollo, duality Artemis, the hebdomad Athena, and the first cube Poseidon, bears a resemblance to the statues and even to the sculptures and paintings

> with which their shrines are embellished . . . but Isis and Osiris were enamoured of each other and consorted together in the darkness of the womb before their birth. Some say that Arueris came from this union and was called the elder Horus by the Egyptians, but Apollo by the Greeks.[53]

If Isis was a lover to her brother in the womb, then her counterpart Artemis seems likely to have similarly experienced a prenatal loss of virginity. Neither Plutarch nor his literary predecessors commonly express any such suspicion, but apparently the common folk did, therefore the references of modern scholars to traditions that she was not perpetually virginal. Barbara G. Walker lists Artemis and Isis among the goddesses who copulated with their twin brothers "even in their mothers' womb." She also repeats but does not source the legend that Apollo copulated with or ravished Artemis on the Altar at Delos; so, too, does Félix Guirand in the *Larouse Encyclopedia of Mythology*. Elsewhere Walker even endows Artemis with motherhood when she references her identity as Artemis Caliste, or Ursa Major, the Great She-Bear, and mother of the Arcas, who is Ursa Minor, the Little Bear.[54]

THE RIVALRY OF APOLLO AND ORION

Artemis's determination to remain virginal, or at least unmarried, was protected by an irrevocable gift from Zeus, but being unmarried is not exactly the same as being virginal, and the gifts of the gods are not always as they seem. Artemis apparently had at least one flirtation that went so far as to arouse her brother's jealousy. Ancient and modern mythographers have suggested that Apollo, fearing his sister might surrender to Orion, a male hunting companion, tricked her into killing him. H. J. Rose and other mythographers have provided numerous irreconcilable accounts of how and why Artemis killed Orion and whether she did so accidentally or on purpose. Robert Graves says that Apollo, fearing she might "prove susceptible" to the allure of Orion, "the handsomest man alive," tricked Artemis into killing him. Bullfinch went further, reporting without giving his source that Orion "dwelt as a hunter with Diana, with whom he was a favorite, and it is even said she was about to marry him."[55]

Alberta Randall says, "The power of their brother-sister union was often mobilized covertly to eliminate potential rivals for either one's affection. Apollo's course of action suggests that jealousy was more the motivating passion underneath his scheme." Perhaps Apollo had nothing to fear, thanks to Zeus's promise, and it may be that Artemis's chaste fidelity was never in jeopardy, but the gifts of the gods often contain a sting of irony, and those who receive them often have regrets. Artemis may have come to find her celibacy burdensome, and in any case, the virginity of a goddess is easily restored. In any case, if Artemis and Apollo were indeed lovers in their mother's womb, Zeus's gift was somewhat belated and, at best, restorative.[56]

The pagan gods survived and thrived well into the Renaissance, as Edgar Wind, Jean Seznec, Douglas Bush, and others have observed, and over the centuries, the attributes of the gods were mingled with those of various pagan gods and Christian saints. A delightfully sensuous harmonizing of the characteristics of Artemis and Apollo with those of Adam and Eve was achieved by Renaissance master painter Louis Cranach the Elder, friend and frequent portraitist of Martin Luther. Cranach and his son, Louis Cranach the Younger, are less familiar to modern audiences than their Italian contemporaries and less familiar than their German contemporary, Albrecht Dürer, but their studio was prolific in its production of sensual paintings on classical and biblical subjects. Sometimes these combinations, which the Cranach studios produced in prodigious numbers, revealed a paganistic eroticism that was not confined to Roman Catholics despite the protests raised by puritanical Protestant reformers, most prominently Luther himself.[57]

In the course of several portrayals of these Olympian twins and numerous portrayals of Adam and Eve, Cranach mingled the attributes of these two sibling pairs. In each of these, Artemis is seated on a stag, one of her traditional symbols, and stags appear prominently in several of Cranach's paintings of Adam and Eve. In several of Cranach's paintings, Apollo bears the attributes of a hunter, but Cranach's studio also produced one painting, presumably of Adam and Eve with the infants Cain and Abel, in which the adult male is a hunter with a slain lion at his feet. Christian and pagan symbolism are intentionally mingled in Cranach's works as they are in those of his Italian counterparts. In this regard, Botticelli's

Primavera comes to mind with its richly ambiguous suggestions of Eden. For example the Adamic figure beneath the apple tree, wearing the winged sandals of Hermes, at first appears to be reaching for an apple, until one sees that he is probing the branches with his staff entwined with a serpent.

Cranach's *Apollo and Diana*, as it's titled, in the collection of the British royal family is easily mistaken for Adam and Eve, as its curators have noted. "Prince Albert bought the painting as Adam and Eve, which is understandable since the protagonists have no obvious attributes and as nude types are very like those of Adam and Eve in the Garden of Eden."[58]

The male figure is bearded, which is normal for Adam but out of character for Apollo, who is traditionally portrayed as beardless in contrast to the elder gods, Zeus and Poseidon. Nonetheless, this Adam possesses the traditional attributes of a hunter—a bow, arrows, a quiver—which this Artemis representation lacks, along with her usual vigorous athleticism. Her body is soft and fleshy, softer than the Aphrodites in several Cranach paintings. Additional ambiguity is lent by the attitudes and facial expressions of Cranach's characters. In the royal family's portrait, they seem to ignore one another's presence, but in other representations by Cranach, Artemis and Apollo exchange gazes that seem to transcend brother-sister affection. In one depiction, the seated Artemis is apparently attending to a thorn in her foot, which might be seen as symbolizing Adam and Eve's impending mortal vulnerability, although it also accords with traditional portrayals by other artists of Aphrodite in the act of removing a thorn from her foot.[59]

While resisting any tendencies to syncretism, John Milton could not resist evoking images of Artemis (Delia) and her attendant nymphs (Delia's train) in *Paradise Lost*, comparing their legendary beauty to that of Eve in her unfallen state.

> like a Wood-Nymph light,
> Oread or Dryad, or of Delia's train,
> Betook her to the groves; but Delia's self
> In gait surpassed, and Goddess-like deport,
> Though not as she with bow and quiver armed.[60]

Cranach had already divested Artemis of her bow and quiver a hundred years before Milton and, with apparent relish, accentuated her similarities to Eve. His good friend and admirer Martin Luther expressed discomfort with mingling Christian and pagan symbolism. Some Protestants in our day find Roman Catholic "Mariolatry" uncomfortably close to goddess worship and view it as a remnant of pagan myth and practice. Barbara Walker and Maria Warner have noticed some of these elements of pagan mythology in Mariolatry.[61]

"Tristan & Isolde" by John Duncan (1912)

– CHAPTER SIX –

ROYAL SIBLING INCEST AND THE AVUNCULAR TRANSMISSION OF KINGSHIP

MATRILINEAL KINGSHIP, which transmits royal privilege and power through the sister rather than the consort of the king, guarantees the purity of the bloodline, along with the certainty of royal lineage, while expanding the kinship network. Thus, in exogamous societies, avuncular succession through the sister's son can carry all the benefits of royal incest without the disadvantages. Most scholarly treatments of matrilineal succession focus on Africa and Asia to the neglect of Indo-European cultures. A once-influential theory of matrilineal succession was developed by Johann Bachofen, who asserted in *Mutterrecht* that promiscuity characterized all primitive societies, an idea that cannot be supported. Nor can his pontification that the replacement of matriarchy by patriarchy is an essential step in human progress. Nonetheless, Bachofen's errors do not undermine his observations. The historical existence of matrilineal institutions is undeniable, and prior to DNA testing, matrilineality was more conveniently ascertained than patrilineality. The idea that all "primitive" societies showed traces of a matrilineal past was accepted by Friedrich Engels, Lester Ward, Charlotte Perkins Gilman, Emile Durkheim, and W. E. B. Du Bois, among others.[1]

Royal incest is usually discussed in the context of ancient Egypt, Hawaii, or Peru. These acknowledged exceptions to the universal incest taboo were attested to, as we have seen, by Plato, Aristotle, Aquinas, Darwin, and Freud. An abhorrence of sibling incest has been expressed universally in every society—except when it pertains to royals and divinities.

Livy, the Roman historian, reported that Celtic patriarchal leadership was passed down matrilineally through the sisters of chieftains.[2] Another Roman historian, Tacitus, commented on the sanctity of the sister-son relationship among the virile barbarians of Europe's primeval forests, where Germanic tribesmen regarded their matrilineal nephews as their closest kin.[3] European travelers noticed an avuncular tradition when first encountering the "noble savages" of Africa's pristine *Urwald*.[4]

The assertion that the marriage of brother to sister existed as a means of keeping wealth within royal families is specious and unconvincing. Exogamy, as Aquinas and others have noted, is socially and politically desirable and efficient in practical terms to maintain and increase wealth. With exogamy arrives exigencies regarding "dowry" and "bride price." While dowry customs vary among cultures and classes, they sometimes have the function of increasing family property or securing it by expanding the investment in a network of political and military alliances and religious obligations. An alternative explanation for the practice of "royal incest" is that it provided double insurance for the purity of the royal line. The identity of mothers is more certain than that of fathers. The king in a matrilineal dynasty might marry his sister in order to guarantee his son's position in the line of succession rather than leaving things to chance. The sister's son is always his blood relation, but his wife's son may not be. In ancient Egypt, by fathering his sister's children, the king could claim his nephew as his biological son, thus doubly reinforcing his claim to be not only the king but also the father of kings.[5]

SIBLING INCEST IN MEDIEVAL STORIES

Adultery and incest, often combined, were prominent and recurrent motifs in medieval epic tradition from Dante to Thomas Malory. Broad definitions of incest, imposed by the medieval church, were reflected in the prohibition of marriage between in-laws, as Elizabeth Archibald has noted.[6] Dante's encounter with Francesca and Paolo di Remini in *Inferno* led to his passing allusion to Tristan and Isolde. Since these legendary transgressors were related to their partners by marriage, all were damned for the sin of adultery compounded by incest. Tristan and Isolde's tragedy, the paradigmatic example of romanticized anti-social behavior, occupies a considerable portion of Thomas Malory's *Le Morte d'Arthur* and mirrors Lancelot and Guinevere's adultery. Most versions of the Arthurian legend attribute the downfall of Camelot to adultery and incest. Both Lancelot and Tristan behave in violation of the barbarian code of *Kriegertreue*—fealty to the warlord, which Tacitus called *comitatus,* recalled in Anglo-Saxon poetry. Tristan, therefore, behaves in violation of traditional warrior code and Christian doctrine.

Tristan and Isolde

If one entertains the speculation of some scholars that Tristan's mother was King Marc's sister, the legend becomes even more complicated, for that makes Tristan himself the product of sibling incest. This hypothesis has attracted the attention of Elizabeth Archibald and Claude Evans, who cite the work of André de Mandach.[7] With the collaboration of Eve-Marie Roth, and at the suggestion of a vaguely referenced "*érudit français,*" Mandach pursues this notion and, on the basis of painstaking investigation, arrives at the following:

> It has been suggested to us by a French scholar that Tristan was the fruit of clandestine amours between Marc and his sister. The pregnancy of his sister led Marc to marry her to a Breton chief named Rivalen de Léon. If one believes the Tristan of Thoma, the baby was born in the course of voyage over the English Channel. Both Rivalen and his mother were killed by a usurper shortly after he came into the world.
>
> Tristan would have grown up in Lénois with Governal as his patron. In the course of a voyage, he arrived at the court of King Marc of Cornwall, where he spent his youth. The kin loved him "as a son" perhaps not at all ignorant of his origin. He would not have any plausible reason to divulge to Tristan the ambiguous secret of his birth.[8]

Sibling incest would certainly magnify the anti-social behavior that is central to the saga of Tristan and Isolde. This same complication is preserved as folk tradition in the fifteenth-century Danish ballad *Tistram og Jomfru Isolt*, an admittedly obscure transmogrification of the legend that makes Tristan and Isolde twins separated in infancy. Their mother, on learning of a prophecy that they were destined to become lovers, sends Isolde off to be brought up in a faraway kingdom; Tristan eventually woos her without realizing she is his sister, and they consummate their love. There are several different versions of this ballad, most of them ending in the tragic deaths of the lovers, as one might anticipate, but medieval scholar Paul Schach has discovered a rendition in which "the most profound and poignant love tragedy of the Middle Ages has been '*zersungen*' into an insipid jingling *marchen* with a happy ending."[9]

Gottfried von Straßburg's *Tristan* alludes to Adam and Eve in a scene, "the structure of which is modelled on the Fall and the expulsion from the Garden of Eden," as Annette Wolfing has noted.[10] There is perhaps an indirect allusion in that Tristan and Isolde consummate their passion after drinking an enchanted potion, which may be a reminder that the fruit of Eden's tree has rightly or wrongly been viewed as an aphrodisiac. Alfred Lord Tennyson and Richard Wagner, who recycled the story of Tristan and Isolde, made no obvious comparisons between adulterous transgression and original sin. Tennyson's *Idylls of the King* did not romanticize infidelity or incest but portrayed Tristan and Isolde as consumed by guilt and recrimination.

Le Morte d'Arthur

It is well known that historical figures Charlemagne and William of Normandy were conceived out of wedlock, so too the fictitious King Arthur. Geoffrey of Monmouth's enormously mythical *Historia Regum Britanniae* (ca. 1136) asserts that Uther Pendragon disguised himself with the aid of Merlin the magician to deceive and impregnate Igraine, wife of the Duke of Cornwall, to engender Arthur, the future king. Thomas Malory elaborated this fiction in his *Le Morte d'Arthur* (1485), reiterating the adultery motif and seasoning it with incest by having Arthur impregnate Morgause, the wife of King Lot, although unaware she was his half-sister. Matters are complicated by the fact that her name is sometimes spelled "Morgawse" and elsewhere given as "Morcades." In the 1981 film *Excalibur*, Morgause is confounded with Morgan La Fey, who deliberately seduces him, and Arthur, under a spell at the time, is unaware of their relationship. In Malory's and all subsequent versions, the product of that union is the villain Mordred, who was both Arthur's son and his nephew. Mordred carries on the family tradition of adultery and incest when he seduces Queen Guinevere, his father's wife, thus his stepmother, and usurps the throne.

In the darkest versions of this myth, Arthur orders a "slaughter of the innocents" when Merlin reveals he is destined to die by the hand of Mordred. The recurrent themes of murder, incest, and adultery in the Arthurian and other medieval romances reveal a persistent demand for the sentimentalization of sexual transgression in the Western tradition from the Middle Ages to the present day. It also reveals the persistence of the sibling incest motif in classical, Hebraic, and Germanic mythologies.

THE STORY OF CHARLEMAGNE AND ROLAND

A reverse cognate of the legendary King Arthur's accidental incest is the fable of Charlemagne's "unspeakable sin," his fictional affair with his sister, Gisele, that produced the hero Roland, both his nephew and his son.[11] The legend is of interest only as a literary artifact and is not taken seriously by historians. Gisele would have been in her early twenties, and the semi-fictitious Roland no older than twelve when he died at Roncevaux.

At the time of his birth, Charlemagne's parents were united informally according to the barbarian custom of *Friedelehe,* and their marriage was later solemnized by the church. Charlemagne's first partnership was his *Friedelehe* union with Himiltrude, which produced a daughter, Amaudru, and a son, Pepin the Hunchback, whom Charlemagne acknowledged but considered unfit to become his successor. The relationship with Himiltrude was informally dissolved around the time of his first Christian marriage to Desiderata, canonically annulled after a year, which produced no children. His first successful and enduring marriage to Hildegard of the Vinzgau lasted twelve years and produced nine children. His second enduring marriage was to Fastrada, with whom he had two more children. He is known to have had at least four concubines, with whom he produced at least nine additional children.

There is no historical basis for the legend that he was the father of the hero Roland; it is intriguing as literary myth but dismissed as so absurd that most historians find it unworthy of comment. Charlemagne was certainly no saint, although he was canonized in 1165 by antipope Paschal III to gain favor with Frederick Barbarossa, but the Catholic Church has not recognized this canonization. This may or may not have been due to his sexual conduct, which was decidedly Old Testament. Like his father, Charlemagne paid little heed to the Christian prohibitions on concubinage and extramarital sexual relations. The Bible prohibited sexual relations with or coveting "thy neighbor's wife" but did not prohibit men from polygamy, and it actually approved the exploitation of women taken as prisoners of war. The Christian church officially condemned sex outside of marriage, but males of the warrior caste paid little heed to the frowns of the clergy, and concubinage was socially acceptable for males in medieval Europe, just as it had been for the ancient Hebrews. The medieval church's definitions of incest could be even stricter than the ones in Leviticus, although the Pope had the power to set aside certain of these restrictions.

The myth of Charlemagne's incestuous relationship with his full sister Ghisla—her name is variously given as Ghisela, Gillen, Gisela, Gisèle, or

Gisla—has its roots in the legendary "*Péché du Charlemagne*," the "sin so great that he feared to confess it." Roland is identified as Charlemagne's nephew in *La Chanson de Roland*, but not as his son, although various allusions to the legend are preserved in other works of the imagination. Several texts refer to visions of Charlemagne in hell for an unnamed sin of the flesh that was so abominable he could never bear to confess it, but there are legends that he eventually confessed his sins, did penance, amended his life, and was paying his dues in purgatory.

One fiction speaks of his miraculously receiving absolution after the sin was revealed by an angel who descended from heaven while Saint Giles was celebrating mass and presented the saint with a parchment revealing that Charlemagne's sin was incest with his sister, who was pregnant with his child. The sin would be forgiven if he did not persist, and the missive instructed him to take good care of the child who would serve him in his hour of need. This legend is preserved, or at least alluded to, in a stained glass window in the Chartres Cathedral and a fresco in the Saint-Jean-Baptiste du Loroux-Bottereau Church. There is also an illustration of this miraculous event in a psalter that belonged to Lambert le Bègue. While the aforementioned literary and iconic representations derive from the thirteenth century or later, the legend of Charlemagne's secret sin has been traced to 824, when Belgian mystic Wetti of Reichenau experienced a vision of purgatory, where an animal tore at his emperor's genitals.[12]

Aside from its other aspects of implausibility, the tale clashes with the fact that St. Giles lived—if he ever existed—two centuries before the time of Charlemagne. Einhard's *The Life of Charlemagne* refers to Gisele only briefly and only as a woman of extraordinary piety, who, after two broken betrothals, entered the convent at Chelles Abbey, where she eventually became abbess. Little more is known of her other than Einhard's report that Charlemagne was very devoted to her. Barton Sholod, who investigated the matter with diligence, alluded to Charlemagne's extraordinary protectiveness regarding his daughters and his sister, and the fact that he never arranged marriages for any of his daughters.[13] Sholod also observes that Gisele "was an active member of the court in spite of her duties as an abbess."[14]

A scandalous legend that Gisele was the mother of Roland apparently arose in the thirteenth century, most notably in the *Karlomagnus Saga* (ca. 1230). Inspired by the legend of the unmentionable sin, the story may or may not have existed prior to that date in oral tradition. It was circulated in such fourteenth-century texts as *Le Myreur des Histoires* by Jean d'Outremeuse and in the anonymous Chanson de Geste, *Tristan de Nanteuil*, which says "*Que ce fut le péché quand engendra Roland en sa sœur germaine* [That it was a sin when Roland begot his full sister.]" All of the foregoing, however, are literary concoctions, as is the *Chanson du Roland*, which mentions no incest.[15]

The literary traditions that make Charlemagne the father of Roland all render him conscious and culpable of his sin. Joseph J. Duggan identifies the legend's numerous sources, including "the fragmentary Occitan version of the Song of Roland known as *Ronsasvals*, Charlemagne himself mentions, in his regrets over Roland's body, that he has sinned with his sister."[16]

Beau neveu, je vous ai eu par mon grand péché de ma sœur et par mon erreur. Je suis ton père et ton oncle également et vous êtes, cher seigneur, mon neveu et mon enfant.	Fair nephew, I have had you through my great sin with my sister, and by my fault. I am equally your father and your uncle and you are, dear knight, my nephew and my child.

As Duggans observes, no version of the Roland saga is historically valid. The only historical record of Roland's existence is a brief mention by Einhard regarding the Spanish campaign of 778, from which he withdrew after achieving very little success. On returning to France, his army was ambushed while passing through the Pyrennes, but there is no detailed contemporary account of the attack or where exactly it occurred. Einhard mentions "Roland, the lord of the Breton March, along with many others died in that skirmish." Nothing else is said of Roland or of any relationship to Charlemagne. While Stefan Weinfurter, in his *Karl der Grosse: Der Heilige Barbar*, devotes some attention to the mythical figure of Roland and his special status among the sons of Charlemagne, he reveals no interest in the "fair nephew" legend. Éric Vanneufville takes pains to demolish the literary myth, pointing out that Gisele was not born until 757, and Roland would have been perhaps a child of ten in 778 at the time of the ambush.[17]

Novelists have pounced on the imaginative opportunities presented by the myth, and Laure-Marie Lapouge expands on it in her *Moi, Ghisla, Soeur de Charlemagne*, presented as a first-person narrative that exploits Einhard's *lacunae* regarding the lives of the principals. Thus, Lapouge does not assign to Roland his traditional heroic role in the *Chanson de Roland* as commander of Charlemagne's rear guard, at the battle of Roncevaux, a matter of spurious historicity to begin with. She arranges for Roland to be killed in the ambush, but as a boy of ten in the company of his foster father. There is no need for her to preserve the heroic mythology of Roland's final battle; she is concerned only with the legend of Charlemagne's mourning the death of a son who is also his nephew. She undertakes, furthermore, the task of presenting this as a story of romantic love and preventing her invention in a manner that departs from convention: "In the end, I intended that this story of forbidden love would have nothing to do with what is presently evoked almost automatically by the word incest, nowadays connected above all with rape and pedophilia, and therefore to a power relationship of one over the other and hence to violence imposed by one on the other."[18]

Her stated intention was to fashion Ghisla as a character who gradually matures, to portray her as maintaining a relationship of equality with her brother—"*rester l'égal de son frère*"—and to avoid the conception of violence imposed by strength over weakness usually evoked by the word incest. In an interview, Lapouge remarked in passing that she never intended to write a story of "incest intergénérationnel" between father and daughter, which would be emblematic of the abuse of power by parental authority. A brother and sister are more or less equal, in the author's view, although problematized by the fact that, in her relationship with Charlemagne, Ghisla must deal not only with a brother but with an emperor, "a person of great stature, a powerful masculine protagonist." The relationship is consensual, but she is forced into sexual relationships with other men to conceal the paternity of the offspring resulting from her illegal and antisocial relationship with her brother. She also admits to an unspecified number of other affairs despite which she convinces the reader, and apparently Charlemagne as well, of her certainty regarding the fathering of her children.

In one conversation, she wonders whether suspicion might be aroused when Charlemagne chooses Ghisla instead of his wife to accompany him on a diplomatic mission. Charlemagne responds that he requires her assistance since she reads Latin with ease and can decipher Greek. She accompanies her imperial brother on many of his travels, and he arranges for them to sleep together. Ghisla eagerly becomes sexually active at the age of twelve, and both Charlemagne and the reader are asked to believe that she has complete control over her reproductive activities. She conceives Roland at the age of nineteen, and she tells us that both Roland and her daughter, Juliana, are the children of Charlemagne despite her promiscuity and her marriages of convenience. When she tells him she is again pregnant, he insists that she marry Roland to provide a pseudo-father for the daughter she is expecting, and she goes along with the charade. When she subsequently asserts her right to take Ganelon as a lover, he gives his silent consent but also conveys signs of jealousy.

Charlemagne trusts her timing, never doubting her word that the children are his own, and she boasts that he prefers them over his legitimate children. Ultimately this royal incest is impossible to conceal, and when Ganelon tells her he knows all, does not judge, and loves her nonetheless, she is astonished:

> *Comment avait-il devine? Je le savais suffisamment fidèle pour taire ce secret à tout jamais. Mais s'il avait compris, d'autre, sans doute, avient aussi entrevu la vérité. Comment Charles et moi avions pu être näifs a point de croire que nos perpétuelles manoevres resteraient inaperçues?* (293, 296)
>
> [How had he guessed? I knew he was sufficiently faithful to conceal the secret forever. But if he had understood, others had doubtless also guessed the truth. How could Charles and I have been so naive as to believe at all that our perpetual maneuvers could remain unperceived.]

There have been other novelistic treatments of Charlemagne's supposed sexual intrigues, but Lapouge's fiction has a purpose.[19] She conceived Ghisla as a pubescent rebel and invented her collaboration with Charlemagne as a life of incest and adultery. The work incorporates a great deal of pseudo-history and presents a satire on the the fictional lives of Isolde and Guinevere and the real life of Eleanor of Aquitaine. The extraordinarily daring aspect of Lapouge's fable is the shockingly unconventional license she takes with Charlemagne's life. Lapouge makes Ghisla's autobiography a device for theorizing about the secret power of medieval women of the warrior caste. Ghisla and Charlemagne are confrontational lovers who manipulate one another throughout the novel, and Ghisla constantly insists that the relationship is equal. She pressures Charlemagne into granting her a divorce from her first husband, then, after sleeping in his embrace fully clothed—*tout habillé à mes cotes*—he awakens momentarily from his sleep and, tightening his embrace, murmurs, "You are my light—*ma lumière*—Ghisla."

In the end, Ghisla confesses, not without irony, to what she calls her only "veritable fault," the confidence that God and the Savior will understand and pardon "the love from which they have never fled." She justifies her unrepentant relationship with her brother by citing the description he reveals of his life's work—the construction of roads and canals, of cathedrals, monasteries, palaces, and hospices, and the promotion of education—his project to renovate the world, to restore knowledge, to reconstitute the glory of Athens and the grandeur of Rome, an immense work, which, despite all discouragements, he will never renounce. She tells us that Charlemagne has dedicated everything to their child Roland, who died at Roncevaux:

> *"C'est pour Roland," m'a-t-il dit un jour. Notre enfant disparu est la pierre angulair, du monde que je veux créer.*
>
> ["It is for Roland," he said to me one day. Our lost child is the cornerstone of the new world I want to create.]

She projects a vision of a new world, but its cornerstone is Roland, who symbolizes her code of honor and her worldview that are barbarian at the core, with only a thin Roman Catholic veneer. The novel's emergent theme is the primeval feminism that is revealed in an outburst by Bertrada, the Iron Queen, the mother of Ghisla and Charlemagne. Her brother is the true and legitimate king of the Franks, because he is the son of the sovereign mother of the Merovingian Clan. She explodes vehemently against the "aberration" of paternal succession asserted by Clovis, the first Christian king, and invokes the ancient law as the only law—"before the Christians imposed their principles"—the only law that guarantees the preservation of the royal blood and the aristocratic caste.

> "I speak of power," Bertrade declares, "the manner of its transition, and the role of women. . . . In the old days . . . it is your son . . . Roland who would be the future king of the Franks . . . and if you had a son with the king, who in this case is your brother, it is that child who would be the sole heriter. . . ."
>
> Ghisla manages to respond to this tirade with a forced laugh. "If I understand, the system is an incitement to incest."
>
> Amused by this reflection, Bertrand answers, "*Theoretiqument, oui.*"[20]

Lapouge has employed daringly unconventional methods to focus our attention on matrilineal power by linking it to royal incest—the only variety of sibling incest social scientists presently seem to admit has ever existed. Barbara G. Walker's *The Women's Encyclopedia of Myths and Secrets* has perhaps exaggerated the predominance of ancient royal incest, but there is unquestionably deep insight in her observations:

> Brother-sister incest was customary in ancient ruling families, when it was felt that a king and queen should be offspring of the same mother, so the true line of succession would not be weakened. Egyptian pharaohs married their sisters as a matter of course because their thrones were inherited through the female line. One pharaoh with only one son and one daughter suggested to his wife that the children might marry outside the family. The queen angrily rejected the idea: "Dost thou wrangle with me? Even if I have no children after those two children, is it not the law to marry them one to the other?"[21]

Exogamy—the intermarriage of two different clans—clearly has potential benefits in terms of enriching the biogenetic heritage of any tribe, and exogamy also brings with it several socio-political benefits, for it is a mechanism for combining and increasing the wealth of the families that unite their fortunes. Exogamy expands kinship networks and enriches the political, economic, and social contacts of two families, as well as their military alliances. These obvious material benefits of exogamy call into question the traditional hypothesis that "royal incest" was practiced to conserve wealth. Lapouge provides a more convincing explanation for royal incest when she speaks through Bertrada, the mother of Ghisla and Charlemagne:

> *"On ne sait jamais si les pères sont les vrais péres."*
> [One never knows if the fathers are the real fathers.]

Matrilineal succession assures the royal children are truly royal, for as Bertrada sees it, only the "mére dominant" can know the certainty of royal blood.

JOHN GOWER AND THE "TALE OF CANACE AND MACHAIRE"

The character of Aeolus is described as "dear to the gods" in *The Odyssey*, but his status in Greek mythology is complicated. Homer implies that he is a man, although he displays supernatural powers when he gives Odysseus an ox-hide bag containing all winds but the west. Over the centuries, Aeolus occupied an indefinite position somewhere between god and mortal. According to one myth, he was a son of Poseidon, and, at least potentially, a demigod. Like Polyphemos, also a son of Poseidon, he possessed limited supernatural attributes, but in other accounts, he was merely the son of Hippotes, a mortal man. Gustav Schwab calls him a god, and Robert Graves speaks of "the divine status of Aeolus's daughters and sons." Therefore, his character evolves, as do the characters of other mythical figures over the centuries. His myths are combined, becoming complicated, contradictory, and transmogrified in oral and written reiteration.

Although the Aeolus of Homer's brief interlude is not described as a god, merely as king of the island of Aeolia, he is endowed with a godlike privilege when he benevolently promotes the marriage of his six sons to his six daughters, thereby abrogating the mortal taboo of incest. Centuries after Homer, Euripides modified the already ancient legend of Aeolus and his children into a play that has been lost. According to scholarly consensus, Ovid based his version of Aeolus on Euripides's play, which blended several conflicts.

The reports of Aeolus's views on sibling incest are as contradictory as the reports on his divine status. In their authoritative account, the editors of the Loeb Classical Library cite Homer's reference to his promotion of six incestuous marriages but report the obvious linkage to Euripides's drama, the Aeolus that survives today only in fragments. Presumably Euripides was familiar with its legendary setting in which Macareus, one of Aeolus's sons, fell in love with and impregnated his sister Canace. Without revealing this to his father, Macareus convinced Aeolus to allow all the sons and daughters to intermarry, and Aeolus decreed that the brothers should draw lots to see which brother would marry which sister. The story resembles the previously alluded to rabbinical myth that Adam offered a similar proposition to Cain and Abel. As in the case of Cain, fate did not favor Macareus, and he was denied his favorite sister. When Canace gave birth to Macareus's child, an enraged Aeolus sent her a sword with an order to kill herself and ordered the death of the child by exposure.

Against the background of this legend, and with full knowledge of the incestuous dynamics within Aeolus's family, Ovid wrote his own tragedy of Canace and Macareus centuries after Euripides's tragic presentation of Aeolus's wrath.

John Gower presents the "Tale of Canace and Machaire" within the episodic framework of his *Confessio Amantis,* an admixture of serious moralizing and satirical irony, conveyed in a tone that is at times almost sacrilegious and bordering on the heretical. It is presented as a confession and dialogue between a central character, Aman, and his Confessor, a priest of Venus, also identified as Genius, and provides moral counseling through a series of episodes in which Christian and pagan values are occasionally at odds. C. G. Macaulay, the admirable editor of the 1901 edition, views the entire work as "grotesquely absurd," because Gower's Confessor is portrayed as both a Catholic priest and a devotee of Venus. At times, he presents one set of Christian principles against another through fables that seemingly illustrate some moral lessons to the neglect of others.

Gower tells us Genius's motive is to present an example of how the passion of "melancholy" can provoke rage and vengeance. He narrates how King Eolus (a version of Ovid's and Euripides's Aeolus) had a son named Machaire (Euripides's Macareus) and a daughter named Canace (unchanged from Euripides's telling), who were raised together from infancy, and how, at puberty, Cupid's fiery arrow penetrated their hearts so that Canace was impregnated by her own brother, leading the father to such an excess of rage and fury that he orders his daughter's death. The speakers throughout these narratives may sometimes appear naive and humorless, but Gower was a man of learning and a canny court politician, but it is now conceded that Gower's moral positions and those of Genius, Gower's literary persona, were not always self-evident. It has been claimed that Gower's contemporary, Geoffrey Chaucer, disapproved of his presentation of incest based on the words of his Man of Law in the Canterbury Tales.[22] Gower's purpose, however, is to express dismay at the tragically unrestrained passions of all three characters: father, son, and daughter. Their tragedy is, after all, set in motion by the tyrannical Eolus's closeting of a pubescent son and daughter in the same chamber. Gower's masterpiece is further complicated by the tricky introduction of Cupid's intervention, and his assertion that the siblings are following nature.

Gower's Canace and Machaire remind us of Adam and Eve, for they are as much a product of Genesis as of Ovid. Gower's irreverent commentary on Genesis evades many readers. The isolated young couple is not tempted by a loathsome serpent or by his imaginary Cupid; they are victims of their solitary confinement. Genius neither ignores nor dismisses the incest taboo, but since he is ignorant of Darwin and Westermarck, he does not attribute it to instinct. He presents the mutual attraction as something more than carnal lust that is a natural reaction to extreme circumstances. Although C. G. Benson and other scholars have expressed some discomfort with this, C. G. Macaulay and other specialists in the field have not only noticed but seemingly shared Gower's compassion for his subjects. Elizabeth Archibald writes,

> I agree with Macaulay's comment that "In spite of the character of the subject, it must be allowed that Gower tells the story in a very touching manner"; but he goes too far, I think, in arguing that for Gower "there is nothing naturally immoral about an incestuous

> marriage", other than the Church's disapproval (note on *CA* 3. 172). It is certainly true that Gower shows no horror or disbelief at the idea of a brother and sister feeling desire for one another.[23]

According to Benson's sampling, literary scholars who read the "Tale of Canace and Machaire" demonstrate no remarkable "third party *Inzestscheu*" and tend to view the sibling lovers sympathetically. Medievalists deplore but are deeply moved by the hypothetical situation of pitiably neglected children huddling together in isolation. Such a situation was unlikely in the Middle Ages, when brothers and sisters were so often separated in early adolescence. Parents commonly exported their teenagers to be trained or disciplined in other households. This custom, along with the practice of early marriage, minimized the possibility of sexual experimentation between siblings beyond the stage of infantile erotic play.[24] James A. Schultz notes that in medieval romances and studies of German nobility, "one half to one third of the daughters who married did so when they were between twelve and fifteen."[25] Girls were usually under pressure to become sexually active—to "be fruitful and multiply"—in early adolescence. Margaret of Provence and Eleanor of Aquitaine, for example, were married to kings of France in their early teens to guarantee production of male heirs.[26]

Achibald correctly notes the absence of "horror or disbelief" in the voice of Gower's narrator, but we must never lose sight of the fact that Gower presents the story of Canace and Machaire within a framed narrative and in the words of a persona who, as Benson correctly observes, shares his disapproval. We must remind ourselves, however, that framed narratives are deceptive, and misunderstandings are frequent in discussions of love. Gower's fable is presented through a secondary narrator whose moralizing tone can hardly be seen as a defense of sibling incest, to which he never gives approval, albeit he does not seem horrified by the idea that Canace and Machaire can and do fall in love, nor does he express disbelief.

Gower is neither so naive nor so heretical as to pretend he has resolved the perennial dichotomy of determinism and free will. There is more than a hint of the inevitable in this story of two adolescents confined by their father in an infantile Garden of Eden. The "falle" and "misdede" of these youngsters seem almost predestined by Nature, and the whisperings of Cupid, the God of Love. Mighty forces at work, both natural and superhuman, but Gower makes no mention of Eolus's special relationship to the gods, nor does he allude to the ambiguities in the tradition that makes him a promoter of sibling marriage.[27]

> Ther was a king which Eolus
> Was hote, and it befell him thus,
> That he tuo children hadde faire,
> The Sone cleped was Machaire,
> The dowhter ek Canace hihte.

In G. C. Macaulay's analysis in the 1901 edition of *Confessio Amanti*, Genius, both a priest and a devotee of Venus, explains to Amans that "These two grew up together in one chamber, and love made them blind, so that they followed the law of nature, and saw not that of reason." We cannot deduce Gower's and Macaulay's intentions. My purpose is to note the ambiguity and complexity of Gower's presentation, as Macaulay so obviously did when he observed "the grotesque absurdity when the Confessor occupies himself in demolishing the claims of Venus; to be accounted a goddess, and that too without even the excuse of having forgotten for the moment that he is her priest."[28]

The Confessor's discourse approaches the heretical and is not entirely anachronistic. He seemingly hints at times at inevitability, and while any suggestion of predestination seemingly antedates Martin Luther's doctrines by a century, Christian theologians had problematized the matter since ancient times.[29] Gower does not deprive his characters of free will or culpability, but there is without question a tone of inevitability in the story of Canace and Machaire, and there is a dichotomy within the poem between nature and reason. The young couple are subjected to an extraordinary trial, because, from infancy, they are confined and isolated, presumably by their father, and always within the same chamber.

> Be daie bothe and ek be nyhte,
> Whil thei be yonge, of comun wone
> In chambre thei togedre wone,
> And as thei scholden pleide hem ofte,

They dwell together day and night in close cohabitation, right up until they reach the "lusti age,"—let us say the age of Romeo and Juliet, or of modern high school freshmen—and they play innocently enough,

> Til thei be growen up alofte
> Into the youthe of lusti age,
> Whan kinde assaileth the corage
> With love and doth him forto bowe,
> That he no reson can allowe,

This is the crucial point at which the Confessor first alludes to the "lawes of nature," and we must surmise that either Gower or his Confessor is ignorant of—or has chosen to ignore—Plato's dictum that the law of nature is sibling incest aversion. The Confessor seems to accept Aristotle's and Aquinas's premise that fatal attraction between the children of Eolus is natural and inevitable given the circumstance of their constant enclosure "by daie, and eke by nyhte," with no guide other than Nature.

> Bot halt the lawes of nature:
> For whom that love hath under cure,
> As he is blind himself, riht so
> He makth his client blind also.
> In such manere as I you telle
> As thei al day togedre duelle,
> This brother mihte it noght asterte
> That he with al his hole herte
> His love upon his Soster caste:
> And so it fell hem ate laste,
> That this Machaire with Canace
> Whan thei were in a prive place,
> Cupide bad hem ferst to kesse,

I recognize and share in the perplexity that Macaulay revealed in his 1903 edition of *Selections from the Confessio Amantis,* for there is a roughness in the genius with which Gower sketched his framework. Macaulay admitted to some dissatisfaction with the characterization of the Confessor, "who as a priest has to expond a system of morality, while as a devotee of Venus; he is concerned only with the affairs of love." I thoroughly agree, but I would add that the Confessor, in this instance, is concerned primarily not with the misbehavior of adolescents but with the cruelty of a god-like father who confines his children in a "privy place," then terrorizes them with diabolical judgments and sentences of death. Cupid is not the serpent in this garden; Canace and Machaire had already fallen in love before he "bad hem ferst to kesse." The driving force is not the winged boy, but Mother Nature, personified.

And after sche which is Maistresse
In kinde and techeth every lif
Withoute lawe positif,
Of which sche takth nomaner charge,
Bot kepth hire lawes al at large,
Nature, tok hem into lore
And tawht hem so, that overmore
Sche hath hem in such wise daunted,
That thei were, as who seith, enchaunted.

At this point, Gower employs the word "falle," which is so easily linked to the fall of Adam and Eve, and again alludes to their temptation when he speaks of them as birds caught in a "net which in deceipt of him is set." He alludes mystifyingly to "lore" of which the reader has some "remembrance." Is there any other "lore" in the reader's "remembrance" than the story of Adam and Eve's original "falle?"

And as the blinde an other ledeth
And til thei falle nothing dredeth,
Riht so thei hadde non insihte;
Bot as the bridd which wole alihte
And seth the mete and noght the net,
Which in deceipte of him is set,
This ikin folk no peril sihe,
Bot that was iking in here yhe,
So that thei felle upon the chance
Where witt hath lore his remembrance.

Canace and Machaire are siblings in the hands of an angry God. Gower's Confessor borders on heresy, if not on blasphemy, for Eolus is none other than the cruel and angry God of Genesis. Eolus has placed his children in a Garden of Eden that is really a chamber of horrors. The forbidden fruit of their love does not originate in the whispering of Cupid; it arises from the law of Nature and the situation in which Eolus places them.

So longe thei togedre assemble,
The wombe aros, and sche gan tremble,
And hield hire in hire chambre clos
For drede it scholde be disclos
And come to hire fader Ere:
Wherof the Sone hadde also fere.[30]

As we have seen, there were multiple and contradictory exploitations of Homer's richly provocative episode before and after it was retold in Euripides's lost version. The tale lost no fat in Ovid's retelling, and Gower was entitled to an extension of his own poetic license. He tells us that Machaire feigned a "cause forto ryde" in fear that others would see "he his sister hath forlein," for she had not yet revealed who was the father of the child.

For yit sche hadde it noght beknowe
Whos was the child at thilke throwe.
Machaire goth, Canace abit,
The shich was noght delivered yit,
Bot riht some after that sche was.
Now lest and herkne a wofull cas.
The sothe of which could not be hid,

The reader "muar hearken unto the woeful case," the truth of which could not be hidden when it was made known to the king, who falls into a state of melancholy. We are reminded that the Confessor is telling this tale to illustrate precisely this vice. As Macaulay frames it, the vice is "MELANCHOLY, which lours like an angry beast," and takes possession of Eolus,

And whan that he it understod,
Anon into Malencolie,
As thogh it were a frenesie,
He fell, as he which nothing cowthe
How maistrefull love is in yowthe:
And for he was to love strange,
He wolde noght his herte change
To be benigne and favorable
To love, bot unmerciable
Betwen the wawe of wod and wroth
Into his dowhtres chambre he goth,

We already know the rest of the story, which generally follows other renditions. Eolus sends Canace a knife and orders her suicide, but Gower's Confessor offers additional gore when she thrusts the knife into her heart and the child is "bathende in hire blod. . . . the blod was hot and warm." The imagery is stark and so is the response of the father.

The king cam in the same throwe,
And sih how that his dowhter dieth
And how this Babe al blody crieth;
Bot al that mihte him noght suffise,
That he ne bad to do juise
Upon the child, and bere him oute,
And seche in the Forest aboute
Som wilde place, what it were,
To caste him out of honde there,
So that som best him mai devoure,

The Confessor's depiction of a merciless father abandoning his child to the beasts of the forests reveals that his loyalty is neither to Leviticus nor the teachings of the church; it is to an antecedent law of nature and his goddess of love. The moral Gower conveys through his Confessor is to beware the pitfalls of "Malencolie," which banishes love and leads to wrath. As previous commentators have noted, Gower—or at least his persona, the priest of Venus—shows greater abhorrence for the wrath of Eolus than he does for the incest of Canace and Machaire. Archibald correctly sees this as problematic, and so does Macaulay. Neither can explain Gower's decision to reiterate this salacious legend and reserve his condemnation not for this youthful Adam and Eve but for the father who placed his children in a garden of temptation.

Gower's Eolus is not the Aeolus of *The Odyssey*, who gives his daughters as brides to sons, nor is he the dark and obscure father portrayed by Ovid. While this Eolus retains the attributes of a king and is presented as a king, no reference is made to any power he might have to set aside the "lawe positif" or the societal conventions regarding sibling incest. Both Gower and the Confessor regard sibling incest as immoral, but the Confessor does not perceive it as any more "unnatural" than did Aristotle or Aquinas. Canace and Machaire are victims as much of nature as they are of their father.

C. David Benson observes what the majority of critics have recognized in Gower—a "sympathetic" presentation of the lovers—and Benson stunningly displays the consensus among scholars who, in his view, "regard Canace as more sinned against than sinning, one who merits compassion rather than blame."[31] Benson argues correctly that the "Tale of Canace and Machaire" is concerned with teaching the importance of controlling passion through reason. He focuses on the furtiveness of the brother and sister's behavior as indicating their awareness that it is wrong.

> [T]heir passion is carried out in secret, inspired by irrational desire, eventually recognized by all (including the couple themselves) as wrong, and disastrous in its consequences. Gower does not invite our sympathy for the couple so much as our horror at the sin they have committed and the evil it produces. The furtiveness of the affair is indicated when the poet notes that brother and sister first kiss in a "prive place" . . . and they are compared to the blind leading the blind, who fear nothing until they "fall," perhaps a reference to the Fall of our first parents.

But the "honor killing" of daughters is an abhorrent crime that persists in some societies, and very few English professors would be in accord with Benson's "hint that Eolus's condemnation by Genius (and most modern critics) is excessive." Benson redeems himself by the painstaking care with which he presents the positions of his opponents, and he reveals his silent accord with them, for, in spite of himself, he shows that Gower does indeed "invite our sympathy for the couple," as proven by the wealth of scholarly opinion that Benson so honestly assembles. Gower's moralizing does not focus on the reckless transgression of the adolescent lovers, whose passion, according to the Confessor, is inspired by nature.

The moral indictment is directed at the unnatural wrath of a cruel parent suddenly forced to witness, perhaps even to recognize, the horrific situation he has created by ignoring what can happen if "youthe of lusti age . . . al day togedre duelle." Familiarity supposedly breeds incest aversion according to the doctrine of Westermarck, but in Gower's tale, the opposite occurs, and the father's subliminal suspicion of his complicity is proven by the violence of his reaction.

> And whan that he it understod,
> Anon into Malencolie,
> As thogh it were a frenesie,
> He fell, as he which nothing cowthe
> How maistrefull love is in yowthe:
> And for he was to love strange,
> He wolde noght his herte change
> To be benigne and favorable
> To love, bot unmerciable
> Betwen the wawe of wod and wroth

Canace and Machaire, like Adam and Eve, are siblings in the hands of an angry God, and I accept Benson's hint at a "reference to the Fall of our first parents." The reference is necessarily oblique and deliberately veiled, however, for Gower could not openly declare that the Father of Genesis was supremely irrational or that, for the sake of a mere fruit, he fell "anon into malencholie, as thogh it were a frensie." Eolus is unreasonable and unjust, caught "Betwen the wawe of wod and wroth [wave of madness and wrath]." Gower was certainly aware of Aeolus's traditionally ambiguous status, somewhere between God and man. The Confessor safely condemns the imaginary demigod and bypasses the question of forbidden fruit. Eolus is deprived of any justification and condemned for failing to understand "how maistrefull love is in youthe."

María Bullón-Fernández suggests that the "Tale of Canace and Machaire" is more than an incest poem, and she pushes it toward a more daring conclusion with her assertion: "By choosing her own lover and becoming pregnant, Canace takes some control over her own body, and by writing a letter, she tries to take control over her own life. These two assertions of independence, though, are finally thwarted by the absolute control of a tyrannical father."[32]

Al full of wraththe in his entente,
And tok the conseil in his herte
That sche schal noght the deth asterte
As he which Malencolien
Of pacience hath no lien,
Wherof the wraththe he mai restreigne
And in this wilde wode peine,
Whanne al his resoun was untame,

The shock, pain, and disappointment experienced by a parent when their child, especially a daughter, partakes of a forbidden sexual experience is known in all societies, ancient and modern, and all too often it has resulted in an "honor killing." The extreme forms of endogamy and exogamy—incest and miscegenation—have been punishable by death under moral, religious, and civil authority. Many living persons are ready to justify the murder of a daughter for "choosing her own lover," as Bullón-Fernández and other feminists might put it. Canace's "choice," if choice it is, of her brother for a lover is extremely uncommon. She acknowledges that she has transgressed both societal norms and parental authority, but she never repudiates her love.

Canace presents her case in a letter that expresses her undying devotion to her brother and their child:

And yit with al myn hole herte,
Whil that me lasteth eny breth,
I wol the love into my deth.

Bot of o thing I schal thee preie,
If that my litel Sone deie,
Let him be beried in my grave
Beside me, so schalt thou have
Upon ous bothe remembrance.

Most modern readers are perhaps more shocked than Gower's audiences at the expression of these thoughts, but medieval historians, literary scholars, and students of comparative religion often regard the subject matter with scholarly detachment. Scholars are aware of Aristotle's and Aquinas's opinions that incestuous impulses between siblings are neither unnatural nor unknown. Of course, Aquinas refers to these impulses as a "species of lust" that must be resisted and repressed for social expediency and religious reasons. Freud inadvertently concurred with Aquinas on this point, albeit his perspectives on sibling incest are occluded by his obsession with the Oedipus complex. By contrast, contemporary social scientists usually conform to the views of Plato, Darwin, and Westermarck that incest aversion as innate and biogenetically predetermined, although Shor and Simchai, writing in the *American Journal of Sociology*, warn against against both social and biological determinism.[33]

The question of Canace and Machaire's culpability, which arises occasionally in scholarly literature, does not seem to have been Gower's main concern. The "Tale of Canace and Machaire" is not set in the real world of fourteenth-century England, albeit it cannot be isolated from the prevailing moral values of that society. Scholars have disagreed over Gower's perspective on those values, because he speaks ironically through a mystical persona. The tragedy of Canace and Machaire unfolds within a world peopled by fantastic characters created by a fertile poetic imagination that intermingles pagan and Christian elements. While the composition purports to be didactic, it reveals the lack of conformity among medieval Christian moralists on matters of destiny and free will.

Original sin wasn't invented by Jews and Christians; the idea existed before Sophocles. The conundrum of determinism versus free will dominated Greek tragedy long before it was rediscovered by Augustine or Luther. Joseph Duggan has deftly shown how "intentionality" has little if anything to do with the retributive justice of God in medieval literature and religion:

> The Middle Ages knew two radically different types of sin. The first was the sin for which one's personal intention was irrelevant, namely Original Sin, committed by Adam and Eve in the garden of Eden when they ate the fruit of the knowledge of good and evil, which according to Christian doctrine resulted in human concupiscence.[34]

Although God or the gods may appear neutral or even supportive, tragic heroes and heroines always fail in their struggle against destiny. Human beings aren't entirely "masters of their fates." If their misfortunes are not predetermined by an oracle, they are triggered by a serpentine stepmother, or a magic potion, or a wager between God and Satan. Even those tragic figures who do not intentionally sin may be fated to soil themselves by profanation. Whether or not they have deliberately overturned the pitcher, they must weep for having spilled the milk.

The book of Job admonishes silence before the judgments of God, for his justice is beyond human comprehension. Abraham Lincoln, tormented by the horrors of his Civil War, could only repeat the words of the psalmist: "The judgments of the Lord *are* true *and* righteous altogether."[35] Voltaire dismissed Leibniz's contention that this world represents "the greatest good that the wisdom of God permits him to know and which his goodness causes him to choose." But many persons find consolation in the sentiments of Bach's Cantata:

Was Gott tut, das ist wohlgetan.
[Whatever God does, that is well done.]

It is a statement of submission to God's will and an affirmation of His justice. What God does is rightly, justly, and perfectly done; perhaps an accidental affirmation of Gottfried Wilhelm Leibniz's contemporary assertion that all is for the best in the best of all possible worlds.

"Gregorius" by Friedrich Wilhelm Gubitz (1839)

– CHAPTER SEVEN –

GREGORIUS: AN IMITATION OF CHRIST, NOT OEDIPUS

THE MEDIEVAL fiction of Pope Saint Gregorius by Hartmann von Aue was never intended as a retelling of the myth of Oedipus, the King of Thebes, who unwittingly killed his father and married his mother. It is, first and foremost, a Christian parable of salvation by "the wonderful grace of God."

Gregorius is conceived in the illicit but willful embrace of two royal siblings who are not yet in their teens.[1] The remorseful brother dies while on a penitential pilgrimage to the Holy Land. The sister swaddles the baby in the finest silks and sets him adrift on the ocean in a small chest with twenty marks of gold and an ivory tablet inscribed with the nature of his conception. The coffer is salvaged by a fisherman, whose find is immediately detected by the abbot of a nearby monastery, who commits the child to the fisherman's foster care. For seventeen years the abbot presides over the boy's education and eventually gives him the tablet, which reveals his sinful origins but not the names of the sinners. Gregorius embarks on a knightly quest for his identity and unknowingly wins his mother's hand in chivalric combat. On discovering this act of unwitting contamination, Gregorius undertakes a double penance, both for his parents' conscious offense and his own unconscious abomination. He has himself chained to a rock on a desolate shore for seventeen years until he is miraculously chosen to assume the chair of Peter. As Pope in Rome, he pronounces his mother's absolution and assures her that her penitent brother is in heaven.

Modern readers may be tempted to overlook the fundamentally Christian essence of Hartmann's storytelling and be diverted by its close but imperfect analogue to the tragedy of Oedipus, along with Sophocles's dramatization and Sigmund Freud's adumbration of that myth. While Gregorius's inadvertent violation of his mother is horrifying, it cannot bear the same moral burden as the act that made it possible in the first place. Hartmann, like Sophocles, spares us the sordid details of maternal contamination but presents the original sin of the brother and sister with sensuous finesse. His entire poem alludes to Adam and Eve's vicarious guilt and redemption by the suffering servanthood of Christ, the Son of Man.[2]

Numerous renderings of the Gregorius legend have been curated and brilliantly displayed by Brian Murdoch, with particular attention to Hartmann's *Gregorius in dem Steine* (*Gregorius on the Rock*) (ca. 1190) and Thomas Mann's *Der Erwählte* (1951). So far, Murdoch has identified at least one hundred primary versions of the Gregorius story, rendered in several languages, including a version from the popular *Gesta Romanorum* in its original Latin and some of its influential translations.[3] *La Vie du Pape Saint Grégiore* (ca. 1150) is a work in medieval French of unknown authorship, presumably a source for Hartmann's *Gregorius.* The Gregorius chapter of the anonymous *Gesta Romanorum* exists in several undated and non-identical manuscripts, the earliest of which is circa 1342. Significantly, the title of the Latin work offered no hint of

Gregorius's marriage to his mother but alluded subtly to the original sin of his parents.

> *De mirabili divina dispensatione et ortu beati Gregorii papae* [Of the Wonderful Grace of God and the Birth of the Blessed Pope Gregory]

Theodore Grasse's 1842 translation of the *Gesta Romanorum* into modern German was reissued by Hermann Hesse in 1914; once again, Gregorius's fable bore a title that referred neither to his marriage nor to his time on the rock but drew attention to his exceptional beginnings.

> *Von der Geburt des seligen Paptes Gregor*
> [Of the Birth of the Blessed Pope Gregory]

Otto Rank mentioned several accounts of the Gregorius legend in his *Das Inzest-Motiv*, but in faithfulness to Freud's Oedipal framework, he relegated its sibling incest to mere incidental status. He deformed the fable's plot, tone, and setting, detaching it from its biblical moorings and its medieval Christian atmosphere and lashing it to the Oedipus myth—a classic Freudian *Verscheibung.* Rank's immediate pivot away from the emotions of the brother and sister is to be contrasted with Hartmann's compassionate focus on the authenticity of their enduring love. The thoughts and emotions of the sister displayed throughout the saga are completely ignored. There can be no simple psychoanalytic explanation for Rank's shying away from the sister as the object of sexual desire; his only sister died in infancy before he was born. He easily interpreted the story's combat scene "as a substitute for parricide" in accord with the fundamental Freudian dogma of the libidinal urge in every man to kill his father and marry his mother.

Anita Geurrequ-Jalabert expresses skepticism regarding "the vain research for the 'origins' of the tale and its connections (or absence of connections) with the Oedipus of antiquity."[4] Brian Murdoch posits that the emphasis scholars place on Oedipus "is not particularly enlightening and need not be pursued" and correctly notes that "Gregorius is not an Oedipus, medieval or otherwise." Brian Clark observes that "Freud's adherence to the Oedipal tale limited his vision into the abundant myths that told of the brother-sister marriage as well as the love and Eros between opposite-sex siblings." Under the provocative title, *Gregorius: A Medieval Oedipus Legend,* by Edwin Zeydel and Bayard Morgan, the authors state, "While agreeing that Hartmann was unfamiliar with Sophocles, we would point out that variations of the Oedipus legend as such were known in the Middle Ages."[5]

Sibling incest, not patricide, is the original sin in the Gregorius legend, and in Hartmann's version of it, both brother and sister participate with pleasure and intent. Their misdeeds are, therefore, unlike those of Oedipus, whose patricide is an unwitting but necessary antecedent to maternal incest, which is equally unwitting. Gregorius is obsessed with guilt, initially that of his parents, but later intensified by his unwitting abomination. While the Oedipus legend is a drama of decline and hubris essential to his undoing, Gregorius is motivated by a sense of guilt, and his exaltation by the sanctifying grace of humility is an entirely different story.

THE SISTER'S CULPABILITY IN GREGORIUS LEGENDS

The sister's role and the degree of guilt are problematic features of the Gregorius legend. Initially, she is a rape victim, but in all versions, a portion of the eventual guilt is given to her. Tertullian characterized women as sources of seduction and occasions of sin: "You are the devil's gateway: you are the unsealer of that tree: you are the first deserter of the divine law: you are she who persuaded him whom the devil was not valiant enough to attack. You destroyed so easily God's image, man. On account of your desert——that is, death—"[6]

In every Latin text of the *Gesta Romanorum*, the girl is initially innocent of compliance, and she attempts to reason with her brother, but her entreaties are met with passionate disregard.

> *Quomodoeumque fiat, voluntatem meam adimplebo.*
> [However that may be, I will have my way]

The Swan-Hooper English translation of 1905 did not transmit that line, but it was present in Grasse's German translation of 1905 as the strongest indictment of the brother as a rapist. Without reference to this omission, Murdoch nonetheless maintains that "The Swan-Hooper translation changes the character of this passage entirely and effectively removes all blame from the girl."[7]

> Tempted by the devil, he gave way to the most horrible desires; and firally, in spite of the pleading of the wretched girl, violated every law both human and divine.[8]

Indeed the sister confronts her brother with the unequivocal accusation, "I bear the weight of thy most fearful wickedness," but the story continues, more equivocally, "They were then both confessed, and their contrition was perfect as sincere." They make a second confession to the ancient knight, the trusted retainer of their departed father, and to him, "they revealed amid a flood of tears their crime." Thus, even in the Swan-Hooper translation, the sister is not entirely free of guilt, even though this version omits her internal struggle as she fatefully decides not to cry out for fear of public disgrace.

In the Hartmann and Old French versions, the sister's exercise of free will is presented less ambiguously. Having convinced herself she is entrapped in a tragic choice between two unacceptable alternatives—the lesser of two evils—either submission to her brother or crying out and arousing the servants, she rationalizes that the latter would result in his disgrace. She might have explained away her cries with the half-truth that she'd had a "nightmare." She justifies her decision, however, with the same sophistry employed by the culpable mothers of Marguerite de Navarre's *L'Heptaméron* and Horace Walpole's *The Mysterious Mother.* In 1914, Carl Keller compiled a "parallel text" of the Middle English Gregorius legend from archival sources—a strong but not singular variant that makes the youthful duchess an accomplice under duress.[9]

> Sche Þouȝt ȝif I loude grede
> Þen shal my brothir ben fullych schent
> And ȝif I lat him do this dede
> Our*e* soules schul ben to peyne dempt
> Þe werste Þat [sche] was to do

Sche lay wel still *and* no word nolde speke
But sufferde hym his wil Þo
Ꝥo was seynt Gregory be ȝete

Providence allows the girl's free will to be tested, for while she is capable of the proper moral judgment, she fails the test by keeping silent and does "Ꝥe werste Þat was to do." The devil gloats at his success, but, as the author of the French *Vie de Saint Grégoire* interjects, he "wist nought" what he did. The unholy moment of Gregorius's conception is providentially transformed into the *saintisme engendrement* of the French version, similarly expressed in Middle English.[10]

Out of Þe holy engendrure
Þe stori sayth he wist nouȝt

While the sister never initiates sex in any version of the legend, she is attributed varying degrees of guilt in each. In every version, there is no question the girl is raped, but Hartmann's text says she eventually takes pleasure in the sin, and both Hartmann and the French *Vie de Saint Grégoire* make clear that she eventually confesses to guilt. Later, in the *Gesta Romanorum*, she addresses her brother in a manner that implies mutual responsibility: "*nos non sumus primi, qui graviter deum offenderunt* [we are not, alas, the first who have grievously offended God]." Later, Hartmann refers to the sorrows of the sister for "the pain she carried from the sin / That she committed with her brother."[11]

Initial intentionality on the sister's part is not a factor in the *Gesta Romanorum,* where the young emperor is guilty of taking his sister against her will, despite her resistance. The influential edition by Hermann Hesse says:

> *Die Prinzessin aber weinte bitterlich und wollte sich nicht zufrieden geben, der Kaiser aber tröstete sie, so gut er konnte, und liebte sie merkwürdiger Weise immer mehr.*
>
> [The princess cried bitterly and would not be consoled, but the emperor conseled her, as well as he might, and in remarkable fashion loved her ever more.][12]

The allusion to the incestuous rape of Tamar in the biblical narrative of Samuel 13 is unmistakable. What is "remarkable" is the continuation of love of the young emperor for his sister in contrast to the hatred Amnon directs at Tamar immediately after his violence. Like the story of the rape of Tamar, the *Gesta Romanorum* departs from the tradition of Genesis that portrays women as seducers. One notes that Eve seduces Adam with a delectable fruit and that Lot's daughters seduce their father with wine. As we have seen, the early Christian church was obsessed with the idea of woman as the occasion of all sexual sin. The *Gesta Romanorum,* however, follows Samuel 13 in making the sister the victim.

The French *Vie de Saint Grégoire*, Hartmann's *Gregorius,* and the *Gesta Romanorum* accentuate the boy's emotions, and he shows remorse, attempts to console his sister, and, "in remarkable fashion, loved her ever more." Notably, in every version of the Gregorius legend, the sister eventually comes to think of herself as having offended God. This reflects an ancient, pre-Christian notion that contamination need not be associated with willful transgression. The guilt that stems from an act of profanation is not confined to the perpetrator, the victim may also bear it. Original sin is transmissible, from parents to their children or from a king to his subjects. Penalties can be imposed upon whole nations due to the sins of a few.

Thus, in every account, the guilt of the rapist brother is eventually shared by his sister, who expresses her own need to confess and do penance. It is deplorable to modern readers of the *Gesta Romanorum* that the victim becomes a participant in her own rape. This is far more sinister than mere "victim blaming," for it marks an insistence on making woman the eternal vessel of sin, just as the early Christian fathers made Eve the vehicle of an indelible original sin. A virtuous woman must resist a seducer or the violence of a rapist, and Gottfried reminds us that, according to the law of Leviticus, a woman who resists insufficiently removes at least a portion of the guilt from the rapist and places it on herself.

A victim-blaming definition of rape is established in Deuteronomy 22:24, which demands that the woman must "scream for help," otherwise the Mosaic law recognizes no rape. The French storyteller is not so pitiless as to suggest that the princess has consented in her silence but laments, nonetheless, that "this is the worst thing she could have done."

Hartmann does not reiterate this sentiment; nonetheless, in his version, the sister, despite her initial resistance, eventually takes pleasure in the affair. She does so in the Hesse translation of the *Gesta Romanorum* as well, but neither the Latin nor the Swan-Hooper translations mention her taking pleasure. Murdoch clearly finds her participation ambiguous and inserts a question mark into his discussion.[13] There is no question, however, that the sister feels the need to confess. Thus, she is counseled by the old retainer in *Gesta Romanorum,* "You know that a heavy sin was committed between you and your brother." Sheema Zeema Buehne, in the introduction to her English translation and in the text itself, presents the siblings as co-participants, so too does Volker Mertens in his modern German translation. The Zyedel-Morgan translation into English presents the most striking assertion of the sister's eventual acquiescence.[14]

> The devil's lustful urgency
> Filled her with this sinning:
> She found herself beginning
> To share her brother's passion.

In her ultimate confession of guilt, the sister admits that she was "tempted by the devil," but she does not mention any devil in the Grasse translation of 1842. As for her brother, it reads simply, "*eine grosse Versuchung* [a great temptation]" overcame him. This contrasts with the Swan-Hooper English translation of 1905, in which the devil plays a substantial role as the igniter, if not the source, of the boy's indecent passion and abominable act.

> Tempted by the devil he gave way to the most horrible desires; and finally, in spite of the pleading of the wretched girl, violated every law both human and divine. Her tears, if tears could have retrieved the ignominy, had been enough: she wept bitterly, and refused all comfort; although the emperor attempted to console her, and evinced the excess of grief and love.

This seems to remove all ambiguity regarding her lack of sinful intent, although "intentionality" is necessary for pollution, contamination, or defilement, either in ancient Greece or Israel. Under Mosaic law, sexual contamination occurs without any act of will, as in the case of menstruation in women and nocturnal emissions for men.[15] The question of guilt in Christian theology has never been one of consent or complicity. All persons are born with the stain of the original sin and, therefore, are burdened with the inherited guilt of the first parents. Atonement and salvation can be attained only by Jesus, the second Adam.

Eroticism is an indispensable element of the Gregorius legend. In the German, Old French, and Latin versions, there is graphic sexual dialogue between the brother and sister, but nothing of the sort occurs later between the mother and son. Regarding the sister's agency in the bedroom scene, there are varying degrees of ambiguity, but in all versions, Gregorius's ordeal represents vicarious atonement, not only for his unintentional self-contamination, but for what he presumes to be both his parents' willful transgression. The story of Gregorius is therefore a Christian allegory that reiterates the vicarious atonement of Jesus for the sin of Adam and Eve, and Gregorius's self-imposed Christlike mission is vicarious atonement for the sin of both his parents. It is more than incidental that he affects their redemption, not only by his vicarious suffering, but by his vicairate authority in his role as pope, for by the year 1200, every pope was endowed with the title, "Vicar of Christ."

HARTMANN VON AUE'S *GREGORIUS*

By the time Hartmann wrote *Gregorius,* there had been ten popes and antipopes named Gregory. The narrator's prologue apologizes for the sordidness of this spurious legend but coyly asserts it would be wrong to suppress it since the telling might prevent sinners from despairing of salvation and thus persisting in their misdeeds. Nonetheless, Hartmann cautions that no one should draw the false conclusion that God's patience outweighs his justice. The correct moral to be drawn is that a sinner can be saved under one condition: "*ob er die riewe begat und rehte buoze begat* [if he knows contrition and rightly does penance]."

Hartmann's narrative begins as a tale of extreme passion between a twin brother and sister, so alike in form and bearing and "so ravishing fair, there beauty is beyond compare."[16] Their mother dies in childbirth, and ten years later, the father too is stricken ill. Seeing death approaching, he assembles his nobles and commends to them his soul and the care of his children, and expresses regret that he has not made better preparations for the future of his daughter. His dying command to the boy is to watch over his sister, as is his brotherly duty, which, in medieval terms, would imply the charge to arrange a suitable marriage. Curiously, the children, barely ten years old, are seemingly left alone to manage their own affairs, although, as previously noted, it was uncommon in the Middle Ages for siblings to remain in the same household after puberty.[17]

Despite his youthfulness, the boy assumes the care of his sister with extraordinary devotion and gives her everything she asks for. They are inseparable companions, whether sitting at a table "or elsewhere," as the poet delicately puts it, for their beds are placed so close together that they can gaze at one another. In this, the devil sees an opportunity, and after the brother's protective love for his sister is transformed into sexual passion, he invades the bed. At first she resists his embrace, but fearing the disgrace that would come from crying out, she submits to his superior strength and is impregnated that night. In Hartmann's rendition, the sin eventally becomes mutual, and the sister joins her brother in relishing the act.

der tiuvelsschünde luoder
begunde si mêre schünden,
daz in mit den sünden
lieben begunde.

"The devil led them further so that the sins began to delight them" is found in Brian Murdoch's and in other translations and relates to both brother and sister.[18] Hartmann does not carry us into the devil's mind or his self-deception; he does, however, present the sister as a participant in her brother's fall, when she says, "*swîge ich stille/sô erât des tiuvels wille* [If I keep silent, the devil's will is done]." Thus, in Hartmann's rendition, she at first consents passively to Satan's design and later participates actively with her brother in a mutual transgression.

The sister's acquiescence is implicit in Shema Buehne's modern English verse translation: "They yielded and began to feel / Pleasure in their sinful way." Karl Pannier's modern German translation interprets them as mutually yielding to the devil's prompting, repeating the sin until they are mutually "*Froh*," rejoicing in it. In the *Gesta Romanorum* and its standard English and German translations, the sister begins as a non-compliant victim but eventually confesses to sharing in the brother's guilt when she says, as she does in the influential Hesse edition, "*Wir sind nicht die ersten, welche Gott schwer beleidigt haben* [We are not the first who have heavily offended God]."[19]

The sister's affection for her brother is by no means diminished by his initial violence, and in Hartmann's and the Old French versions, brother and sister continue to address one another in terms of endearment. The dramatic dialogue between them when the girl announces she is pregnant are particulary revealing in the French version. When the girl announces she is pregnant, the boy's immediate reaction is to fall semi-conscious on his sister's bed. In one text of the Old French version, he wishes she were dead, perhaps mercifully, although Murdoch considers this reaction "curious."[20] In the French version, to a lesser degree than in Hartmann's, the brother seems to suffer more through his sister's anguish than his own. At this point, the sister becomes mistress of the situation, first helping her brother to his feet, then rejecting any consideration of abortion or infanticide: "Brother think no evil thoughts, for you know that I will never allow any harm be done to the fruit that God has laid in my womb."

In both the Old French and the Hartmann versions, the sister is endowed with authority as she counsels her brother to be brave and cease weeping like a woman. It is she, in the French version, who has the idea of calling on a loyal retainer of their father, although in Hartmann's rendition, it is the brother who makes this decision. In both cases, the judgment of the old retainer is that they must separate.

Were it not for a fear of God, Hartmann tells us, the brother and sister would have endured the world's scorn, but at the advice of an old retainer, the brother embarks on a penitential crusade. In Hartmann's version, unable to endure separation from his sister, he dies of a broken heart before reaching the Holy Land. Hartmann devotes two sections of the poem (lines 639–656 and 789–857) to describing the young lovers' grief at being torn apart. His sympathy for the pain of their separation is remarkable and resembles that which Gower shows for the plight of Canace and Machaire. Hartmann emphasizes her heartbreak at the enduring intensity of their tragic love, the sadness of their separation, and the sister's dual bereavement of "*ir bruoder und ir man*," her brother and her husband.

The grieving sister, at the advice of the old retainer and his wife, places her baby in a small coffer and sets it adrift on the sea. This scene is reminiscent of the story of Moses, whose mother hid him in a papyrus basket among the reeds of the Nile. The fable of Gregorius has him wrapped in fine fabrics and accompanied by a tablet bearing the details of his noble ancestry and ignoble birth. The infant is drawn from the waters by fishermen, who marvel at the contents of the casket, but their discovery is witnessed by the abbot of a nearby monastery, at whose behest the child is adopted by one of the fishermen and remains under the abbot's guardianshp so the boy receives a classical education.

Hartmann's *Gregorius* detours from the brother-sister narrative with the brother's death in self-imposed exile and proceeds to relate the boyhood experiences of Gregorius and his unwitting return to the land of his birth. These details are essential to his narrative in that they reveal how the father is reflected in the strength and beauty of Gregorius, who proves his congenital nobility as he effortlessly develops the skills of horsemanship and knightly combat. Thus, Gregorius defeats his foe but spares the life of his mother's unwanted suitor and, unaware of her identity, takes her as his wife. On discovering his unwitting entanglement in this abomination, he exiles himself to live in isolation and poverty, counseling his mother to undertake similar penance. He has a fisherman chain him to a rock in the middle of a lake and throw the key into the water.

After seventeen years of penitential atonement for his parents' original sin and his own inadvertent incest, Gregorius is miraculously released from his rock when the key is discovered in the belly of a fish. The rock, the key, and the fish are symbols of the papacy. Due to a divine revelation, Gregorius is chosen to be pope, in which capacity he pronounces absolution for his deceased father, his repentant mother, and himself. Catholics interpret Matthew 16:18-19 as endowing the church and the chair of Peter with the apostolic power of remission of sin: "And I say also unto thee, That thou art Peter, and upon this rock I will build my church;

and the gates of hell shall not prevail against it. And I will give unto thee the keys of the kingdom of heaven: and whatsoever thou shalt bind on earth shall be bound in heaven: and whatsoever thou shalt loose on earth shall be loosed in heaven."

Hartmann's *Gregorius* is a love story with the happiest of all conceivable endings. It ends with the brother and sister saved by their son, Gregorius, who occupies the throne of Peter. This is not a Greek tragedy but a "divine comedy," a practical joke with Satan as its gull and, of course, a *divina commedia* in the sense that Dante employed that term. It is a dream of the Middle Ages that begins a nightmare but ends as an allegory on the triumph of the brother and sister over the stain of their original sin, which is constantly compared to that of Adam and Eve. Gregorius's mother resembles Eve and ultimately she resembles the Virgin Mary, because she is the mother of her own redeemer, represented on earth by the Vicar of Christ. While she does penance for her incest, she is perpetually devoted to the love that inspired it, and in her marriage to Gregorius, she reiterates that devotion, for Gregrorius is her brother's reincarnation. She falls in love with him for a second time as his embodiment in their son. She and Gregorius are reunited and happily live out their lives together in Rome. Afterward, they ascend to heaven as saints. Gregorius remits the sins of his father, giving him eternal life.

WALPOLE, NAVARRE, AND THE REVERSE GREGORIUS

Reverend Jeremy Taylor, a Puritan clergyman of the seventeenth century, recounted, with apparent credulity, an incredible narrative that reversed the Gregorius legend's sequence of events.[21] A supposed case in Venice implicated a young man who "did ignorantly lie with his mother. She knew it but intended it not . . . she was surprised and gotten with child." On realizing her condition, she sent him to travel abroad. Upon his return, he discovered a beautiful young woman in the house, fell in love, and was determined to marry her. The mother attempted to dissuade him, saying the girl was a beggar's child whom she had rescued from the streets out of charity. If he married the girl, he would dishonor the family and break his mother's heart. It was all to no avail. "The gentleman's affections were strong and not to be mastered, and he married his own sister and his own daughter." After the passage of a year or two, the woman, driven by bitings of conscience, confessed

> and asked whether she were bound to reveal the case to her son and daughter, who now lived in love and sweetness of society, innocently, though with secret misfortune, which they felt not. It was concluded negatively, she was not to reveal it, lest she bring an intolerable misery in the place of that which to them was no sin; or lest upon notice of the error they might be tempted, by their mutual endearment and their common children, to cohabit in despite of the case, and so change that into a known sin, which before was an unknown calamity; and by this state of the answer, they were permitted to their innocence, and the children to their inheritance, and all under the protection.[22]

"Speak now or forever hold your peace" is part of the marriage rite in the Anglican Book of Common Prayer intended to address matters of this sort. Taylor describes this extremely bizarre instance according to the precept that the time for speaking had come and gone. He does not seem to offer this anecdote in the overtly anti-papal spirit in which Martin Luther and others alluded to similar cases.[23] At least in this instance, Taylor resisted the impulse to accuse the Catholic Church of arbitrary positions on marriage dispensations—the position of the confessor was identical with his own: sibling incest is an abomination destructive to the social order, but the mother was justified in holding her peace and allowing her children to remain ignorant.[24]

There are several variants of this story, involving a noblewoman who was culpable, albeit in varying degrees, of conceiving a daughter with her son and thereby causing a double abomination. In some of these renderings, only the mother knows the truth; in others, the son and daughter eventually experience the shock of recognition. Some versions can be traced, directly or indirectly, to the thirtieth nouvelle of Marguerite de Navarre's *L'Heptaméron* (1558): "A young gentleman, of from fourteen to fifteen years of age, thought to lie with One of his mother's maids, but lay with his mother herself; and she, in consequence thereof, was, nine months afterwards, brought to bed of a daughter, who, twelve or thirteen years later, was wedded by the son; he being ignorant that she was his daughter and sister, and she, that he was her father and brother." Only after the marriage had been consummated did the mother discover that her son had married none other than their own daughter. In deep depression and overcome with remorse, she went to the Legate of Avignon to confess the enormity of her sin. The Legate consulted with several doctors of theology, who advised the lady to say nothing to her children, who, acting in ignorance, had committed no sin, and that she must do penance and keep her silence for the rest of her life. As for her son and daughter, "never were there husband and wife more loving, nor yet more resembling each other; for she was his daughter, his sister and his wife, while he was her father, her brother and her husband. And this exceeding love between them continued always; and the unhappy and deeply penitent lady could never see them in dalliance together without going apart to weep."[25]

L'Heptaméron presents another dismal story concerning a woman regarded by her neighbors as living a "marvelously austere life," residing with her brother, a priest, who "was loved and reverenced by his parishioners, who held him for a holy man." When she became pregnant, the people of her village accepted her explanation that this could not have happened "unless indeed it were the work of the Holy Ghost. . . . and deemed her a second Virgin Mary." Count Charles of Angoulême heard rumors of this and, disregarding the peoples' superstitions, put the priest in prison, where "not without serious remonstrances . . . he made confession of his wickedness, and told how he had counselled his sister to speak as she had done." The law took its course, and the brother and sister were burned together, but only after "the sister had been delivered [of] a fine male child . . . And all the people marvelled exceedingly at finding beneath the cloak of holiness so horrible a monster, and beneath a pious and praiseworthy life indulgence in so hateful a crime."[26]

Ellen Pollak references *L'Heptaméron* but has more directly linked several British narratives of the seventeenth and eighteenth centuries to a popular version of the double incest legend widely circulated in the anonymously published short story *Eleanora* (1751). In this exceedingly violent and cruel rendition, after the siblings Orestes and Cornelia are married and have several children, the mother addresses a letter to the son, commanding, under penalty of her curse, that it "not be opened till after I am interred." The reader of *Eleanora* must hang in suspense for several pages before the mother is finally disposed of and poor Orestes is allowed to open the letter.[27]

> He then began at the Top, and read a Sort of Direction, in the Words following. "To my dear Son Orestes, the Father of my Daughter Cornelia . . . Judge you, my dearest Son, my Orestes, once my sole Joy, now my sole Confusion, with what a trembling Hand, and tortur'd Soul, thy miserable Mother must sit, down, to disclose the Foulness of her Crimes, to the Offspring of her own Bowels; himself, though innocent, an Actor in .the most abominable Sin of Incest. Incest in me, my Son, while thou art (though not free from Fornication) involuntarily involved in that bestial Mixture . . . The Issue of it, one Daughter, your present Wife Cornelia.[28]

The benumbed Orestes shares the letter with Cornelia, who is so overwhelmed that she collapses, and after a "few minutes laboring for breath," she succumbs to "a suffocation in her throat," which "entirely prevent[s] all further respiration." Momentarily immobilized, Orestes studies the body of his dead sister-daughter-wife, then proceeds to action. Wailing, "O my Children! my Children!" he first shreds and swallows the letter that would have condemned them to "Prejudice" and then stabs himself, "falling close at the feet of Cornelia."

Horace Walpole's play, *The Mysterious Mother,* presents another lurid story with a cruel and deliberately anti-Catholic element. The Countess of Narbonne takes the place of her servant in her son's bed, and the young Count Edmund unknowingly impregnates her with Adeliza, the daughter, who is fated to become wife and sister to her own father. Edmund departs on a "holy war" against the Turks while his sister-daughter, Adeliza, is gently reared and educated. Upon his return, Edmund discovers and falls in love with his beautiful sister. They are secretly married by the evil monk, Benedict, who has guessed the countess's guilt and plots her downfall. When the countess, reeling with the shock of recognition, confesses all and kills herself using her son's dagger, Edmund resolves to return to his wars in hopes of finding death. He commits Adeliza, whom he has presumably already deflowered and thus rendered no longer marriageable, to a nunnery. Walpole admits in a postscript to having learned of a similar story in *L'Heptaméron* of Marguerite de Navarre, where, at the advice of a bishop, the truth is never revealed, citing that he claims not to have known this until "sometime after I had finished the play."[29]

JOHN I, COUNT OF ARMAGNAC, AND THE LAW

The foregoing fictions subordinate the sibling relationship to the mother's guilt, with varying degrees of blame placed on the Catholic Church. A celebrated ecclesiastical case contained one element of the Gregorius legend but lacked the complicating factor of parental incest. A young brother and sister of the nobility were orphaned and living together in isolation. John I, Count of Armagnac, forced a priest to marry him to his sister and was arraigned before the papal court on charges of unnatural lust. Richard A. McCabe provides an overview of the trial in which he reports the interesting defense of the Bishop of Arras, who requested sympathy for the orphaned siblings who turned to one another for comfort in the absence of their parents. "Familiarity bred love, love passion, and then they thought of marriage. He made careful inquiries whether a brother might marry a sister. He called in consultation jurists and the greatest theologians. He was told that such a union could not be except by the indulgence of the pope, who did sometimes grant dispensation."[30]

Of course no such dispensation had ever been granted, and a document purporting to sustain such a possibility was proven a forgery. Although both specious and irrelevant, the case was nonetheless cited by supporters of a papal dispensation for the marriage of Henry VIII to his cousin in the fourth degree, Catherine of Aragon. The power of the pope to loosely interpret marriage laws provided enemies of the papacy with convenient evidence of papist presumption. There is, however, no record of the papacy ever tolerating, much less condoning, a marriage between a brother and sister, and there was never a Pope Gregory who granted posthumous absolution to his own father for the mortal sin of incest.

"Romeo and Juliet" by Frank Dicksee (1910)

– CHAPTER EIGHT –

FORD'S *'TIS PITY SHE'S A WHORE*

GIOVANNI AND Annabella, the protagonists of John Ford's cruelly farcical tragedy, *'Tis Pity She's a Whore,* have been compared to Adam and Eve as unique companions in a wilderness, but they live in an environment of civilized violence and deceit. Voltaire, who famously described Shakespeare's *Hamlet* as "*une piece grossière et barbare*" should have saved his comment for this piece, which culminates with the murder and mutilation of the sister's body by her "brother unkind." The plot, in summary: Brother loves sister; brother impregnates sister; brother kills sister, then cuts out her heart and presents it on his sword to her husband as a birthday present. The brother is then killed by some of the various assassins who lurk throughout the entire drama. In the opinions of most critics, Ford is not lacking in literary talent or skill despite the luridness of his subject matter, which is justified, by generous critics, as an effort to illustrate the failure of a decadent society—"papist," of course —to enforce even the most universal of moral standards. Its other characters are presented as ineffectual, lascivious, stupid, cowardly, cruel, or cynical.[1]

This sadistic spectacle is often compared, and perhaps too facilely, to Shakespeare's *Romeo and Juliet*. True enough, both works center on adolescent star-crossed lovers, and both works feature a friar and a maidservant in supporting roles, but the obstacles facing the two couples are drastically different. Romeo and Juliet are separated by accidentals, the peculiar customs of their time and place, and a long-standing feud between their two families. Thus, they have gained a veritably universal audience's perpetual sympathy and affection. By extreme contrast, Giovanni and Annabella, having violated a putatively universal taboo, can evoke no such sympathy. They stimulate the usual "third-party reactions" of horror and amazement by their theoretically impossible violation of the *Inzestcheu* instinct, supposedly activated by Westermarck's unbreakable law. Nonetheless, Lisa Hopkins's observation on the play merits serious consideration.[2] "Most obviously it looks back to *Romeo and Juliet*. Romeo and Juliet are young, idealistic lovers, each is clearly the best possible partner that their society has to offer for the other, but the feud between their families means that their union is too radically exogamous for the small Italian city in which they live."[3]

While there is much truth in this, some readers might object that, despite their youth, Giovanni and Annabella do not come across as idealistic. Furthermore, there is no evidence they have been deprived of other youthful and attractive contacts or that unusual circumstances have produced an unusual closeness, as in the instances of Gregorius's parents or Canace and Machaire. Ovid and Gower describe a slowly mounting passion between their sibling lovers, one having roots deeper than mere physical excitement. Ford was probably unacquainted with Hartmann but almost certainly aware of Ovid and possibly Gower, who explains the incest in terms of their isolation.

Giovanni, in his first appearance on stage, proclaims the naturalness of his attraction to his sister, Annabella, but he justifies it only with a description of her physical charms, which he expresses in the conventionally artificial language of courtly love:

> Must I not praise
> That beauty, which if framed anew, the gods
> Would make a god of, if they had it there;
> And kneel to it, as I do kneel to them?

Boyishly, and obviously in vain, he seeks to gain the approval of his erstwhile teacher, Friar Bonaventura, who has endowed him all too well with the elements of scholastic *disputatio.* His excessive "devotion to his book" will be commented on later by his father, and his perversion of Thomistic arguments has been noted by Simon Barker, who believes that Ford may have encountered them in the paraphrasis of Aquinas in John Florio's 1603 translation of Montaigne's *Essais*. Giovanni may well have grasped at Aquinas's passing acknowledgment that it is "natural that a man should have a liking for a woman of his kindred," removing it from its context and converting it into a theological sophism that is both desperate and bizarre.[4]

> Are we not therefore each to other bound
> So much the more by Nature; by the the links
> Of blood, of reason; Nay if you will have 't,
> Even of Religion, to be ever one,

Later, he repeats the same naturalistic argument to Annabella: "Wise Nature first in your Creation meant to make you mine." The scholastic reference to Nature is unnecessary, for as Annabella tells him, she has "never fought; what thou hast urged." But Giovanni must seemingly repeat his sophomoric argument to convince himself. The friar refuses to address his sophistry and appeals to his emotions, reminding his former student that inevitable and eternal damnation awaits him if he persists in his folly. Bonaventura cannot offer the solution to their problem that Friar Laurence presents to Romeo and Juliet, the sanctioning of their sexual union through the sacrament of matrimony; he can only seek to dissuade him. By contrast, the counterpart to Juliet's nurse, Annabella's tutoress, Putana, schools her charge in cynicism and consoles her with cynical and sarcastic commentary once the transgression is complete.

Havelock Ellis rightly described the protagonists as "passionate children" and as "a boy and girl." Nonetheless, unlike Gower's Canace and Machaire, they do not convey impressions of innocence and naivete. Ford's drama disregards the classical and medieval conventions of the sibling incest narrative, which displays the brother's and sister's naivete. In other respects, they are indeed reminiscent of their Renaissance cognates, Romeo and Juliet, but mainly because they are Italian and Catholic. They are driven by passion for several months, in the course of which Annabella is impregnated, and in her desperation, she is driven to marry one of her several unappealing suitors, Soranzo, a cowardly and corrupt nobleman who soon discovers her pregnancy. Soranzo's loyal servant discovers the name of her lover through Putana.

Religious belief is more than incidental to the play, and significantly the opening lines are spoken by Friar Bonaventura, who introduces atheism in the play's opening dialogue and likens Giovanni's skill at disputation to "striving how to prove There was no God; with foolish grounds of Art." In his final dialogue with Annabella, Giovanni confesses to atheism, and with apparent ease, he casts aside all worries of damnation. But not so Annabella, who still believes in heaven and hell and bears the additional burdens of her pregnancy, her continuing love for Giovanni, and her forced deception of her husband. Bonaventura eventually hears Annabella's confession but continues terrifying the poor girl with his description of hell:

> a black and hollow Vault,
> Where day is never seen; there shines no Sun,
> But flaming horror of consuming Fires
> A lightless Sulphur, choked with smoky fogs
> Of an infected darkness; in this place
> Dwell many thousand, thousand sundry sorts
> Of never dying deaths; there damned souls
> Roar without pity . . .
> There stands these wretched things.

> Who have dreamt out whole years in lawless sheets
> And secret incests, cursing one another.

Giovanni describes his sister's lost chastity as "this pretty toy called Maidenhead," and his words to Annabella contain no promises beyond the pleasures of the hour. The immaturity, if not the innocence, of Giovanni and Annabella may be surmised, but they never seem to plan for a future together, not even one that is naive and unworkable. Even the most meticulously constructed works of art may contain accidental and intentional ambiguities, but Ford does not make the most of those. He fails to exploit opportunites to engender ambivalence, if not sympathy, in the hearts of his audience. Amid the confusion of plots and subplots, Ford leaves obscure his definition of "love," a word that, especially when defined as sexual passion, may refer simultaneously to the sacred and the profane. In their brief colloquies, Giovanni and Annabella are not provided with the advantage of defending their passion.

The fundamental question of whether their love is natural is implicitly at the heart of the tragic situation. If we pity Giovanni and Annabella, it is because we see them as teenagers, in many respects still children, who recognize and rebel against adult hypocrisy. Nonetheless, despite resenting adult authority, they are in need of adult support. Thus, Giovanni hopelessly and desperately attempts to gain Bonaventura's approval, and Annabella flounders in the quagmire of Putana's bad counsel. When they are alone, the brother and sister engage in childish conversations in the conventional language of young love, but this triteness within the anomalous setting of a familiar relationship renders their words impossible and absurd. Giovanni's rhapsodies for Annabella's physical charms seem out of place, and normally a Renaissance mistress would respond to them with artful coyness and playful derision.

Although Giovanni has been away at university, perhaps for two or three years, we may assume he and Annabella spent their childhood and preadolescent years in close association. Their fatal attraction cannot be explained in terms of the hypothetical "genetic sex attraction," which is said to erupt when siblings—separated at birth and before the presumably innate instinct of incest aversion can be activated—are suddenly reunited. That is to say, there can be no Westermarck effect when a brother and sister first become acquainted as virtual strangers after reaching sexual maturity. Giovanni and Annabella's initial conversation helps us understand they have been socialized together within a nuclear family, and their relationship is being renewed after a relatively brief separation. This is no precipitous "genetic sex attraction." Their attraction resembles a friendship that starts in childhood between next-door playmates and evolves into a romance. Giovanni says, "I have too long suppressed the hidden flames," and she responds, "what thou hast urged, My captive heart had long ago resolved."

While temporal references such as "long suppressed" and "long resolved" in the mouths of younger persons most often refer to relatively short-lived experiences, we may assume that Giovanni and Annabella's mutual attraction has been developing for some time. They embark with amazing alacrity on their sexual adventure as if suddenly releasing long-repressed energies that both complement and collide with normal sibling affection. On one level, their initial conversation seems impossibly like an exchange between persons meeting for the first time. The only indication of a long-standing relationship is their exchange of references to their mother.

> ANNABELLA: On my knees,
> Brother, even by our Mother's dust, I charge you,
> Do not betray me to your mirth or hate,
> Love me, or kill me Brother.
> GIOVANNI: On my knees,
> Sister, even by my Mother's dust I charge you,
> Do not betray me to your mirth or hate,
> Love me, or kill me Sister.

Their mother's memory is again briefly recalled when Florio, the siblings' father, queries Annabella in a later scene:

> FLORIO: Where's the Ring,
> That which your Mother in her will bequeathed,
> And charged you on her blessing not to give 't
> To any but your Husband? send back that.

Annabella: I have it not,
Florio: Ha! have it not, where is 't?
Annabella: My brother in the morning took it from me,
Said he would wear 't Today.

These invocations of the mother's name, and the transmission of her ring stand among the few dramatic indications that Giovanni and Annabella's love exists in some realm beyond their sexual urges, but otherwise, Ford provides few concrete illustrations of filial affection or romantic love before the final scene. On stage, a director has considerable freedom to shape the characters according to his or her will. Ford has allowed for great freedom of interpretion so the characters may easily be represented as Lisa Hopkins describes them—"idealistic lovers." The situation invites a stage director to present conflicting sentiments, ranging from a purely selfish and salacious lust to a love that transcends its erotic level of expression.

Annabella's situation is more tragic than Giovanni's, for she must confront the double dilemma of her pregnancy and deceiving her husband in a forced marriage. Her eventual repentance arises from both the material and the spiritual consequences of her actions. Due to his apparent lack of contrition and the selfish and vengeful nature of his passion, Giovanni dies beyond all hope of redemption. In Annabella's confession scene, the friar urges her to repent, and she consents to marry Soranzo. Perhaps it is Giovanni's confidence that Annabella has been shriven, since he has overheard her confession to a priest, that allows him to take her life, saying,

Pray Annabella, pray; since we must part,
Go thou white in thy soul, to fill a Throne
Of Innocence and Sanctity in Heaven.
Pray, pray my Sister.

Annabella: Then I see your drift, Ye blessed Angels, guard me.
Giovanni: So say I,
Kiss me; if ever after times should hear
Of our fastknit affections, though perhaps

> The Laws of Conscience and of Civil use
> May justly blame us, yet when they but know
> Our loves, That love will wipe away that rigor,
> Which would in other Incests be abhorred.
> Give me your hand; how sweetly Life doth run
> In these well colored veins! how constantly
> These Palms do promise health! but I could chide
> With Nature for this Cunning flattery,
> Kiss me again — forgive me.

Annabella fully realizes the intent behind her brother's parting words only after he thrusts his knife. We have not heard Bonaventura pronounce his *ego te absolvo,* but with her dying breath, she seemingly expresses some hope of escaping eternal damnation, as she utters her most pathetic lines, an appeal first for his salvation and then for her own.

> ANNABELLA: Forgive him, Heaven—and me my sins; farewell.
> Brother, unkind, unkind! Mercy great Heaven—O!—O!

Only in this scene do we witness anything resembling a love story, and these transgressors of the Darwin-Westermarck code are not influenced either by unusual circumstances or supernatural whisperings. Sympathy is engendered in the narratives of Ovid, Hartmann, and Gower by the gradualness with which the author delivers a love story, but *'Tis Pity She's a Whore* is not a love story. It presents neither the actors nor their audience with any of the moral or artistic ambiguities contained in other sibling narratives. Giovanni and Annabella, unlike Adam and Eve or Hansel and Gretel, are not the victims of wretched parents, a wicked witch, or pagan gods; they are the creations of a sadistic author heartlessly playing God with helpless puppets in an anti-Catholic parody.

"Allegorical Portrait of Urania, Muse of Astronomy"
by Louis Tocqué (1750)

– CHAPTER NINE –

THE PRESENTATION OF NATURE IN SIBLING NARRATIVES OF THE EIGHTEENTH CENTURY

IN *UNNATURAL Affections*, George Haggerty observes in passing that "Sibling incest is unusually common in the eighteenth-century novel." As others who pursue this matter, he presents evidence from the works of Daniel Defoe, Sarah Fielding, Henry Fielding, Sophia Lee and Charlotte Dacre, and further alludes to "a range of novels too numerous to mention." Particularly interesting is Haggerty's investigation of a "number of incest cases in the notorious annals of the Old Bailey," but these dealt exclusively with the molestations of young girls by their fathers or by older boys, and he found "none in which the sibling relationship functioned."[1]

In agreement with Haggerty, Stefani Engelstein observes an "explosion of literary interest in sibling incest in the eighteenth century. . . . Although scenes of intergenerational incest persisted . . . , the far more predominant form of incest in literature beginning in the mid-eighteenth was that between siblings."[2] This burgeoning is marked by Delarivier Manley's 1709 tragedy of Polydore and Urania, Montesquieu's 1721 tale of Apheridon and Astarte, and Daniel Defoe's *Moll Flanders.* Much of this interest echoes the discourse on nature, posed by the ancient authors, perplexing the fathers of Christianity, and causing discomfort to the doctors of the medieval church.

Classical and medieval definitions and debates over what constitutes a natural attraction are recurrent in eighteenth-century prose and poetry, and are accompanied by moralizing explorations of the "natural" limits and obligations of brotherly-sisterly affection. Delarivier Manley, Sarah Fielding, Daniel Defoe, and Baron Montesquieu are the most frequently mentioned authors of sibling incest narratives in the Age of Enlightenment. To this list we might add Voltaire's *Candide,* where an omniscient narrator explains that Cunégonde and Candide are probably first cousins although suspiciously close to being half-siblings.

The concept of natural law is frequently problematized in ancient, medieval, and early modern discourses, where an incestuous relationship seems almost inevitable due to physical and psychic proximity and energizes the putative conflict between the laws of nature and societal conventions—sometimes observed by an omniscient narrator, other times presented in a soliloquy by one of the characters.

DELARIVIER MANLEY: "POLYDORE AND URANIA" FROM *THE NEW ATALANTIS* (1709)

Delarivier Manley's early eighteenth-century fable of Polydore and Urania is a chapter in her political satire, *Secret Memoirs and Manners of Several Persons of Quality, of both Sexes, From The New Atalantis.* It places the inevitable suffering of a young brother and sister within the context of the debate over human nature. Manley is concerned with defining "Nature," a term Raymond Williams calls "perhaps the most complex word in the language." "Polydore and Urania" can be approached as a free-standing short story and a precursor to the Nature-Nurture controversy in today's discussions of the Westermarck effect. The story can be isolated from its satirical tone, oblique political references, and its framing in *The New Atalantis.* Its arrows of feminist anger are aimed at the repressive society, which demanded the arrest and trial of its author, and on British cultural hypocrisy, especially Whig attitudes. Despite its criticism of *The Tatler,* it won the admiration of that periodical's editor, Richard Steele, and the endorsement of other such influential whigs as Lady Mary Wortley Montagu and moderate Jonathan Swift.[3]

While assertively feminist, the work centers on a female villain and her female victim. The principal males are a faceless baron and a grief-stricken teenaged boy. Manley intended to make the point that social conventions could mold one girl into a monster and make the other a criminal, albeit a pitiable one. Ellen Pollak has correctly observed that this treatise problematizes the meaning of innocence, to which I add that it illustrates the primeval opposition between Knowledge and Nature confronted by Eve. I would also add that Manley reiterated the presumed natural/artificial dichotomy that drew the attention of Locke, Hobbes, and other notables.

The suggestion that sibling incest can arise from natural instinct was presented in Gower's "The Tale of Canace and Machaire," and Manley's narrative framework is intermittently reminiscent of *Confessio Amantis.* Like Gower, she employs allegorical figures and personifies idealized traits; Gower personifies Love, and Manley endows Justice, Virtue, and Intelligence with voices. Her frequent employment of the word "Nature" and her references to instinct override the Platonic presupposition that incest aversion is automatic. In her view, the commands of natural instinct without moral education can lead to antisocial behavior. Her nuanced references to Nature and instinct anticipated, and were more complicated, than Montesquieu's approaches to the same question in his tale of Apheridon and Astarte.

Urania and Polydore are twins and orphans, brought up in isolation, and they, too, are interdependent. Deprived of all moral education, they direct their initially innocent emotions toward one another. "Never was any affection so great as that of Polydore and Urania; he was all of the Sex she was permitted to converse with. . . . In this reserve from the other Sex Urania had attain'd to her Fifteenth Year," her irresponsible guardian having "suffered an impious passion to grow up with her; A fatal tenderness for the too lovely Polydore; he burnt with the same criminal Desires." Their "hourly converse" is described in Manley's oppositional terms as "tender and abominable," especially in the words of Polydore,

> Why, my enchanting Sister (would he say) must Human laws and Customs take place of Nature's? Why is it not permitted me to marry *Urania?* Why must she have any husband but Polydore? Oh how happy wou'd it be four us were we to resign our too much valu'd Reason (which is not born with, but taught us) for that happy Instinct, that forbids not the *Brothers and Sisters* of the *feathered kind*, to indulge their Appetites to each other? They pair; they breed; and know no Kindred; no Law but Love. Would it not be the same in the *Human-kind,* if themselves had not made the Prescription? Nature forbids it not; or rather gives a more indearing *gusto* to those born of the same *Blood.*

The reader marvels at the rhetorical skills of Polydore and his pretend knowledge of avian reproduction, but verisimilitude was not the author's goal; her purpose was to place a pair of siblings in an untended garden of emotions. As noted previously, she employs the word "nature" liberally throughout the narrative, sometimes ironically and sometimes to emphasize a distinction between instinct and civilization. In other words, she posits, as did Hartmann and Gower, the dangers of isolating siblings and abandoning them to their instincts. The result accorded with Aquinas, warning that blood relations living "in close touch with one another" are not indifferent to one another's attractiveness, and that "venereal intercourse" is necessarily prohibited by laws and customs and reinforced by their guardians. Thus, she offers the following advice in the voice of personified Virtue:

> Young Maids of *Fashion* cannot be watch'd with too much Delicacy; their *Complexions, Constitutions*, ought to be confidered; the more

> Amorous shou'd be deny'd all heightnings of the Passions . . . But above all, endearing Intimacies and private Converſations, with the nearest Relations, a Brother not excepted; lest (as in the Caſe of Urania) the Sex prevail, and too much leiſure give 'em opportunity to exert their Temper.

Manley has employed the device—unconventional in her epoch—of referring to males as "the sex," but she is conventional in placing her tale of Polydore and Urania within the traditional discourses on sex and natural law. Augustine and other church fathers addressed and found discomfitting that sibling incest could not be declared unnatural. Manley's tale cannot be disassociated from its prominent medieval antecedents, cultural roots, or successors of the Age of Enlightenment. It advances the oppositional discourse of nature versus culture later addressed by Shelley and Byron. Tijana Miletic observes that "Incest blurs the boundaries between the social and the antisocial and is closely related to friendship. The term itself carries a charge similar to the notion of adultery explored by Denis de Rougemont."[4] Denis de Rougement touches on the medieval discourses and definitions of incest as imaginatively as Foucault, who addresses but cannot possibly resolve the question, previously addressed by Aquinas and subsequently by Freud and Westermarck, of whether incest aversion is inborn or socially acquired. In reading Manley's Juvenalian satire, *The New Atalantis*, we are presented with the challenge that accompanies all readings of satire, the untangling of sarcasm from heartfelt assertion. Neither she nor her literary personas are free of ambiguity respecting the connection between the natural and the artificial in human nature.

Professor Pollak has appropriately situated Manley's tale of Polydore and Urania within her analytical constructs of guardianship and education. We have also observed the theme of neglected guardianship in Gower's "The Tale of Canace and Machaire," and the theme is present in the catastrophically imperfect guardianship of a brother for his sister in Hartmann's *Gregorius*. The idea remained popular throughout the Renaissance and Enlightenment. Urania and Polydore are orphans under the guardianship of their uncle, a baron whose role in the narrative is incidental. It is his wife, the baroness, Manley tells us, who is responsible for the children's fall. At first she brings them up with the care she bestows on her own children, but she comes by degrees to perceive Urania in a different light.

The baroness recognizes a responsibility to make Urania a suitable marriage but eventually realizes that her ward's superior beauty raises her prospects above those of her own daughter. Little is said of Urania's education, only that she is strongly influenced by her older cousin Harriet, described as, "Tall, Well-made, Genteel, Agreeable, Precise, a Devotee, fraught with Precepts of outward Honour, an affectation of Virtue, unfathomed Hypocrisy, fire in her Constitution, frost in Conversation." Harriet teaches her that virtue consists only of "outward behavior." Polydore receives the benefits of a tutor, who is competent only in the formal sense, "one of those who was a right *Pedant;* had nothing of the *fine Gentleman* in *himself,* or Man of *Honour;* and knew not how to infuse them into *others;* his Business seem'd only to teach him the *Languages;* not to give his Mind the *Ornaments* of *Virtue;* he understood 'em not; his own narrow Education forbid it."

Manley's attitude toward Urania's interaction with her cousin and Polydore's with his tutor is a mixture of pity and horror, and while she shows compassion for these creatures of her literary imagination, she never calls any of them guiltless. The moral of her story is that "Persons of Condition" must be careful in choosing "those People to whose Conduct they commit the Education of their Children." Polydore and Urania, raised in a serpent-infested Eden, are soon expelled even from this imperfect refuge, for they arrive at puberty in a state of confusion respecting the relationship between nature and culture. Urania is corrupted by her cousin, and Polydore by his tutor, with the idea that morality is no more than social convention. Thus, Polydore initiates the incest with a naive natural law argument, and Urania is susceptible to it. Manley has predisposed the reader to consider this as sophomoric sophistry, yet she has difficulty addressing the long-standing and complicated discourses to which Pollak alludes regarding whether incestuous impulses are stimulated or repressed by nature.

> These Lovers so young and so guilty knew enough of Nature, only to know, there was still something *criminal* and *delightful,*

> *something* that was repugnant to the Laws of Honour and Custom. They would often consult about leaving the *Baron's* House, to retire themselves into an unknown corner of the *Globe.* There in some little Cottage, to consummate their wishes, where guiltless of Commerce with Kindred of *Acquaintance*, they might be all to themselves; *Polydore* the Husband of *Urania* and *Urania* the Wife of Polydore. . . . The ardent Brother would learn to dig or plough for his adorable Sister; and the too loving Sister milk or spin for her beloved brother.

The delving and spinning in the above passage is almost certainly an allusion to the words of John Ball, executed for his role in the peasant's revolt of 1381:

> When Adam delved and Eve Span,
> Who was then the gentleman?

Imagining their flight from civilization as a return to Eden, "They talk'd of Toil and Hardship, as Indearments and Happiness." To Manley's readers, this fantasy would have exemplified Ball's misguided counsels of anarchy and social disorder "inspired by a spirit of hell," as John Gower put it.[5] Adam and Eve were not guiltless, and Manley's narrator censures the siblings' "crime" and their "guilt." Her readers would have recognized, and regarded as sophistry, the argument that "Human laws and Customs take place of Nature's." They viewed sexual and social anarchy with equal negativity. Nonetheless, Manley was a critic of society, and she viewed Polydore and Urania as the victims of their guardians' abdication of responsibility.

No wonder "the eager watchful Brother found an unguarded Moment to complete his *Happiness* without the Forms of Marriage, or any binding Obligation but Love." The guilt is equally shared, and of this, Manley leaves no doubt. "Tis hard to say which was the most *Ardent;* which the most Guilty." No sooner have they drunk of this "delicious Poison, but Urania proved the effects of it! a guilty Pregnancy," but this does not "disturb their joys." They pursue their pleasures until they are caught *in flagrante* by Harriet, who has suspected them for some time, and is delighted with this opportunity to assure their ruin, declaring she will immediately tell the baroness. Urania throws herself at Harriet's feet with fruitless entreaties, and Polydore reminds her of scandals concerning several aristocrats reputed to or known to have slept with, and even engendered children by, their sisters, but to no avail.

The baroness is informed; the siblings are separated, and Urania is committed to the care of "an old *Lady* who had trod the Paths of Honour unblamably, without that nicety of Temper, of condemning in others those little Levities more pardonable in the First morn of Life." By introducing this character into her plot, Manley adds an additional level of ambiguity. Urania's new preceptor is entirely sympathetic; she spares nothing in the way of "tender Exhortations . . . to recall the Young Wanderer into the road of Honour" and weeps "Tears of indulgence over her growing infamy." The result is Urania's awakening "from the Lethargy of Love to a sense of Glory," but this has the opposite effect of bringing "Ease to her tortured Soul." Manley's opinion of the "old Lady" is obscure; she has conjured up a character whose "tender exhortations" have the poisonous effect of engendering despair, the unpardonable sin that closes the path to repentance. The unintended consequence of her counsel is to undermine all hopes of the salvation through the atonement Hartmann provided his sinful lovers.

Urania is cruelly bereaved of her love for Polydore, and what was once a tender love gives place to "a serene Horror, and fixt Despair," which Manley seems to share, for she presides over Urania's downfall with the *Inzestscheu* of a "third-party-observer." Her gaze is not fixed solely on the sinners, however, but on the combined social and moral forces that brought about their downfall. The occasion of sin was furnished by their guardians, who carelessly overlooked the impulses of "Nature," which led the isolated siblings into incest. Their ultimate destruction is delivered by social and moral forces—especially those marshalled by the seemingly sympathetic and tenderly weeping, but ultimately destructive, "old Lady." The forces of nature and society are arrayed against Urania, who despairingly resolves to die in childbirth, knowing she will face eternity with a grievous sin on her soul: "Murder the *Innocent,* the unborn hapless Infant, who possibly might perish with her for want of Assistance. At this she would have strange Meltings, and potent Strugglings with her *Resolutions,* the *Mother-Tender-ness* came upon her so that meritorious *Tenderness,* common to all the Female-kind, and only less to be found in the Human! where *Reafon,* if not destroys, yet weakens *Instinct.*"

With the onset of labor pains, Urania falls into "strong Convulsions, in which she is so happy as to lose her Understanding, fatal to the infant." She dies the following morning and is interred with her child, and Polydore, upon being informed of his sister's misfortunes, falls into a "dangerous Fever" and, "in the Epilepsie," raves "incessantly of his charming Sister."

Manley does not portray Polydore as a carefree Lothario, driven by lust alone. Intentionally or not, she fashions him as a reincarnation of the tragic adolescent of Hartmann's *Gregorius*, who dies en route to the Holy Land. Polydore resolves not to survive without his sister and enlists aboard a warship, intent on engaging in battle against a strong squadron of Venetians. Polydore displays admirable, indeed heroic, qualities, as his actions bespeak courage and despair when he attempts twice to board the enemy until, riddled by a volley of small arms fire, he falls at length at the admiral's feet. Polydore's body is interred "with all the marks of Honour, that so great a Courage seemed to merit."

The culmination of Polydore and Urania's aborted plot to recapitulate the story of Adam and Eve shares structural elements with Gower's "The Tale of Canace and Machaire" and Hartmann's *Gregorius*. In each of these instances, the brother and sister are left in a situation of interdependency, either because they have been orphaned or because their guardian has neglected responsibility. Manley, unlike Gower and Hartmann, does not interject supernatural agencies such as Cupid's arrows or the devil's promptings. This is not the story of a "fortunate fall," or of a redemption either in this life or the hereafter. Manley terminates her moral fable by recounting a rumor of Harriet's entrusting her honor to a seducer and anticipating her comeupance. Perhaps there will be a divine retribution against Harriet, but no hope of redemption is offered to her victims.

The prominent role assigned to "Education" in Manley's fable reveals an ideology that contrasts the natural with the artificial, and contrasts the anarchy of human instinct to the ordered necessity of "Law and Custom." It uproots the certitude of Plato's declaration that the incest taboo is instinctive, and asserts that sexual morality requires cultivation. The *laissez-faire* governance of the baroness results in a catastrophic sexual anarchy that might have been envisioned in Thomas Hobbes's dystopia of ungoverned passions. Manley declares the necessary role of education in laying down prohibitions against this crime against honor and society. The nature-nurture controversy she works out in *The New Atalantis* is exemplified in but not confined to the sibling incest narrative. The moral of Manley's narrative is articulated by her personification of Virtue, who says: "I am tenderly touch'd at the Misfortune of this young unhappy Beauty; her Fault was without *Excuse*, and to be detested and avoided: But does it not severely retort it self upon the Baroness, for giving her so careless an Education?" This reveals Manley's Tory thinking, her opposition to letting nature run its course and expresses her firm conviction "that Nature in it self was never yet so Bright, but that it wanted the Refinement of Education."

SARAH FIELDING: *THE ADVENTURES OF DAVID SIMPLE*

In Sarah Fielding's novel *The Adventures of David Simple,* David has been cheated out of his inheritance by his brother but fortuitously regains it and sets out with the resolve "To travel through the whole World rather than not meet with a real Friend." In due course, he encounters other unfortunates—Cynthia, Valentine, and Camilla—who have suffered cruelty and exile by their relatives. Provided with a surrogate sister in the person of Cynthia, David exchanges her for Camilla, and a double marriage ensues. The novel's first volume ends with the two couples planning a utopian existence together. Fielding chooses to make David's life in the second volume one of tragedy and disappointment, but at least presents Camilla and Valentine as innocents and provides them with appropriate marriage partners.

As we have seen, some authors, like Gower and Manley, imply that the impulse toward sibling incest is innate but antisocial and rightly suppressed by legal and religious mandates. However, one must ask, if such appetites are so "unnatural" and so inevitiably punished, how can siblings indulge such appetites? Pollak suggests that with a little imagination, Freud and Westermarck can be reconciled, and she alludes to

Ruth Perry's study, "Incest as the Meaning of the Gothic Novel," which employs the term "*cri de sang*." Better yet, one might term it a "call of the wild" that howls in the background of civilization's discontents. Conflicting impulses are embedded in human sexuality.

The Western literary tradition, while overwhelmingly condemning sibling incest, occasionally betrays ambivalence in an author's handling of the guilty participants. Haggerty argues that "In some cases, especially in *David Simple* and other novels by women, sibling relations seem not ony transgresssive, but even to a certain extent, ideal." In almost all fiction that involves fully consummated sibling incest, the results are unhappy. Aside from the Gregorius legend, the most striking deviation from this rule is delivered by Montesquieu in the early eighteenth century.[6]

MONTESQUIEU'S APHERIDON AND ASTARTE: "MY SISTER, MY BRIDE," NO GIFT OF THE MAGI

Montesquieu's fable of Apheridon and Astarte, an episode of his *Persian Letters,* is a love story, telling of a brother's undying affection for his sister, described as both natural and erotic, eventually overcoming all artificial obstacles and reversing the usual pattern in such tales of unhappy endings. The first-person narrator, Apheridon, opens with a declaration that he was barely six years old when he discovered he could not live without his sister. It seemed only natural that they should marry, since their religion permitted a "union already formed by nature." The love is justified by invoking the ancient Zoroastrian Magi, whose natural religion is "perhaps the most ancient of religions in the world."

Montesquieu was certainly aware of the references to the sister as lover and bride in Song of Solomon, and he would have known of the Jewish and Christian traditions that interpreted these references as metaphorical. He was alluding to Western perceptions of ancient Near Eastern poetic traditions: Persian, Egyptian, and Hebraic. He would have been aware of additional brother-sister marriage references in the book of Tobit, retained in Roman Catholic Bibles. In context, it is self-evident that the references in Tobit are metaphorical; as such, they demonstrate that marriage is poetically sacralized by its elevation to the level of the love between a brother and sister. I present herewith passages from the Douay Bible, which remains the preferred translation for many conservative Roman Catholics.[7]

> Raguel said to him, ". . . She is given to you according to the ruling of the scroll from Moses, and it has been decided in heaven that she be given to you. Receive your sister! From now on you are her brother and she is your sister.[8]
>
> And after that they were both shut in together, Tobias rose out of the bed, and said, Sister, arise, and let us pray that God would have pity on us.[9]
>
> And now, Lord, thou knowest, that not for fleshly lust do I take my sister to wife, but only for the love of posterity, in which thy name may be blessed for ever and ever.[10]

Montesquieu's library contained numerous copies of the Catholic Bible containing these passages from the book of Tobit, omitted from Protestant Bibles as "apocryphal."[11] These references to brother and sister are symbolic; both literally and contextually, they are to be understood as signs of tribal kinship, reinforcing the spiritual kinship established by marriage. The book of Tobit can be used reasonably enough to demonstrate that such biblical terms of endearment as "my sister, my love" in Song of Solomon does not imply incest. But literary references to love between brother and sister can be ambiguous, as in Egyptian poetry. Thus, the editors of college textbooks hasten to explain to undergraduate readers that, in these instances, the terms "brother" and "sister" are no more than poetic metaphors.

Montesquieu would not have had access to the Mesopotamian texts, but he alluded to a common belief that Zoroastrians had practiced brother-sister marriage, and he was equally conscious of Pharaohanic traditions and the references in the Song of Solomon. He was as aware as we are today that the most ancient of love poems, whether Sumerian, Egyptian, or biblical, employ the metaphor of affection between brothers and sisters to express the sublimest ideal of romantic passion, and Montesquieu seized on this ideal for his fable of Apheridon and Astarte, which is otherwise just an ordinary love story. He was no subscriber to the pejorative Christian tradition that referred to Zoroastrianism as the "foul Persian creed." Montesquieu's speaker replaced that slur with the transcendentalist notion that Zoroastrian religion was not only "the most ancient" but the most in accord with nature. Whether or not this was accurate, it expressed the Enlightenment doctrine that the Law of Moses did not always accord with the law of Nature.

Montesquieu's first-person narrator, Apheridon, tells us that from earliest childhood, he could not bear separation from his sister, Astarte, for even a moment. His father would have liked to see them married according to the precepts of their ancient religion, but unfortunately, Persia was under Muslim rule, which prevented all consideration of such "holy alliances." Therefore, the father, perceiving the danger, placed the sister in the king's harem under the service of the Sultana, thereby necessitating her conversion to Islam. Eventually the Sultana, becoming jealous of her beauty, married her off to a eunuch, who kept her under constant guard. However, Apheridon was allowed to visit her and present her with the holy book of our lawgiver, Zoroaster. After reading it, she agreed to elope with her brother, and they fled to a remote region.

> We were living together in this remote abode without witnesses, repeating ceaselessly that we would love each other for ever, awaiting the opportunity for some Gheber priest to perform the marriage ceremony prescribed by our holy books. Dear sister, I would say, how holy is this union: nature had united us; our holy Law will unite us further. Finally a priest came to quell our amorous impatience: in the peasant's home he performed all the ceremonies of marriage.

Soon thereafter, they leave Persia for Georgia, but this is not the end of their vicissitudes, for after a year, their money being exhausted, Apheridon departs on a fruitless effort to seek assistance from relatives. He returns not only with empty pockets but finds Astarte had been abducted by invading Tartars, "and as they found her comely, they took her, and sold her to some Jews who were going to Turkey, and left only a small daughter to whom she had given birth some months earlier. I followed these Jews, and caught up with them three leagues from there." To purchase her freedom, he sells himself and his daughter to an Armenian merchant, to whom Astarte then offers herself for the freedom of her husband and her daughter. The Armenian is a kind man who grants them their freedom after a year's service. With a loan from an old friend of their father, Apheridon establishes a business in Smyrna, a cosmopolitan commercial center at the time, and brother and sister lived happily ever after.

Montesquieu's Apheridon and Astarte are not the victims of a cruel father but of an understandably solicitous one. In the course of their adventures, it is almost possible to forget they are brother and sister and their romance is a relatively mild challenge to the Mosaic prohibitions imposed on Christians, Jews, and Muslims. In fact, their unhappy interactions with Jews and Muslims and their salvation by the kindly Armenian do not occasion any discussion of love and marriage in general. Montesquieu's romanticized presentation of a union "*formée par la nature*" contrasts sharply with Denis Diderot's bizarre exercise some years later in his *Supplément au voyage de Bougainville* (1771-1773). To serve ideological ends, Diderot manufactured and imposed upon the Tahitians his own entirely fictitious sexual anarchy and promulgated, at least rhetorically, the "naturalness" of wholesale promiscuity, and seemingly derided the incest taboo. Diderot's presentation must strike contemporary anthropologists as bizarre.

> **Missionary:** But incest! The crimes, the enormous crimes . . . Even the unions of brothers and sisters I have no doubt that they are very common.
>
> **Villager:** Yes! And very approved.

There is no record of any society so unrestrained as the one fabricated by Diderot, a society in which a hypothetical villager might disavow any conception of an incest taboo. Such a view, as we know, would contradict all historical observations. The description demonstrated an excess of literary license; it was a polemic against the hypocrisy of a Christian Europe that sent Christian missionaries to Tahiti while adhering so imperfectly to its own moral standards. It was a contrast to the romantic portrayal of endless love in Montesquieu's romance of Apheridon and Astarte. Diderot's fiction implied that sexual anarchy was humanity's natural state, while Montesquieu's idealized monogamous sibling marriage in terms of natural religion. Absent from both their treatises was the traditional justification for the incestuous marriages of Adam and Eve's children, which Aquinas labored to reconcile with natural law.

"The Poet's Vision, Canto I, Laon and Cythna"
by William Huggins (1852)

– CHAPTER TEN –

ROMANTIC MOVEMENT EXTENDS NATURAL LAW ARGUMENTS OF ENLIGHTENMENT

THE PROBLEMATIC natural law retained its centrality in treatments of sibling incest throughout the romantic movement, when authors frequently sentimentalized the topic. As previously observed, medievalist Elizabeth Archibald has pointed to sharp differences in medieval portrayals of sibling and parental incest, and the distinction, as Thorselv noted, was present in romanticism.[1] Percy Shelley presented father-daughter incest as the mark of tyranny in *The Cenci*, but idealized the relationship of his sibling principals in *Laon and Cythnia* as the apotheosis of love. Alan Richardson generalizes that a "paradoxical view of sibling incest as both ideal and aversive" is characteristic of the romantics, and sees in Samuel Coleridge, an example of "intellectual inconsistency on the subject." Nonetheless, it is noteworthy that Coleridge and other romantics—notably Shelley and Montesquieu—rejected the position that sibling incest aversion is natural, spontaneous, and biologically driven. In fact, Coleridge resorted to the traditional observation of Aquinas that the children of Adam and Eve could not have obeyed the divine commands of fruitfulness and multiplication if sibling incest had been inherently unnatural and repulsive.[2]

The Romantic Movement resurrected the brother-sister trope of the Bible's Song of Solomon and the love poetry of ancient Egypt, Persia, and Mesopotamia, when the love between brother and sister was a metaphor for love between kindred bodies and souls. In the discourse of "like attracts like," sibling incest has been displaced by homoeroticism in recent times. The idealized love of brother and sister was once considered so sacred it must be reserved for royalty, gods, and such favorites of the gods as Homer's children of Aeolus in the eighth century BCE. Four centuries later, Plato declared sibling incest naturally repulsive, only to be contradicted eight centuries later by Aquinas, who said it was potentially "too ardent." The Romantics were, therefore, inheritors of conflicting traditions in their treatments of sibling passion.

The question of whether it is nature or society that suppresses sibling eroticism was recurrent in British Romanticism. Peter L. Thorslev and Alan Richardson suggest authors were sufficiently squeamish enough on sexual matters to avoid representations of physical incest between full siblings. This might be either because the sister must satisfy the audience by remaining chaste, or because the lovers had no actual biogenetic bond. Characteristically, however, Romantic literature, like its medieval precedents, rejects the notion that close association in childhood spontaneously triggers aversion. Prior to the rise of Darwinian anthropology, there prevailed an almost universal assumption that childhood intimacy could easily engender the intense romantic ardor represented in the works of Manley, Chateaubriand, and Montesquieu. This seems reasonable enough, otherwise no one would ever marry the girl next door.[3]

Thorslev notes the sibling incest theme in Chateaubriand's *René* and the likely influence of Jacques-Henri de Saint-Pierre's *Paul and Virginie*, "one of the most popular novels of the close of the eighteenth century . . . are not, in fact, brother and sister, but they were raised as if they were by their widowed mothers . . . as infants they lay in the same crib and were even suckled upon occasion at the same breast," alluding to the medieval notion of "milk kinship," once considered an obstacle to marriage. Thorslev observes of pre-Romantic depictions of sibling ardor that "These incestuous loves are in every case both mutual and idealized, although some of these works may seem ludicrous today, accustomed as we are to sexual abnormality in our literature."[4]

Thorslev made the preceding observation in 1965, and conceptions of "sexual abnormality" have been drastically altered since then. As of this writing, society rightly condemns coercion, abuse of authority, the exploitation of underage minors, and some instances of adultery. Modern courts and police agencies currently enforce stricter definitions of rape, abuse, and victimization than those prevailing in the mid-twentieth century, if only in some respects. We note the automatic contemporary reflex to define incest strictly in terms of power abuse by persons in positions of power or authority. This is supplemented by the presupposition that sibling incest is invariably duress committed by an older and stronger male. Thorslev's line of thought must appear strange indeed to many persons who were still in their infancy when he wrote them in 1965: "The first and most obvious of these implications is that sibling incest, as exonerated, made sympathetic, and even idealized by these three poets, is the ultimate expression for the Romantic Movement of the tradition of courtly or 'romantic' love."[5]

LORD BYRON'S *MANFRED* AND *CAIN*

Innuendos concerning brother-sister dyads have long obsessed students of the Romantic Movement. When I started graduate school in 1965, one heard coy suggestions concerning William and Dorothy Wordsworth, Charles and Mary Lamb, and Percy and Elizabeth Shelley, but most frequently discussed were the rumors of Byron's having an incestuous affair with his half-sister, Augusta Leigh. This, along with other scandals, occasioned his ostracism and permanent departure from England in 1816. So far, there is no direct evidence in support of an affair with Augusta, and Byron's biographer, John S. Chapman, who is more than suspicous, asks, "Why all the bother? After all, Augusta was only a half-sister, so the relationship—if it occurred—could have been no more than demi-incest. In terms of human genetics, it varied only slightly from the successive first-cousin marriages common among the British aristocracy of the time and almost a regular practice among royalty."[6]

The most commonly cited evidence is indefinite, drawn from a letter Byron wrote to Augusta on April 25, 1814, which some scholars interpret as a subtle admission of something extraordinary, but it is difficult to find anything incriminating in the following often-reproduced lines.

> Oh! but it is "worth while"—I can't tell you why—and it is not an "Ape" and if it is—that must be my fault—however I will positively reform—you must however allow—that it is utterly impossible I can ever be half as well liked elsewhere—and I have been all my life trying to make some one love me—& never got the sort that I preferred before.—But positively she & I will grow good—& all that—& so we are now and shall be these three weeks & more too. – – –

The protagonist of Byron's dramatic poem, *Manfred,* implores the "Witch of the Alps" to resurrect his sister, Astarte, whose death is attributed to the consummation of an incestuous love. Manfred alludes to a hypothetical deadly sin, and many readers interpret this as relating to an incestuous relationship.

> . . . Thou lovèdst me
> Too much, as I loved thee: we were not made
> To torture thus each other, though it were
> The deadliest sin to love as we have loved.

Whether the poem makes it clear that Astarte was Manfred's sister has been questioned, and it is unclear whether an incestuous relationship between her and Manfred is implied. Joseph Lew argues that Byron naming the heroine Astarte indicates an allusion to Montesquieu's tale of Apheridon and Astarte.[7] The critical tradition of discovering incest in *Manfred* calls to mind the critical tradition of discovering incest in Edgar Allen Poe's short story, "The Fall of the House of Usher." In both narratives the possibility is conceivable, perhaps even likely, but indefinite, and so, too, is the mythology surrounding Byron and Augusta.

In response to the allegations about Byron's private life, Harriet Beecher Stowe expressed outrage in an *Atlantic Monthly* article of September 1869 entitled "The True Story of Lady Byron's Life" and treated the matter at greater length in her book, *The Byron Controversy,* published the following year. Stowe's stated purpose was to defend Lady Byron from attacks she had endured for separating from her husband in the wake of his ostracism and departure for the continent. Rumors of Byron's potential incest were widespread, but Stowe was denounced in the press for openly mentioning the unmentionable.[8] She argued that Lord Byron had denounced himself "with all the sophistries of his powerful mind. He repudiated Christianity as authority and asserted the right of every human being to follow out what he called 'the impulses of nature.'" The word "incest" appeared only once in Stowe's *Atlantic Monthly* essay, but the word "nature" appeared nineteen times, for Byron, in mentioning the "impulses of nature," had drawn her into the ancient controversy over whether the primeval intermarriage of Adam and Eve's children accorded with natural law.

Stowe had no difficulty finding evidence of Byron's depravity in "one of his dramas the reasoning by which he justified himself in incest." It was in his drama, *Cain,* where Adah, Cain's sister and wife, speaks of her marriage to Cain and speculates on the future marriage of their offspring. Adah says: [9]

> Must not my daughter love her brother Enoch?
> . . . O, my God!
> Shall they not love and bring forth things that love
> Out of their love? have they not drawn their milk
> Out of this bosom? was not he, their father,
> Born of the same sole womb, in the same hour

With me? did we not love each other? and
In multiplying our being multiply

It bears endless repeating (because most readers of Genesis refuse to see it) that scripture does not say Cain became "a fugitive and a vagabond in the earth." God reversed his curse and gave a special mark, effectively a blessing, to Cain, who settled with his wife and built a city. The couple did not end their lives in barbarism or desolation. Cain and his wife suffered no more than other notorious couples of the Bible. David gained Bathsheba through adultery and murder, but the union brought forth "Solomon in all his glory." Abraham delivered Sarah, his sister-wife, twice to the harems of other men, and he profited handsomely in both instances. A modern reader might ask whether Sarah and Bathsheba had any freedom of choice, but the Bible does not allow either to address their compliance. Cain's wife was endowed with no voice in the canonical books, but Byron decided she must be allowed to express herself.

As much as she despised Byron, Harriet Beecher Stowe fully appreciated "the sophistries of his powerful mind." She was not, however, willing to bestow on him any praise for one of his more interesting achievements—his decision to give voice to a biblical personage who is usually nameless and almost always shadowy. Cain's wife had been endowed with numerous names by ancient authorities, both Jewish and Christian, but Byron endowed her with both a name and a voice, and that voice was strong and sympathetic. Byron was gifted enough as a mythographer to end *Cain* on a note of agony, with Adah's mourning the loss of one brother while shouldering the burden of the other's torment.

Adah:
A dreary, and an early doom, my brother,
Has been thy lot! Of all who mourn for thee,
I alone must not weep. My office is
Henceforth to dry up tears, and not to shed them;
But yet of all who mourn, none mourn like me,
Not only for thyself, but him who slew thee.
Now, Cain! I will divide thy burden with thee.

PERCY SHELLEY'S WITCH OF ATLAS AND *LAON AND CYTHNA*

Less direct than the accusations concerning Byron and Augusta are innuendos related to Percy B. Shelley's closeness to his sister Elizabeth during childhood and adolescence, but there is no evidence of any erotic relationship. In 1810, they published a small volume of poetry together, which certainly relates to Shelley's poetic idealization of affectionate and intellectual companionship between siblings. Shelley later attempted to arrange a liaison between Elizabeth and his friend Thomas Jefferson Hogg.[10] This is not to deny a possibly autobiographical component to his fascination with incest and unconventional marital relationships, which were aspects of his belief that artificial conventions should not proscribe natural impulses. Nonetheless, while he romanticized sibling eros, he equated paternal incest with tyranny and saw it as justifying patricide in his drama, *The Cenci.* Shelley, like Montesquieu, proclaimed the naturalness of sibling romance directly in *Laon and Cythna,* implicitly in his description of "coy" lovers in "The Witch of Atlas," and again more directly in his shorter lyric in "Love's Philosophy."

> No sister flower would be forgiven,
> If it disdained its brother;
> And the sunlight clasps the earth,
> And the moonbeams kiss the sea:
> What are all these kissings worth,
> If thou kiss not me?

Byron and Shelley's association during their sojourn in the Swiss Alps leads to the unavoidable intimation that Shelley's poem "The Witch of Atlas" bears a relationship to Byron's "Witch of the Alps." Byron invoked his witch in *Manfred*, which he composed in the summer of 1816; that same summer, Shelley composed his poem "Mont Blanc," referencing the "still cave of the witch poesy." Shelley's Witch of Atlas may thus be perceived as the embodiment of his poetic imagination in service to his philosophy of nature and his utopian political ideals. She is close to Nature but not a personification of Nature; she is a creative force and a Promethean trickster goddess whose "many pranks" disrupt "the code of Custom's lawless law" and undermine the authority of priests and kings.

The witch can "write strange dreams upon the brain," bringing together "timid lovers, who had been so coy. They hardly knew whether they loved or not." The uncertainty of these lovers and the implicit secrecy of their lovemaking is reminiscent of Zeus and Hera's youthful encounters "which their parents knew not of." They seem to occupy the same household, sleeping in proximity as do Gregorius's parents, whose "beds stand so close [*ir betten stuonden also nâ*]," they easily approach each other. Incited not by the devil's temptation but inspired by Shelley's "Witch Poesy," they seem like sleepwalkers.

> Would rise out of their rest, and take sweet joy,
> To the fulfillment of their inmost thought;
> And when next day the maiden and the boy
> Met one another, both, like sinners caught,
> Blushed at the thing which each believed was done
> Only in fancy—till the tenth moon shone;

This describes no ordinary tryst, for it is clear these hesitant, "timid lovers" spend their nights close enough together that they need not venture abroad "to take sweet joy." Like Homer's stealthy Olympians, they are enabled in their clandestine meetings by domestic proximity, and the youngsters blush "like sinners caught" when inevitably they meet the next day. And when the proof of their love becomes evident with the tenth moon, the maiden and the boy do not suffer the unhappy fate of Gower's Canace and Machaire or the difficulties encountered by Montesquieu's Apheridon and Astarte. Shelley offers the youngsters his assistance in the Preface to *Laon and Cythna,* helping them "break through the crust of those outworn opinions on which established institutions depend." Thus, like Montesquieu, he appealed to the innocent state of nature in which Adam and Eve's children were fruitful and multiplied, and "therefore to the most universal of all feelings." His Witch of Atlas breaks through what are "only crimes of convention" and presides over a marriage in which nature triumphs over artifice.

And then the Witch would let them take no ill:
Of many thousand schemes which lovers find,
The Witch found one,—and so they took their fill
Of happiness in marriage warm and kind.

The poet's ominous allusion to the "many thousand schemes" would seem to recall the shock and horror of "sinners caught" in the dilemmas of Hartmann's Gregorius legend, in Gower's story of Canace and Machaire, and in Manley's tale of Polydore and Urania. Shelley's witch allows the lovers to "take no ill," from the schemes that prevent a happy ending. In a lengthier poem, *Rosalind and Helen,* Shelley presents the typical outcome when siblings become lovers.

A fearful tale! The truth was worse:
For here a sister and a brother
Had solemnized a monstrous curse,
Meeting in this fair solitude:
For beneath yon very sky,
Had they resigned to one another
Body and soul. The multitude,
Tracking them to the secret wood,
Tore limb from limb their innocent child,
And stabbed and trampled on its mother;
But the youth, for God's most holy grace,
A priest saved to burn in the market-place.

Although the relationship of the "timid lovers" under the aegis of the Witch of Atlas arrived at "happiness in marriage," as the course of sibling love never ran smooth, but this was due to artificial conventions in opposition to nature. Montesquieu appealed to the legendary natural religion of Zoroastrianism in defense of Apheridon and Astarte and tacitly to the unions of brothers and sisters in Genesis. Shelley and Montesquieu followed Diderot in portraying sibling unions as natural in the abscence of religious and legal obstacles. As if anticipating and rejecting Westermarck's hypothesis, Shelley presented *phlilos* and *eros* as naturally intertwined and held it to be self-evident that romantic love arises spontaneously between persons who grow up together.

And such is Nature's modesty, that those
Who grow together cannot choose but love,
If faith or custom do not interpose (VI:XL)

While consistently radical in his attitudes toward sibling incest, Shelley was less supportive of male homosexuality. He published *A Discourse on the Manners of the Ancient Greeks Relative to the Subject of Love*, which was tolerant respecting nonsexual affinities but expressed disgust for physical homosexual contact with such terms as "ridiculous," "detestable," "disgusting," and "gross." As David Conner observes in his translation of Plato's *Symposium*, Shelley altered or expurgated the positive references to homosexuality.[11] His hostility was possibly rooted in his boyhood experience at Eton, where a tradition of muscular homoeroticism persisted into the twentieth century. At Eton, he was nicknamed "mad Shelley" due to his resistance to "fagging," a system in which younger boys were required to act as servants to the older boys, sometimes involving physical and/or sexual abuse.[12] Boarding school homosexuality and father-daughter incest were both relegated to the realm of power abuse, and the institutionalization of the unnatural by church and state. Eton, Oxford, and the Church of England exemplified the violation of nature by social institutions and motivated Shelley's publication of *The Necessity of Atheism* in 1811, as was consistent with his rebellion against a cruel and capricious God who presented His truth "through a glass darkly" and punished His children for seeking knowledge.

Shelley's most controversial exploration of the sibling incest motif was in *Laon and Cythna*, which he revised and republished as *The Revolt of Islam*. The similarities between the poems' sibling lovers Apheridon and Astarte, the brother-sister protagonists of Montesquieu's *Persian Letters*, has been observed by Joseph Lew, Alan Richardson, and others. Montesquieu's hero and heroine must overcome the impediments to their marriage imposed by Islamic laws and customs, and Shelley's title, if not its content, suggests the same obstacle. Neither work implies that the sibling incest taboo is peculiar to Islam, and despite Shelley's title, the poem's references to Islam are purely incidental. His publishers, who were certainly not Muslims, insisted on revisions because they recognized its offensiveness to a largely Christian audience. Thus, as John Donavan notes, Shelley, "By contriving to replace five occurrences of the word 'sister' and three of 'brother', as well as two related phrases suggesting a blood relation, Shelley writes the incest between the lovers Laon and Cythna out of the poem."[13]

Even in its revised form, however, the work defended the naturalness of a love affair that had arisen during childhood between two persons raised as siblings. Richardson notes that both versions contained an incidental reference to England's "inbred monsters," (Canto 11:22), but in that context, the words were no more than a gratuitous swipe at the British aristocracy; they were by no means a condemnation of sibling romance, which Shelley justified philosophically in several instances. He defended its employment as an artistic device in a letter to Maria Gisborne, where he wrote "incest is like many other incorrect things a very poetical circumstance."[14] But shock was not its only value, nor was "poetical circumstance" its only justification. Shelley offered a more encompassing philosophical rationalization in the original preface to *Laon and Cythna*, where he endowed incest with a universal moral value.

> In the personal conduct of my hero and heroine, there is one circumstance which was intended to startle the reader from the trance of ordinary life. It was my object to break through the crust of those outworn opinions on which established institutions depend. I have appealed therefore to the most universal of all feelings, and have endeavored to strengthen the moral sense by forbidding it to waste its energies in seeking to avoid actions which are only crimes of convention. It is because there is so great a multitude of artificial vices that there are so few real virtues. Those feelings alone which are benevolent or malevolent are essentially good or bad. The circumstance of which I speak was introduced, however, merely to accustom men to that charity and toleration which the exhibition of a practice widely differing from their own has a tendency to promote.* Nothing indeed can be more mischievous than many actions innocent in themselves which might bring down upon individuals the bigoted contempt and rage of the multitude.
>
> * The sentiments connected with and characteristic of this circumstance, have no personal reference to the Writer.

The first noteworthy alteration to the poem was in the preface, eliminating its asterisked footnote. The second was in Canto 2, when the lovers were originally introduced as siblings:

> I had a little sister, whose fair eyes
> Were loadstars of delight, which drew me home
> When I might wander forth . . .

But the first of these lines was removed and replaced as follows:

> An orphan with my parents lived, whose eyes
> Were loadstars of delight, which drew me home
> When I might wander forth . . .

He also dropped from the lovemaking scene in Canto 6:39, 2694, its final line that "linked a sister and a brother." In both versions, however, Shelley was bound by the convention that the worldly happiness of sibling lovers cannot long endure. Montesquieu gave his story of Apheridon and Astarte a happy ending, allowing them to become married, have a child, and live happily ever after. Shelley's Laon and Cythna, like the parents of Hartmann's Gregorius, can attain happiness only after death and transfiguration. Their idyllic existence at the poem's opening is disrupted almost immediately, and it is unclear whether their love is consummated before Othman's tyrant minions abduct Cythna. Like Montesquieu's Astarte, Cythna endures confinement in a seraglio, but unlike Astarte, she must endure sexual assault by her captor. Whether or not Othman is successful in raping her has puzzled some, but not all, readers. Cythna later tells Laon that Othman, "aghast and pale" in the face of her revulsion, has her cast into a dungeon, where, in a half-mad state, she recalls having a baby, but her narrative of this sequence is nightmarish and phantasmagoric.

> Methought I was about to be a mother—Month after month went by, and still I dreamed That we should soon be all to one another, I and my child; and still new pulses seemed To beat beside my heart, and still I deemed There was a babe within—and, when the rain Of winter through the rifted cavern streamed, Methought, after

> a lapse of lingering pain, I saw that lovely shape, which near my heart had lain.
>
> It was a babe, beautiful from its birth,—It was like thee, dear love, its eyes were thine, Its brow, its lips, and so upon the earth It laid its fingers, as now rest on mine Thine own, beloved!—"twas a dream divine; Even to remember how it fled, how swift, How utterly, might make the heart repine,—Though "twas a dream."

Some readers believe the child to be more than a figment of Cythna's delirium, proof that Othman, having taken her by force, is the biological father, while others note Cythna describing the child as resembling Laon, and then retracting everything as "Though t'was a dream." John Taylor Coleridge, a distant relative of the poet, wrote a caustic review of both versions for *The Quarterly Review,* noting Othman's persistent evil "to whom this model of purity and virtue *had borne a child.*" Carlos Baker seemingly believed that Othman was "repulsed by the virtuous Cythna" and that he imprisoned her for that reason. By contrast, Lorraine Anne Morris emphatically states that Cythna was "repeatedly raped by the tyrant." Brent Steven Robida sees evidence of at least one rape but confesses to some doubt as to the consequence, saying, "Othman's child was ostensibly conceived when he raped Cythna, yet the child identifies with Laon and accompanies Laon and Cythna in the afterlife to the Temple of the Spirit." Teddy Lynn Chichester is certain of the child's paternity and asserts that Shelley "displaces" Laon with Othman, "the 'sceptred wretch' who rapes Cythna, enable[ing] the young man to avoid violating Cythna's virginity, but he also allows Laon to father a child without actually inseminating his sister-spouse."[15]

If Shelley, who had no qualms about the artistic representation of rape or incest, had reasons for preserving Cythna's virginity and avoiding an incestuous impregnation, he did not make them clear. He gave us ample suggestions of consensual sexual activity between Laon and Cythna prior to her abduction. There is nothing to justify Chichester's use of the term "violating" and plenty to justify Robida's use of the term "ostensible" with respect to Othman's paternity. Cythna and Laon were, as Baker notes, "lovers in their youth," and Laon, who tells us they were together night and day, describes her sleeping in his arms. Many readers have complained of the poet's lack of artistic and philosophical meticulousness in these and other matters, but even those readers, certain that Cythna was passively "impaled" by the "sceptered tyrant," cannot be sure it was Othman who impregnated her.

Neither rape nor incest inevitably results in pregnancy, and there is nothing in the narrative to invalidate Carlos Baker's claim that Othman was "repulsed." Cythna's account of her struggle and Othman's flight is confined to one stanza of mysterious and imprecise language that leaves almost everything to the imagination.[16]

> She told me what a loathsome agony
> Is that when selfishness mocks love's delight,
> Foul as in dream's most fearful imagery,
> To dally with the mowing dead—that night
> All torture, fear, or horror made seem light
> Which the soul dreams or knows, and when the day
> Shone on her awful frenzy, from the sight
> Where like a Spirit in fleshly chains she lay
> Struggling, aghast and pale the Tyrant fled away.

I shall give Shelley the benefit of the doubt and grant that the presumption of this sequence was intentionally ambiguous, both artistically and politically. Laon recounts Cythna's description of the events, and he is as vague in his narrative as she was in her recollection of the pregnancy, the nativity, and the child's physical appearance. Cythna's, Laon's, and the poet's intentions are seemingly to assign at least the possibility of fatherhood to Laon, while questioning the necessity of making him the biological father of a child whose very existence has been thrown, for whatever reasons, into the realm of nightmare fantasy. Cythna relives her experiences in her account to Laon, describing a state of shock and delirium, twice using the word "methought," concluding with "Though t'was a dream." The political intentions of the poet are unclear; we do not know whether his goal was to challenge the traditional sacrosanctity of biological paternity, or to assert the radical legitimacy of a brother and sister having a child together. Perhaps the melding of these objectives was precisely his goal.

John Cordy Jeaffreson noted the ambiguity but maintained, in his perpetually useful 1885 biography, *The Real Shelley*, that the child embodied the poet's complicated intentions.

> . . . to some readers this charming child appears to have been the tyrant's daughter, instead of Laon's offspring. Sir John Taylor Coleridge's memorable article in the *Quarterly Review* shows that, whilst recognizing with repugnance, the incest of Laon's intercourse with his sister, he regarded the child as the issue of the despot's passion. But on this point I conceive the reviewer to have erred through the mystifications and ambiguities of the narrative. To me it is clear that Shelley meant to intimate to careful readers of the monstrous story, that Cythna's child was Laon's daughter. . . . The two actors of the poem, in whom it is sought to interest the reader most strongly, and for whose stainless purity and unqualified goodness the author solicits our admiration, are a brother and sister, whose embraces result in the birth of a little girl, no less lovely in person and mind than her parents. The main purpose of the poem, which has numerous subordinate and minor objects, is to plant the incestuous pair in the reader's affection, and lure him into regarding so exemplary an instance of conjugal affection with sympathy and approval.[17]

Jeaffreson, despite his irrepressible Victorian abhorrence of the poet's unconventional sexual morality, is more candid than most of the poem's more recent critics in acknowledging "the mystifications and ambiguities of the narrative." He admits that the first explicit description of anything sexual between Laon and Cythna does not occur until Canto VI, verse XXXIX, after Cythna has been delivered from captivity. The amorous linkage of "a sister and a brother" is not ambiguous in the poem's original version, which anticipates and challenges the Westermarck hypothesis that sexual indifference is the natural result of early childhood contact.

> There we unheeding sate, in the communion
> Of interchanged vows, which, with a rite
> Of faith most sweet and sacred, stamped our union,—

Few were the living hearts which could unite
Like ours, or celebrate a bridal night
With such close sympathies, for to each other
Had high and solemn hopes, the gentle might
Of earliest love, and all the thoughts which smother
Cold Evil's power, now linked a sister and a brother,

I agree with Jeaffreson that the poem's mystification and ambiguities, especially in its most relevant stanza, result in ambiguities concerning the child's paternity. These may be the result of the poet's neglect of artistic and philosophical discipline, and over the centuries, *Laon and Cythna* has been criticized repeatedly on those grounds. Or the poet may have indulged in a gratuitous swipe at the traditional importance assigned to paternity. It is a comforting thought, however, that following Laon and Cythna's burning at the stake and their resurrection in Elysium, their own child steers the enchanted boat that bears them through the wilderness paradise.

There is no reason to suspect Shelley intentionally alluded to the Gregorius of Hartmann von Aue, although his child of incest, like the child who greeted Laon and Cythna, presided over the beatification of his parents. Shelley's strategy of leaving the paternity of the divine child vague left the poet unable to exploit the full poetic potential of its possibly incestuous conception.

If Jeaffreson and Baker are right, and John Taylor Coleridge and others are wrong, then Shelley's hero and heroine can be seen as cognates of Gregorius's parents and congruent with the tradition of redemption through sin, although Shelley does not configure them as sinners and does not present their child as performing strenuous acts of atonement. Coleridge does not view the child as the product of incest, but his assessment of *Laon and Cythna* deserves serious consideration, if only as an example of the third-party shock and horror usually attached to depictions of consanguinamorous affairs. I take exception to some particulars in his phraseology:

> Mr. Shelley specifies with great *sang froid* the commission of *incest*! . . . marriage he cannot endure, and there would at once

> be a stop put to the lamented increase of adulterous connections amongst us, whilst by repealing the canon of heaven against incest, he would add to the purity, and heighten the ardour of those feelings with which brother and sister now regard each other. . . .

Coleridge cannot accuse Shelley of regarding incest with "*sang froid*," since the poet always approaches the matter with self-righteous passion. He regards father-daughter incest in *The Cenci* with such revulsion as to justify patricide. But like Montesquieu in *Les Lettres Persanes*, he views love and marriage between a brother and sister as ordained by nature but smothered by society. Coleridge likewise misrepresents Shelley's attitudes regarding the institution of marriage. To be sure, Shelley romanticized the sexual interlude between Cythna and Laon without marrying them, but his Witch of Atlas offers "happiness in marriage warm and kind" to "coy," and furtive lovers as an alternative to the "many schemes" so desperate and barbarous resorted to elsewhere in the poetic tradition, such as exposing a child to wild animals, piercing a child's feet and hanging it in a tree, or setting the child adrift on the ocean.

Hansel and Gretel gingerbread house
by Pauli Ebner (1895)

– CHAPTER ELEVEN –

US AGAINST THE WORLD: EXILE AND ANIMAL TRANSFORMATION NARRATIVES

THE GRIMM brothers collected at least twenty-one versions of the sibling exile narrative. Some versions of Hansel and Gretel present symbolic passages through puberty and may represent sexual barriers that emerge between opposite-sex siblings as they reach adolescence. All versions of *Brüderchen und Schwesterchen* stories isolate the children while de-sexualizing the brother as the sister passes from childhood to marriageable age.

What these stories have in common with the story of Adam and Eve is their representation of the universal childhood fear of parental exposure and chastisement. The fable of Adam and Eve instills in the child a terror at the thought of being "unacceptable," which persists into adulthood in forms that invariably go unrecognized by those most susceptible to the terror of being "caught with their pants down." The fables of Hansel and Gretel and of Adam and Eve are parables representing the fear of ostracism. The Grimm brothers published three of these basic horror stories with twenty-one variations on the theme of the cruelly exiled brother and sister.

These fables present problems of translation due to their employment of German diminutive forms; the neutral gender, which always accompanies the German diminutive, can convey a quality of affectionate endearment that cannot be approximated in English when a mother, lover, or opposite-sex sibling makes use of "baby talk." A younger sister might affectionately wheedle or coax an older brother by asking him to "be a lamb" or addressing him in baby-talk. We might translate the Grimms' "*Lämmchen*," therefore, as "Lamby" or "Lambikins," but for "*Fischchen*," we can only resort to "Little Fish."

English has its equivalent forms for Hanschen or Hansel, approximated in English when we replace the name John with diminutives, as in Jack Kennedy or Jackie Robinson. The names Greta, Gretchen, or Gretel easily carry into English, but there is no satisfactory equivalent for the Grimms' title "*Brüderchen*" and "*Schwesterchen*." The common translations "Brother and Sister" or "Little Sister and Little Brother" are unsatisfying nonsense, especially when the fable's burden is to show the transference of seniority from one sibling to the other. In several of these brother-sister narratives, the brother is divested of conventional gender authority and sexuality while the sister passes through puberty. At the outset, she may be depicted as younger, but she ripens dramatically into adulthood and authority, in some cases becoming her big brother's protectress and guardian, thus supplanting the mother, as when Gretel saves Hansel from the wicked witch, who, in some versions, is the stepmother's *doppelgänger*.

Our present concern is with the core features of the story of Adam and Eve and variations in brother-sister exile folklore. The theme, which appears in the stories of Hansel and Gretel and other brother-sister narratives recorded by the Grimm brothers, has variant forms, and each of these has more than one version. This variability means that some more intriguing features may not appear in all the narratives. Furthermore, each Hansel and Gretel story has a complicated publishing history, as do the various cognates, but all have resemblances. Some of these variants follow the siblings into adulthood, and these feature the storytellers' tacit allusions to sexual maturation and its accompanying tensions and taboos.

"HANSEL AND GRETEL"

Like Adam and Eve, Hansel and Gretel are involuntarily exiled, but unlike Adam and Eve, they are exiled through no fault of their own and, therefore, have no cause for shame, nor do they experience shame, not even when they get in trouble for pilfering sweets. But their story, like that of Genesis, reminds children of the power of adults to determine what they can and cannot eat and whether they will be allowed to eat. Their parents give the children pieces of bread before abandoning them, but Hansel crumbles and scatters his in an ineffective effort to mark a trail out of the forest. The children stumble upon a witch's house made of bread, cake, and sugar, which they steal, but only to appease the hunger their parents have not satisfied. The witch seizes the children and then controls their food intake. The witch seeks to fatten Hansel, while Gretel receives more meager fare until she pushes the witch into her own oven. Afterward, the siblings rifle the witch's house and appropriate her valuables, then return to their father, who "had not had even one happy hour since he had left the children in the woods. However, the woman had died." In the 1812 version "the woman" is described as their mother. In the 1840 version, she becomes the *Stiefmutter* to emphasize her character as an alien and intrusive presence. By the 1857 version, she is called simply "the woman" who dies conveniently—and synchronously—with Gretel's shoving her *Doppelgänger* into the oven.[1]

The siblings begin their story as "babes in the woods," but their story is a rite of passage; with their maturation, there is the growth of a sexual barrier between them. It is noteworthy that the siblings encounter no such obstacle on their way into the forest but only after their ordeal with the serpent-witch. The problem of this obstacle is solved by the resourceful and mature Gretel, who sees a white duck (*Entchen*) and implores it to carry them across: "The duckling approached and Hansel sat upon it and asked his sister to sit next to him. 'No' answered Gretel, 'it would be too heavy for the duckling, it must bring us across one after the other. The good animal did so.'"[2]

Gretel, too, is a witch; she reveals she possesses uncanny resources with her power to conjure the duck and her knowledge concerning it. She somehow knows and firmly declares that she and her brother must not mount the duck together, which surprises Hansel. Equally surprising is her rationale; she says the duck is too small to carry them both, but this is as mystifying as the enchantment that enables a duckling to carry either one of them on its back. To emphasize the animal's small size, the Grimm brothers preserved their informants "*Entchen*," often translated as "duckling," and its size is doubly accented by the diminutive "*Thierchen*," small animal. The incident of the water obstacle and Gretel's ability to summon a magical "duckling" to assist in the crossing is missing from some well-known versions of the narrative, along with Gretel's admonition at the water's edge that they must not mount it together. The sole function of this extraneous incident is to emphasize Gretel's newfound dominance, her mandate of sexual separation, and her accompanying function as proprietress of decorum.

"BRÜDERCHEN UND SCHWESTERCHEN"

The Grimm tale of "*Brüderchen und Schwesterchen*" is a more direct allegory than "Hansel and Gretel" of the passage from childhood to sexual maturity. Usually the title is translated, unsatisfyingly, as "Little Brother and Little Sister," which comes across poorly in English. The Grimms preserved the affixation to their names of the diminutive "*chen*" suffix, which cannot imply an age discrepancy; the siblings cannot both be younger than the other. The suffix is intended to awaken the reader's sympathy by stressing their youthfulness, vulnerability, and mutual affection. The terms "*Brüderchen*" and "*Schwesterchen*" cannot be transformed in an English that expresses with equal convenience the idea of the siblings' pathetic vulnerability and the frustrated attempts of each in turn to protect the other from threatening adults. In the end the siblings are delivered from their cruel destinies only by a supernatural intervention.

"*Brüderchen und Schwesterchen*" resembles "Hansel and Gretel" but is vastly more suggestive regarding the biologically predetermined roles and socially designated barriers between the siblings. *Brüderchen and Schwesterchen*, unlike Hansel and Gretel, are not driven from home but choose to leave voluntarily, significantly at the initiative of *Brüderchen*, who takes the initiative: "Brother takes his sister by the hand," saying, "Come, we will go forth together into the wide world." The male sibling initially assumes dominance as he leads his sister by the hand into the forest to escape their cruel stepmother.

Early in the story we learn that the stepmother is a witch who pursues them into the forest, where she presents Hansel with a series of temptations, including tasting the gingerbread, akin to Adam and Eve's tasting of the forbidden fruit. *Brüderchen* is tempted to drink from springs the stepmother/witch has enchanted. At this point, the sister's voice becomes more adult, the leadership roles are reversed, and the sister assumes authority. She suddenly possesses greater wisdom and knowledge than her brother when they come upon the enchanted brook. In effect, she is an "anti-Eve" with her premonition that something is not right: "I bid thee brother, drink not, or you will become a wild animal and rend me."[3]

The original verb used, *zerreissen*, means to rend or tear apart, and may suggest *Schwesterchen*'s hymenal vulnerability.[4] Suddenly, the girl is endowed with an adult awareness of the danger her male sibling represents, but which neither foresaw when he took her by the hand and led her into the forest. *Brüderchen* pays heed to *Schwesterchen*'s premonition, overcomes the temptation to drink, and proceeds with her through the forest, where they come upon a second brook. Once again, *Schwesterchen* counsels the brother to resist his urges, expressing similar fears in similar terms. This time, her premonition is that if he drinks, he will be transformed into a wolf and devour her. In both instances, she fears her brother will ravish her, and he submits to her warnings. Something different happens when the siblings arrive at a third brook, for sister expresses a contrasting premonition. She fears separation from her brother rather than his potential hunger for her flesh:

> *Das Schwesterchen sprach: Ach, Brüderchen, ich bitt' dich, trink' nicht, sonst wirst du ein Reh und läufst mir fort.*
>
> [The sister spoke: Ah, dear brother, I bid thee, drink not, or you will become a deer and run away from me.]

Brüderchen obediently resists the temptations that would turn him into a rapacious beast but not the third temptation, and he drinks from a spring that transforms him into the harmless fawn. In this story, the sister is not a temptress—far from it; she is the voice of conscience that represses his baser animal temptations. Transformed into a fawn, the brother retains his human personality and power of speech, and his sister promises she will never leave him. She ties her golden garter around his neck and feeds him from her hand. In the 1812 version, the siblings make their home in a cave where they live alone and happy for "long years in the woods." In the 1819 version, they do even better and discover a little house, where they live an idyllic life for the "long time that they were thus alone in the wilderness. . . . In the evenings when the sister was tired and had said her prayers, she lay her head upon the back of fawn, her pillow, on which she gently slept. And if only the brother had his human shape, it would have been a grand life."[5]

Here, the Grimm tale presents a woodland idyll of indeterminate length. Time must stop for the interlude to be truly Edenic. *Schwesterchen* lays her head on the back of her virginal fawn-brother in a charming alteration of the medieval iconography in which the fierce, wild unicorn can be tamed only by a virgin and meekly lays its head in her lap. *Brüderchen* is analogous to the unicorn of legend, although transformed into a fawn—significantly not a fierce unicorn, nor the virile stag often placed proximate to Eve in renaissance paintings. What a grand life *Brüderchen* and *Schwesterchen* might have enjoyed, otherwise, alone in the woods, sporting by day and snuggling by night, if only he had retained his human shape. They remain alone in this almost-Eden, dwelling in some versions "for long years" in which there is a transformation from childhood to adulthood.

One fateful day, the woodland idyll is rudely brought to an end as the siblings become aware of the horns of the king's hunting party in the forest. The girl attempts to confine her brother in the cabin but cannot. He tells her that, despite the risk, he feels an irresistible urge to brave the danger of the chase. The storyteller does not explain *Brüderchen*'s impulse to escape from *Schwesterchen*'s comfort, joy, and protective love. He must join the hunt, where he is wounded by the prince who leads the chase. Now the structure of the story changes with the introduction of an adult male figure. The prince pursues the fawn to the cabin, where he discovers *Schwesterchen*, who has become a marriageable woman during her years in the forest. Immediately the prince falls in love; he and *Schwesterchen* are married, and soon they are blessed with a child. Nonetheless, she keeps *Brüderchen* close to her.

At this point in the story, the witch/stepmother reappears. She murders *Schwesterchen* by boiling her to death in her bathtub and replaces her with her own daughter, who, although she is one-eyed and ugly, deceives the prince. The ghost of *Schwesterchen* is *Brüderchen*'s guardian, and even amid her misfortunes, she seems to feel as responsible for his welfare as she does for that of her child. She haunts the castle in the shape of a dove (*Seelenvögel*) who cries in the night, "*Was macht mein Kind? Was macht mein Reh?* [What's happened to my child; what's happened to my deer?]" At the end of the story, the dove-sister and the stag-brother are magically returned to their human forms. The false queen is chased into the forest and devoured by wild beasts, and the witch is cast into a fire and burnt to ashes.

This story is similar in significant respects to that of Hansel and Gretel. In the beginning, *Schwesterchen* seems to be the younger of the two, for the guardian brother takes his sister by the hand and leads her into the forest. But once they enter the forest, as in the story of Hansel and Gretel, the sister assumes seniority and guardianship. *Schwesterchen* becomes the *Brüderchen*'s superego, his authority figure, and his protector for as long as she can. The little sister becomes the little mother: she is the homemaker and provides a safe haven and much more. She is almost but not quite a wife; they are almost lovers, even sleeping chastely together until the entry of the prince. Then she becomes a mother, both to her child and her brother, only to be murdered when the stepmother reenters the picture.

All versions of this story have a remarkable resolution in that the narrator's main interest does not seem to be in restoring the conventional nuclear family. One might expect the conclusion to assure us of the royal family's happiness, but the final line focuses on *Brüderchen* and *Schwesterchen*. We are told that they "lived together until the end."[6] *Schwesterchen*'s prince recedes quietly into the background, and so does her child.

"DAS LÄMMCHEN UND FISCHCHEN"

In a variant of the brother-sister transformation fairy tale, the Grimms describe a brother and sister who remain in the forest and live "happily ever after" in splendid isolation. The title of this *Märchen*, "*Das Lämmchen und Fischchen*" (Little Lamb and Little Fish), indicates the siblings' animal transformations, a metamorphosis effected by their witch/stepmother. We are not told much about this brother and sister except that they are playing a game with other children at the opening of the story. The witch/stepmother works her evil magic at the start of the tale.

> Brother and Sister love one another, but their stepmother is evil. She sees them playing a game with other children, and decides to change them into a lambkin and a fish. After a long while, guests come to the castle, and the stepmother appears and suggests to the cook that he slaughter the lambkin. However the fish swims to the kitchen and holds a sad conversation with the lambkin. The cook is frightened, kills a different animal, and brings the lamb to a good lady farmer. She was the Nurse of the children. She brings them to a wise woman, who blesses them so that they again become human, and takes them to a solitary cabin in the woods. *There they are alone, but happy.*[7]

The connubial bliss which this version terminates is facilitated by the sudden appearance of a good witch, a fairy godmother, who arrives as a *dea ex machina* to restore them to their original forms, then arranges for the brother and the sister to live happily together. In the end, they seem to have become more adult.

There is a cannibalism theme, as in "Hansel and Gretel," as the sister, who has been transformed into a lamb, comes close to being slaughtered and cooked, but she cries out to her brother, and he responds:

> "*ach Brüderchen im tiefen See,*
> *wie thut mir doch mein Herz so weh!*
> *der Koch der wetzt das Messer,*
> *will mir mein Herz durchstechen.*"
> Das Fischchen antwortete
> "*ach Schwesterchen in der Höh,*
> *wie thut mir doch mein Herz so weh*
> *in dieser tiefen See!*"
>
> ["Oh brother in the deepest sea,
> what pain is in my heart!
> The cook whets the knife
> and will stab me through the heart."
> The fish answers,
> "A sister up above,
> what pain is in my heart
> in this deep sea!]

But their happiness in the woods does not occur at the story's mid-section. Unlike *Brüderchen and Schwesterchen*, the children retire at the end to the woods "alone and happy." Both stories, however, place the siblings in a forest paradise, although in one case, it is merely an interlude while in the other, it seems permanent. The common element of the two narratives is the animal transformation and how the brother is restored to his human form by the blessing of a "wise woman."

GRETEL VS. THE WITCH-MOTHER-STEPMOTHER OR WICKED WIFE OF GOD

The anima of the protective sister is archetypal in her own right; no less archetypal than the mother figure, who may be nurturing in some instances but destructive in others. Freud is not wrong in suggesting the sister can function as a symbolic substitute for the mother, but the sister, especially in the Grimm stories, may rival or supplant the mother by assuming her guardian role. The sister may protect the brother by shoving the bad mother into her own hell. If Freud is correct that incestuous drives are innate, the sister is a more fitting wife than the mother because she has the beauty of her youthfulness and shares in the brother's generational conspiracy against authority. There is an implicit rivalry between mother and sister because the mother is an adult authority figure; she is the resented and sometimes hated co-parent, the wife of God, who collaborates with Him in setting rules and administering punishment. Gretel is Hansel's co-conspirator in the revolt against parental authority and the tyranny of the adult world. In fact, Gretel can be seen as defying both the adult world and its cruel God.

The adult-parent archetype in the core brother-sister narrative of the three Grimm stories has variable masculine and feminine avatars. The serpent of Eden is a bewitching adult who usurps authority and appeals to Eve's nascent resentment of the Father's arbitrary power. In the Grimm tales, this serpent undergoes various incarnations from mother to stepmother to witch. In the first edition of the Grimm version, she is the natural mother of the siblings; in later versions, she is transformed into a stepmother, that is to say, a wife of God, who is associated with a serpent. In "*Brüderchen und Schwesterchen*," she is a composite, both the witch and the stepmother. She is the Lamia, the Lilith, who steals and eats children.

In all her various shapes, she is an adult figure who commands an imbalance of power. She is a merciless god who places obstacles in the way of forbidden sweets and cruelly punishes those who nibble at them. She is the wife of God the Father, who exiles children to the forest without food. When Hansel and Gretel approach the sugared house of the witch-stepmother, she simultaneously encourages and represses their desire for sweets. If there is any sexual innuendo in the story of Adam and Eve's forbidden fruit and tree of knowledge, there is also sexual innuendo in Hansel and Gretel's gingerbread house. The adult world places the siblings in a garden of stifled delights, punishes them for tasting them, then exiles them into a wilderness where they cling together for warmth in a divine marriage, a sacred relationship of interdependency.

This divine marriage need not involve actual divinities like Zeus and Hera, and it need not be physically consummated as it is in the case of Milton's Adam and Eve. The divine union of siblings needs only be suggested as in the relationship of Apollo and Artemis. The *hieros gamos* is evident in the *Homeric Hymns*, where Artemis tires of the hunt and "goes to the great house of her dear brother Phoebus Apollo." Here, the poet alludes to their inseparable union in which the sibling's souls are eternally intertwined. The essential quality of their sacred marriage is not in a sexual union but in the perpetual endurance of their sibling relationship.

WAGNER AND THE GERMANIC VANIR

It was from Norse legends that Wagner created the half-gods Siegmund and Sieglinde, the twin children of Wotan, the father of the Walküries, in his opera *Die Walküre.* Wotan, ruler of the gods, has planned this mating of his children, hoping they will produce a heroic son. Sieglinde is inadvertently active in advancing the plot. When Siegmund shows up unexpectedly at her hearth, she drugs her husband, Hunding, and shows Siegmund a magic sword, which their father, disguised as a mysterious Wanderer, has thrust into the trunk of a tree in the middle of her house. Siegmund is the archetypal hero who effortlessly draws the sword. They now recall their childhood together at an indefinite time in their past but not beyond their recollection. The recognition of kinship results in their immediate falling in love.

> *Zu seiner Schwester schwang er sich her; die Liebe lockte den Lenz: in uns'rem Busen barg sie sich tief; nun lacht sie selig dem Licht. Die bräutliche Schwester befreite der Bruder. . . .*
>
> [To his sister hither was he drawn; love lured springtime into our bosoms, where it lay deeply hidden; but now it laughs joyously in the light. As his bride the sister frees her brother. . . .]

They embrace as lovers because they are sister and brother, and the music is an ecstatic celebration of their resolute defiance. As the curtain falls on Act I of *Die Walküre,* Siegfried triumphantly proclaims the lawless heroism of his barbarian tribe: "*Braut und Schwester bist du dem Bruder so blühe denn, Wälsungen-Blut!* [Bride and sister art thou to the brother. Thus shall the blood of the Wälsungs flourish]!"

The sibling's jubilation is abruptly curtailed by Fricka, their father's wife, who accuses Wotan of twice assailing the sanctity of marriage, first by his liaison with the "she-wolf," the mother of Siegmund und Sieglinde, and then by promoting their incestuous union. She rages against the twins' adultery even though Sieglinde never consented to become Hunding's wife. This is of no importance to Fricka; she expresses horror for the benefit of the audience that incest should flourish in the bonding of twins. "*Mir schaudert das Herz, es schwindelt mein Hirn* [It makes my heart shudder, It makes my brain reel]." Fricka's overflowing hostility arises from her understandable sense of being wronged, for the twins' existence is a reminder of her husband's history of infidelity. Another of Wotan's children, Brünhilde, is his favorite daughter. Later in the story, she must suffer for protecting her brother, Siegmund, in combat. Brünhilde distinguishes herself by succoring the pregnant Sieglinde in her exile, and she later becomes the lover of Siegfried, the fruit of her twin siblings' union.

The three siblings, all hated by Fricka, do not share the stage for long, although their interaction is crucial. Siegmund's illicit meetings with both his sisters spell his doom, for it is fated that when a warrior sees the *Walküre* before a battle, it is an omen of his impending death. Brünhilde rebels with her siblings against her parents; her immediate attraction to her half-brother is a preview of coming events, for in the succeeding opera of the tetralogy, she will fall in love with his reincarnation, the hero Siegfried. Brünhilde's half-sister is, in a sense, Sieglinde's other self, with whom she bonds immediately. Sieglinde is already carrying the embryonic hero within her womb. Brünhilde defies Wotan and Fricka in her vain attempt to aid her brother and sister. After failing to do so, she flees to the Felsenberg, where more *Walküres*, her other sisters, are assembled, and Brünhilde reveals her plight and that of Sieglinde, the woman she brings with her:

> Brünhilde: Hear me then quickly: Sieglinde is she, Siegmund's sister and bride: 'gainst all the Wälsungs doth Wotan angrily rage; to strike the brother dead in the fight was Brünhilde's task; but Siegmund held I safe with my shield: Wotan in wrath

then struck him himself with his spear: Siegmund fell; but I fled forth with the wife; and to save her flew I to you that in danger (in fear) ye might hide me from the threatening view.

THE OTHER SIX VALKYRIES: Hence with the woman! danger is here: the Valkyries' shelter dare we not give!

SIEGLINDE: *(on her knees before Brünhilde)* Rescue me, maid! rescue the mother!

BRÜNHILDE: *(raises Sieglinde with sudden determination)* Away, then, fly swiftly, and fly thou alone! I stay in thy stead, draw on me Wotan's anger, by me holding the wrathful one here, whilst thou from his vengeance escap'st.

Third-pary *Inzestscheu* augments Fricka's anger and exceeds Hera's anger at Zeus for begetting Artemis, Apollo, or Heracles. Audiences may sympathize with Fricka's justifiable anger at Wotan's infidelity, but Wagner's sentimental and romantic treatment of adultery in *Tristan and Isolde* does not ordinarily elicit hoots of derisive outrage. Audiences are often charmed and enraptured by Tristan and Isolde's betrayal of the noble King Marc. Thereto, it requires no effort to sympathize with Sieglinde's conspiring against the loathsome Hunding, for her forced marriage to a barbarian has amounted to nothing but repeated rapes. Nonetheless, twin-sibling incest is no solution. Audiences share Fricka's outrage, not at the adultery but at Wotan's scheme to unite the brother and sister as lovers, and when the curtain falls at the end of *Die Walküre*'s first act, shocked gasps and embarrassed titters often ripple through modern audiences.[8]

The fruit of Sigmund and Sieglinde's illicit rapture is Siegfried, the eponymous hero of this opera's sequel, *Siegfried.* We follow his adventures as he slays a dragon and, bathed in its blood, acquires partial invulnerability and the ability to understand the songs of a bird. From this he learns of the sleeping *Walküre* Brünhilde, the half-sister of his parents. Braving a wall of fire, he awakens her and pledges his eternal devotion. Alas, in the last opera of Wagner's Ring Cycle, *Götterdämmerung,* in a scene reminiscent of Tristan and Isolde, he is tricked into drinking a magic potion that makes him forget his vow, and a vengeful Brünhilde betrays the secret of his single invulnerability. Wagner freely adapted elements from the complicated plot of the Icelandic *Völsung Saga*, which tells of how Signy tricks her twin brother into making love to her to conceive Sinfjotli, who, like Wagner's Siegfried, is destined to become a hero and take revenge on the enemies of the clan. The product of sibling incest in Indo-European mythology may be a god, as in the case of Zeus, or a mighty warrior, as in the case of the Irish hero Cú Chulainn. Sibling incest and royal incest may carry blessings or curses, but they are reserved for gods and heroes.

Die Walküre is Wagner's most shocking sibling narrative, but he presents another brother-sister narrative in *Lohengrin,* an opera that contains elements of the exile narrative and the animal transformation narrative. The victim-heroine, Elsa von Brabant, is accused of murdering her younger brother, Gottfried, who mysteriously disappears while they are wandering in the forest. Unlike the resourceful Gretel, Elsa has failed to perform her womanly duty as goddess and protector of her brother. Her innocence must be proven in a trial by combat, and in answer to her prayers, Lohengrin, a knight in shining armor, arrives in a magic boat drawn by a swan. The strange knight agrees to defend her on condition she never ask his name, but in the end, at the insistent prompting of her mortal enemy, the serpentine Ortrude, she breaks her vow. Elsa has now committed the sin of Eve, the sin of desiring knowledge, the sin of Lot's wife, who yields to curiosity.

And now Elsa's husband must depart; he is a knight of the Holy Grail, and the rule of his order is that if his identity be revealed, he must return to the land of heroes whence he came, the holy mountain Monsalvat. Lohengrin summons his enchanted boat, and as he is about to depart, a dove descends from heaven, replacing the swan, who resumes his true shape as Elsa's lost brother, Gottfried. We learn Ortrud, Elsa's chief accuser, is ultimately responsible for all the mischief. Ortrud—a variant of the witches in other fairy tales—transformed Gottfried into a swan.[9]

The dove and swan in *Lohengrin* are as supernatural as Gretel's duck; they belong to the mythological category of the *Seelenvögel,* or Soul-birds, which caught the attention of the Grimm brothers and other students of myth and fairy tale. In cultures around the world, magical birds have plaid crucial roles. The song of a soul-bird directs Siegfried to where Brünhilde the *Walküre* lies sleeping. In one of the later versions of Hansel and Gretel, a soul-bird leads the brother and sister to the witch's house.

"Lohengrin" by Walter Crane (1895)

– CHAPTER TWELVE –

W. E. B. DU BOIS, THOMAS MANN, AND ARISTOTELIAN NARRATIVE

WITHIN THE same three-year period (1903–1906), W. E. B. Du Bois and Thomas Mann produced tragic tales of siblings in a humanly tragic wilderness, each built on decisive and repeated references to Wagnerian opera and containing crucial scenes in which principle characters attend an opera by that composer. Both stories reach their climaxes in scenes centered on the protagonist's relationship with his sister, and each addresses a threat presented by an ethnic outsider with sexual designs on the protagonist's sister.

Thematically, Du Bois's tale, "The Coming of John," makes repeated references to Wagner's *Lohengrin.* The story has a beginning that presents the tragic predicament of John Jones, its hero; a middle, which brings this predicament to a crisis; and an end, which reveals the moral of the story as John realizes he cannot escape destiny. In these respects, the story conforms to Aristotle's model for tragedy as a presentation of the protagonist's prideful struggle against the inevitable, and his final resignation to his fate.

Mann's story, *Wälsungenblut,* which is controlled by intentional references to Wagner's *Die Walküre,* presents a tragic situation but lacks a classic Aristotelian structure. Mann's fable contains the fatal element of an ineluctable taboo and the fears of miscegenation experienced by the male protagonists. Siegmund, by incest with his sister Sieglinde achieves a momentary satisfaction by stealing her presumable virginity from her suitor, Beckerath. This, however, is a closeted triumph, and it does not present the dramatic consequence that accompanies John Jones's righteous wrath, and his obstruction of John Henderson's designs by clubbing him to death. "The Coming of John" is a classic tragedy, constructed around the quest for knowledge and ironic achievement of knowledge through suffering. It evokes pity and fear, accompanied by the shock of recognition as John confronts reality and his inexorable fate.

W. E. B. DU BOIS'S JOHN JONES AND THE FORBIDDEN FRUIT OF KNOWLEDGE

"The Coming of John" is a fable featuring a conversation between a brother and sister concerning the forbidden fruit of knowledge and its consequence of death. It was originally published in 1903 as a short story in Du Bois's *The Souls of Black Folk,* and it reflected American sexual taboos at the time of its publication. The story describes the brother's attendance at Richard Wagner's *Lohengrin* and ends with an allusion to that opera. The structuring of works on African American life on frameworks of classical, Germanic, and Hebraic mythology was a device Du Bois often employed in his poetry and fiction. Classical mythology and Afrocentric themes were blended in his novel *The Quest of the Silver Fleece,* an extrapolation on "that Fleece after which Jason and his Argonauts went vaguely wandering into the shadowy East three thousand years ago; and certainly one might frame a pretty and not far-fetched analogy of witchery and dragons' teeth, and blood and armed men, between the ancient and the modern quest of the Golden Fleece in the Black Sea."[1]

"The Coming of John" was an excruciatingly brutal transplantation of Christian Germanic mythology into the Black Belt of the American South. The story culminated with a significantly altered quotation from *Lohengrin*'s familiar chorus, "Song of the Bride," which is not incongruous but does require explanation.[2]

By the 1930s, Wagner's "Here Comes the Bride" had become a cliché throughout the Western world. Elizabeth Hafkin Pleck notes that Wagner's 1850 composition gained notoriety in 1858 when it was played at the wedding of Queen Victoria's daughter.[3] The tune was fairly well known by 1880 when Mark Twain heard it at Bayreuth. One may suppose Twain referred to it because he assumed most of his readers would know it even if they had never heard of Wagner. But if the song retained any novelty as late as 1880, it was certainly familiar when Du Bois referenced it in 1903. Du Bois was aware of Twain's comment that it was the most recognizable interlude in the opera. Several scholars have attempted to explain why Du Bois alluded to it, and in my view, other elements of *Lohengrin* are equally pertinent.

The eponymous hero of "The Coming of John" reflects the archetype of the long-suffering crusader, a black knight doomed to the same tragic heroism Du Bois saw "painted so beautifully in Uncle Tom."[4] Nietzsche lambasted Wagner for yielding to elements of the Christian slave mentality in *Lohengrin,* but Du Bois exploited the contradictions reconciled in the archetype of the sacrificial god. Like Harriet Beecher's Stowe's Christlike martyr, Du Bois's heroic John was fated to die while struggling to protect a black woman, but John also reflected the apocalyptic Christian rhetoric of Julia Ward Howe, who called for muscular Christian soldierism, "trampling out the vintage where the grapes of wrath are stored." Howe invoked the Christ of the Apocalypse, who fulfilled the prophecy of Genesis: "Let the hero born of woman crush the serpent with his heel." Du Bois enhanced the same mythography of suffering servanthood when he wrote, "Above all looms the figure of the Black Mammy, one of the most pitiful of the world's Christs."[5]

St. Gregory, chained to his rock, was "despised and rejected of men; a man of sorrows, and acquainted with grief,"[6] while John Jones was a "black Prometheus bound to the rock of ages by hate, hurt, and humiliation."[7] These were not the portable icons of American masculinity, but Du Bois fashioned his black hero as a Christlike martyr, the messianic crusader. John, who suffers and dies for his sister, is a young black man who wanders outside the torturous American South into the city of New York, where he attends a performance of *Lohengrin* and encounters a former playmate from his boyhood, a young white man also named John, the son of Judge Henderson, an influential magistrate of their hometown. White John is outraged when Black John is seated next to the young woman he brought to the performance, and at White John's insistence, John Jones is removed from his seat, at which point John Henderson finally recognizes, with indignation and contempt, his former playmate.

Soon afterward, John Jones returns to the South, and we learn that his sister, Jennie, is employed as the Henderson's kitchen maid. John's conversation with his sister and his plans to start a school for Colored children unveil the anguish of tasting from the tree of knowledge.

> Long they stood together, peering over the gray unresting water.
>
> "John," she said, "does it make every one—unhappy when they study and learn lots of things?"
>
> He paused and smiled. "I am afraid it does," he said.
>
> "And, John, are you glad you studied?"
>
> "Yes," came the answer, slowly but positively.
>
> She watched the flickering lights upon the sea, and said thoughtfully, "I wish I was unhappy,—and—and," putting both arms about his neck, "I think I am, a little, John."

The moral of the story is *pathei mathos*—suffering is the price of knowledge. Several days after his conversation with his sister, John has another conversation with Judge Henderson, who permits him to start a school for Colored children, but everything collapses when the judge learns of the incident in New York and John's effort to teach the history of the French Revolution. The judge shuts down the school with peremptory words of dismissal: "John, this school is closed. You children can go home and get to work. The white people of Altamaha are not spending their money on black folks to have their heads crammed with impudence and lies. Clear out! I'll lock the door myself."

In the meantime, John Henderson decides to distract himself with flirtation, and his eye falls on Jennie. He tries to steal a kiss and she resists:

> [John] started to meet his sister as she came from work and break the news of his dismissal to her. "I'll go away," he said slowly; "I'll go away and find work, and send for them. I cannot live here longer." And then the fierce, buried anger surged up into his throat. He waved his arms and hurried wildly up the path . . . but starting as from a dream at the frightened cry that woke the pines, to see his dark sister struggling in the arms of a tall and fair-haired man.
>
> He said not a word, but, seizing a fallen limb, struck him with all the pent-up hatred of his great black arm, and the body lay white and still beneath the pines, all bathed in sunshine and in blood. John looked at it dreamily, then walked back to the house briskly, and said in a soft voice, "Mammy, I'm going away—I'm going to be free."

The story reaches its inevitable conclusion with the insertion of a quotation from *Lohengrin*'s "Song of the Bride," which I once thought incongruous, not realizing Du Bois had altered Wagner's original words: "*Treulich geführt ziehet dahin.* [Led in truth (or troth) and drawn hither]," replacing the word *treulich* (truly) with *freudig* (joyfully):

> Yes, surely! Clear and high the faint sweet melody rose and fluttered like a living thing, so that the very earth trembled as with the tramp of horses and murmur of angry men. He leaned back and smiled toward the sea, whence rose the strange melody, away from the dark shadows where lay the noise of horses galloping, galloping on. With

> an effort he roused himself, bent forward, and looked steadily down the pathway, softly humming the "Song of the Bride,"—
>
> "Freudig geführt, ziehet dahin."

Du Bois transformed the text into a reflection on joyful martyrdom in light of Philippians 2:17, "upon the sacrifice and service of your faith, I joy, and rejoice with you all." If Du Bois's substitution of *freudig* for *treulich* was a Freudian slip, it was a "fortunate fall," because it was well suited to the context and recalled the Afro-Christian song that blends resignation with defiance: "Before I'll be a slave, I'll be dead and in my grave, And go home to my Zion and be free!" The story of John links an American tragedy to *Lohengrin*'s themes of trial by ordeal and heroic deliverance. John's sister parallels Elsa, Wagner's heroine who describes her dream of "a shining knight who approaches armed in light." John is that Grail Knight who becomes the champion of his sister's honor and confronts death with Lohengrin's thoughts at the moment of trial: "God will pass rightful judgment on me, so I shall trust in Him."[8]

THOMAS MANN'S TWIN LOVERS

The principals of *Wälsungenblut* (*The Blood of the Walsungs*), Siegmund and Sieglinde, are self-exiles of a sort in their sheltered *haute bourgeoisie* existence in "super-refined West Berlin [*überfeinerten Berliner Westens*]." Their supercilious mocking attitude and mutual narcissism place them in splendid isolation and lead them to an imitation of their incestuous namesakes, the mythical Ur-Germans, Siegmund and Sieglinde of Wagner's *Die Walküre.* Their father, Herr Aarenhold, of whom they are ashamed and contemptuous, is presented as a shambling collector of crumbling books, expensive but trifling, and their mother as "impossible . . . small, ugly, prematurely aged . . . , shriveled." Their older brother and sister, who also live with their parents, are Kunz and Märit. Kunz appears in military uniform and bears what one suspects is a dueling scar. Märit, a law student of twenty-eight, "goes her own way," austere, ash-blond, with a hooked nose, a contemptuous mien, and a bitter mouth. The twins, Siegmund and Sieglinde, make their first appearance descending a staircase, holding hands as "gracile" as young fawns, somewhat childlike in physique despite their nineteen years. The family is joined at an elaborate luncheon by Sieglinde's fiancé, Beckerath, to whom she seems indifferent. He is embarrassed by his inability to engage in the overly refined, supercilious repartee of the Aarenhold siblings.

That evening, Siegmund and Sieglinde attend a performance of Wagner's *Die Walküre,* and on returning home, they entwine in a lover's embrace on the bearskin rug in Siegmund's room. The final scene of the novella have been controversial, but not primarily because, like the first act of its Wagnerian antecedent, it culminates in sibling incest.[9] Much discussion has centered on Mann's employment of two Yiddish expressions in the final sentence and other markers in the text identifying the principals as Jewish. On first encountering this story in its standard English translation, an Anglo-American audience might not immediately discern the numerous other cloudy, anti-Semitic references ostensibly clear to its original readers. Mann never denied that his novella was "the story of two . . . Jewish twins" who exist in a state of luxury-mocking and painful loneliness ("*üppig-spöttisches Einsamkeitspathos*"). Most readers feel that real-life allusions and self-mockery are easily discoverable in the text. Mann had recently married into the splendidly wealthy and highly cultured family of distinguished mathematics professor Alfred Pringsheim.

Alan Levenson observes that the story can be read as a "cathartic release of pent-up frustration and aggression" after Katja's "long and frustrating" courtship. Paul Levesque accuses Mann of exploiting Jewish stereotypes with "cold blooded calculation." Sander Gilman has examined its anti-Semetic stereotypes and clichés and finds it "as much a critique of the Jew as parvenue in the (mocked) world of German high culture as it is a critique of the Jew as incestuous sibling." Stefani Engelstein argues, however, that Mann's "superficial conformity with anti-Semitic stereotypes is carefully built only to be deconstructed." It was scheduled for publication in the January 1906 issue of *Neue Rundschau,* although the editor Oskar Bie expressed concerns about the ending as too vulgar. The piece drew an even stronger response from Mann's father-in-law, who objected to some of its Jewish stereotypes and the employment of Yiddish colloquialisms, specifically the terms "*goy*" and "*beganeft*" in the final sentence. The story was withdrawn, but attempts at suppression proved futile when it was inadvertently leaked. Rumors of its content circulated broadly, eventually encompassing a legend that Pringsheim had confronted his son-in-law "*mit dem Revolver in der Hand* [with a revolver in his hand]."[10]

Mann's initial impression of visiting the Pringsheim mansion was subtly ambivalent, as expressed in a letter to his brother containing the internal contradiction of both denying and calling attention to the family's "Jewishness:" "No thought of Jewishness arises in connection with these people, one senses nothing but culture."[11]

Despite its superficially admiring terms, the letter made gratuitous reference to Pringsheim's affectation of a golden cigarette case but made no mention of his distinction in the field of mathematics or his condescending attitude toward novelists. According to Klaus Pringsheim's recollection, his father did not consider *Romanschreiben* (novel writing) a *seriosen Beruf* (serious profession). Golo Mann reportedly quoted his father as saying he never liked his in-laws and they never liked him.[12] Mann reportedly read the text to Katje and her mother, and there seems to be no record of her immediate reaction. In her *Unwritten Memories* of 1973, she wrote that if Mann had gained the impression of a forbidden relationship, he would certainly have kept it secret. Mann also shared the text with her brother Klaus, who later wrote of feeling "*ein wenig geschmeichelt* [a little flattered]" rather than embarrassed on recognizing some of his characteristic turns of phrase "in the young hero."

Peter Mendelssohn exhaustively investigated the publication history and the undeniable relationships between *Wälsungenblut* and its real-life counterparts. Rudolph Brettschneider, a Munich bookseller's apprentice, accidentally found and secretly read the galleys, which had been used as packing paper for a shipment of books to his employer. Reports of its content rapidly spread along with rumors it had been written as an "act of revenge" on the Pringsheims in retribution for their condescending attitude toward the author. The first German edition was not issued until 1921 in a private printing of 530 copies with a significant change to its ending, from which the Yiddish expressions, but not the ethnic stereotype, were removed. The French edition, *Sang Reservé* (1931), retained incest and the original ending.[13] The suppression and revision of the work is reminiscent of the publishing history of Shelley's *The Revolt of Islam*.

If Mann intended to attribute the emotional self-exile of the Aarenhold twins to their ethnicity, or if he intended the tortured fragility and isolation of the twins to represent the effects of anti-Semitism under the veil of assimilation, he was exceedingly subtle. Engelstein observes that his understanding was "too tenuous" and intentions conveyed too indirectly. The twins themselves make no direct references to their Jewish heritage, notwithstanding the incongruous insertion of Yiddish vernacular at the story's suppressed first ending. Sieglinde's impending marriage represents not only assimilationism but biogenetic amalgamation. Beckerath himself, and possibly Mann, represent von Treitsche's condescending notion that a limited number of exceptional Jews can be tolerated, if not entirely assimilated, within the German nation. Thomas Mann presents the splendid isolation of his Siegmund and Sieglinde as a reciprocal narcissism, which is bizarre and unexplained, for he never sketches out why they should feel isolated. He never suggests that the attitude of "us against the world" is rooted in a sense of social rejection or exclusion.

The twins are arrogant vulnerable teenagers and insecure, underconfident, and overcompensating know-it-alls. They are the age of college sophomores, and their conversations are embarrassingly sophomoric. They are temperamental adolescents, rebellious in some respects but rigidly conformist in others, excessively conscious of dress codes and changing fashions, and, like many young people, compulsively derisive of those who are out of step. They are rudely dismissive when Beckerath ventures an opinion on the cast of the evening's opera, and they disparage even the way he knots his ties. Their aesthetic opinions are hypercritical, although neither demonstrates a capacity for artistic discipline. Sigmund exposes himself as an indelicate snob when he dismisses Beckerath's opinion that the evening's opera has "an excellent cast." Later they criticize the conductor and the singers with the pseudo-sophistication one might expect from obnoxious high school seniors or college freshmen, and they disturb the audience with their whispering. During the intermission, Sieglinde disparages the refreshments in advance—"I might like an ice," she says, "but it's most probably of inferior quality."

Understandably most of Mann's readers view the Aarenhold twins negatively. Scholar Todd Kontje calls them "self-indulgent, nasty, incestuous little beasts."[14] His concluding terms seem reflective of third-party *Inzestscheu,* the vicarious horror of incest from which scholarly commentators seldom depart. On the other hand, Jules Glenn reacted with the detachment of a professional psycholanalyst to "Mann's remarkably keen understanding of the twinship," in line with his own findings, and "the pair's early and lasting closeness." Nonetheless, Glenn viewed the twins as maladjusted and their relationship as pathological. His literary psychoanalysis of the Aarenhold twins was somewhat influenced by the Oedipus complex dogma of Sigmund Freud and Otto Rank, which is nowadays almost entirely discredited.

Literary scholars almost always assume the relevancy of Thomas Mann's covert sexual inclinations in discussing the overt homoerotic plot of his *Death in Venice*—a practice that accords more with common sense than Aristotelian principles of criticism.[15] Ad hominem observations are by no means irrelevant to literary or social criticism, and I have elsewhere made reference to Arthur P. Wolf's supposition that because Edvard Westermarck was "a homosexual, he may very well have understood better than most the way society responds to sexual behavior." In accord with Wolf's surmise, I have suggested that Thomas Mann's self-revealed, albeit repressed, homosexual disposition could very well have provided him with a superior understanding of society's reactions to additional varieties of sexual experience.

Scholarly discussions of Mann's *Death in Venice* cannot avoid the topic of its homoerotic subject matter or its connection to Mann's privately revealed sexual inclinations. Scholars must also confront the undeniably anti-Semitic stereotypes in *Wähsungenblut* and Mann's private thoughts concerning the Pringsheims. But prominent discussions of *Wähsungenblut* have shied away from mentioning that its theme of sibling incest is presented again in *Der Erwählte*. Sander Gilman and Stefani Engelstein's scholarly discussions of Mann's literary treatment of incest show equal, if not greater, interest in the Aarenhold twins' Jewishness than their romance. Neither scholar approaches what might be reduced, albeit simplistically, to anti-Catholicism in *Der Erwählte* or, for that matter, the novel's incidental deployment of the medieval Jewish money-handler stereotype. It is not surprising, however, that scholars have found sibling incest, due to its universal unattractiveness and presumed rarity, a less important subject for academic discussion than the prominent and persistent evils of ethnic and religious oppression.

"Episode from the 'Gesta Romanorum': The Emporer and the Page"
by Jorg Breu the Elder (1500–1537)

– CHAPTER THIRTEEN –

MANN'S *DER ERWÄHLTE* (*THE HOLY SINNER*)

MANN PRESERVES the structure of the medieval Gregorius legend but enhances selected ingredients and adds a few of his own, such as the character of Friar Clemens, his omniscient first-person narrator. The protagonist's name is changed to Grigorss, and the names Sibylla and Wiligis are provided for the parents of the destined future pope. Mann has Clemens portray Sibylla's erotic interest in her brother with elegance, and her enduring loyalty to his memory with sympathy.

Since Mann presents his teenage sinners as counterparts of Adam and Eve, his Sibylla cannot be a mere victim; she speaks the words of a seductress in the bedroom scene and identifies herself with the mother of God in a later prayer to the Virgin. By endowing Sibylla with such complexity, the author explores such arcane elements of medieval mysticism as the tradition that venerates Mary as both the bride of God and the mother of God. Grigorss, Sibylla's bridegroom, becomes her man of sorrows and finally her redeemer. As the mother of sorrows, Sibylla's heart is wrenched first by the agony and death of her brother, and then again by the suffering of her son for her original sin in the personhood of Eve. Sibylla's love has the power of fashioning a holy trinity of three persons in one love through the metempsychosis of Wiligis into Grigorss and the metamorphosis of Grigorss into Saint Gregory.

Friar Clemens follows Hartmann's precedent and apologizes for his tale of double incest and admits he might have chosen to relate the inspiring legend of St. Benedict and his sister St. Scholastica ". . . how they lived so sweetly and saintly together in the valley of Sublacus . . . and betook themselves, accompanied by three ravens upon a toilsome wandering; bearing all out of love for each other, converting all the heathen whom they still found, flinging down altars to false gods, and the saint himself, among Scholastica's applause, destroying the last temple of lyre-bearing Apollo."

He recalls the legend of how, after Benedict's retirement to a monastery, Scholastica visited and entreated him to continue their saintly conversation until late in the evening. Benedict replied that monastery rules did not permit his absence overnight, so Scholastica prayed for divine intercession, and her prayers were answered with a terrific thunderstorm, making it impossible for her brother to leave and keeping them awake all night engaged in saintly discourse. "Should I not rather in all pious detail recount the tale of Bernard and Scholastica? No, of my own free choice I rather elected this one, because the other witnesses only to saintliness, but this one to God's immeasurable and incalculable loving kindness."

Three days later, Benedict had a vision in which he saw his sister's soul ascending to heaven in the form of a white dove. He had her body placed in a tomb he had prepared for himself, and so their two bodies were inseparable in death.[1] Benedict and Scholastica are twins who sleep together in their tomb; Sibylla and Wiligis are twins so inseparable that they must share sleeping arrangements.

> They were ever handfast wherever they went, at eight and at ten years, and were like a pair of dwarf parrots or love-birds, together day and night, for from the first they had shared a bedchamber high up in the tower where the little owls flew hooting and where their bedsteads stood with straps of salamander-skin on which the cushions lay and bedposts of twisted snakes.

Serpent imagery is significantly reintroduced in a later episode: "They both lay naked under their covers of soft sable in the pale gleam of the swinging lamp and the scent of the amber with which their beds were dusted-they stood, as fittingly, far apart, and between them, coiled round like a snake, slumbered Hanegiff, their good hound."

Clemens describes Wiligis emerging from sleep in their shared bedroom at the age of eleven, "nude like a pagan god" and bathed by the nurses in Sibylla's presence. When he springs from the bathtub, the extraordinary size of Wiligis's *Mannesteil* (male part) is compared to the oversized paws of a young puppy. This peculiarity does not escape the notice of his attendant nurses, who exchange significant glances and remark on his equipment as "*l'espoirs des dames.*" Sibylla observes all from the corner of her eye, taking note of the nurses' exchange, and fumes silently, "He belongs to me!" and if anyone gets fresh with him, "I'll scratch her eyes out!"

THE SEDUCTION SCENE

Friar Clemens is mysteriously conscious of Sibylla's most secret emotions, including her erotic interest in Wiligis, unusual possessiveness, admiration for his physique, and appreciation of his kisses. He knows the content of her prayer to the Virgin and is privy to her secret conversation with her son in the papal confessional. In his semi-pornographic depiction of adolescent eroticism, Clemens presents Sibylla's resistance as "jesting, with voice unjestingly breathless." He describes her mounting arousal and diminishes the ambiguity of her submission as presented in the narratives of Hartmann and his French antecedent. With attention to the "seduction," Christian Luckscheiter inquires, "Is it not worth considering that the seduction in *Erwählten* is reversed?" (*umgedreht*).[2] The insertion of dialogue in Anglo-Norman French, lifted from *Ordo representacionis Ade*, a twelfth-century mystery play, shrouds the scene with mystery "and they murmured what one would no longer understand and is not meant to be understood."

> *N'en frais pas. J'en duit.*
>
> I won't do it. I fear it.
>
> *Fai le. Manjue, ne sez que est. Pernum ço bien que nus est prest.*
>
> Do it! Eat, you don't know what it is. Let us take this good thing which is ready for us to us
>
> *Est-il tant bon?*
>
> Is it so good?
>
> *Tu le le saveras. Nel poez saver sin gusteras.*
>
> You'll find out. You cannot know without tasting it.

In the context of the mystery play, the words of seduction belonging to Eve had been excerpted by Erich Auerbach in his widely read *Mimesis,* which had appeared in the preceding year.[3] Mann's employment of them evoked Siegfried Mandel's criticism, who felt Mann should have paid tribute to Auerbach, a matter Auerbach publicly dismissed. Mann, however, wrote subsequently to Auerbach, acknowledging his debt. The letter, originally in German, was reprinted with Mann's permission as an appendix to an article by Hermann Wiegand.

> Your book with the citation from the came exactly at the moment as I wrote the chapter of the "Bad Children. (A secret magnetism very often allows books to arrive just at the right moment.) The two dozen words that I picked out of the old dialogue, were particularly useful, because in that delicate situation, for the average reader, a half, or totally, incomprehensible murmering was entirely appropriate. I am indebted to you. Mr. Mandel is completely right in that respect. But are they not quite pretty and in this other context astonishingly suitable? The discovery became more or less the invention.[4]

LURE OF THE FALLEN SERAPHIM

The "incomprehensible, murmering" in archaic Norman French "not meant to be understood" was succeeded by Sibylla's ecstatic gasping in modern German, a parody of pornography hyperbole harkening back to the extended commentary on the size of her brother's penis in the bathtub scene. Sibylla long ago staked her own claim on her brother's "*Trutgespiel* [plaything]" and now takes possession of it.[5]

> *O Willo, welch Gewaffen! Ouwe, mais tu me tues. Oh schame dich! Ganz wie ein Hengst ein Bock, ein Hahn! O fort! O, fort und fort! O Engelsbub! O, himmlischer Gesell!*
>
> [O Willo, what a weapon! Ow, but you are killing me. Oh shame on you! Just like a stallion, a he-goat, a rooster! Oh go! Oh go on and on! Oh angel-boy! Oh heavenly friend (or partner)!]

Sibylla cries, "Oh angel-boy," writhing in ecstasy like St. Theresa beneath a smiling, boyish-looking angel's symbolic arrow in Bernini's statue *L'Estasi di Santa Teresa.* Her cry, "Oh heavenly friend," overwhelms any prior suggestion of hesitancy or reluctance and replaces the rape described unequivocally in the *Gesta Romanorum.* Clemens does not claim, however, that his description of this first sexual encounter announces the moment of Gregorius's conception. Clemens attributes the sin to "Valande's wicked counsel" and "the scourge of the flesh under Valande's spur," but unlike previous authors, he makes no references to conception.[6]

Sibylla meditates on the Annunciation as she kneels in the castle chapel before "a beautiful picture of the Blessed Virgin from a good school." Her complicated presentation in the novel is nuanced by references to the divine incest of Christ's conception: "Maria, mild Queen, now help me, holy Magden, sweet one, Bride of God . . . which He so strangely did elect for wonder-honour to select out of thy womb to manifest the man of all on earth the best, namely God's self, who thee for His Mother planned."

Sibylla's prayer to the bride of God and mother of God as she decides to abandon her life of celibacy and accept Grigorss, the reincarnation of her beloved Wiligis as her bridegroom, is: "Are you not weary of ardent ways, / Lure of the fallen seraphim?" These words are from James Joyce's "Villanelle of the Temptress." The Angelus bells inspired the merging of the angel's visit to the Virgin and the visitations of the sons of God to the daughters of men in Genesis. So are the angels of Genesis one with the angel of Luke. Joyce merged the image of Gabriel of Luke's gospel with the sons of God in Genesis 6:2.[7]

Sibylla is a temptress of angels, and Wiligis is likened to the heavenly visitor at the conception of Christ. "Tell me, some Pitying Angel" is a monologue in the accusing voice of the Blessed Virgin, written by Poet Laureate Nahum Tate, set to music and published by Henry Purcell in *Harmonia Sacra* (1693). The alternate name of the composition, "The Blessed Virgin's Expostulation," does not charge the angel with paternal responsibility. Barbara Walker goes too far with her assertion that the name Gabriel means "heavenly husband,"[8]

> Where's Gabriel now, that visited my cell?
> I call, I call: Gabriel!
> He comes not . . .

In every rendition of her saga, Sibylla must twice undergo the pain of parting: "Wiligis she cried . . . and then bethought herself."

THE RECOGNITION SCENE

Sibylla is no victimized Jocasta but a headstrong and never fully repentant animatrix who steals the scene whenever she appears on stage. Unlike Jocasta, suicidal upon recognizing her unwitting contamination, Sibylla participates knowingly and energetically in her first incestuous encounter and responds pragmatically when confronted with her second. She proposes to Grigorss that they continue living together, presenting the public appearance of marriage while privately abstaining from sexual relations. Grigorss dismisses this proposition as womanish nonsense and immediately departs on his penitential pilgrimage.

Sibylla keeps a shadow of her beauty and, as Dame Sibylla, retains her noble bearing. Although divested of most of her wealth, she retains sufficient means to establish a hospital for the poor, and the financial resources to undertake her pilgrimage to Rome. While it is true Sibylla assumes a life of atonement, it is without the wretched self-detestation of Delarivier's "artless Urania." Sibylla is blessed and, in a sense, vindicated like Cain, who prospered without ever expressing repentance for killing his brother. Sibylla never repents of her love for Wiligis. She is forever her brother's keeper, forever tendering the hearth of the love she bears for him and for his reincarnation as the fruit of their love, Grigorss.

THE CHOSEN ONE: CHRISTIAN OEDIPUS OF VICAR OF CHRIST?

I have mentioned several fables in which a son ignorantly seeds his mother to produce a sister-daughter, whom he eventually marries. In these stories, the mother is guilty of initiating the incest in varying degrees. Mann's Gregorius narrative of double incest reveals no direct debt to these legends, although they are a more likely influence than the Oedipus myth. Isabelle François claims that *Der Erwählte* is "obviously an avatar of Oedipus," and certainly by 1951, the year of his novel's publication, Mann would have been exposed to Freud's notorious reflections on the legend. It is not surprising that François sees the work as "an Oedipus reviewed and corrected through the Freudian prism," but I see no evidence of any such "correction," and fortunately, François's reflexive assumption is modulated by the more judicious consideration that "it is equally a Christian reincarnation and "baptized" in the "*quête de preux.*"

Quête de preux signifes something more substantive than the "Quest for the "Holy Grail" a cliché that has lost its favor through overuse. The actual *quête de preux,* in the medieval mind, was the "holy quest" of the First Crusade, the *quête de preux* of Godfrey of Bouillon, who, as liberator of Jerusalem, was numbered among the *neuf preux,* the "nine worthies" of military history.[9] Hartmann is reported to have taken part in the crusade of 1189 or 1197 as a knight and vassal of the Duke of Aue.

In Mann's *Der Erwählte*, as in prior versions of the Gregorius legend, the young Duke of Aquitaine departs on a crusade as an act of atonement, a *quête de preux*, but dies en route to the Holy Land. His son undertakes more than one *quête de preux*. First he embarks on a quest to discover his parentage, again as he fights for the deliverance of a kingdom, then once more when he sets off on a pilgrimage of atonement and performs seventeen years of self-imposed penance for his unintentional contamination.

Elements in Mann's story, especially its symbolic system, are singularly Christian. Gregorius's heraldic symbol is a fish, the symbol of Christ in early Christianity. The Greek letters ἸΧΘΥΣ (for *ichthus* meaning "fish") are an ancient acronym: Ἰησοῦς Χρῑστός Θεοῦ Υἱός Σωτήρ, *Iēsoûs Khrīstós, Theoû Huiós, Sōtḗr* which translates into English as "Jesus Christ, God's Son, Savior." Significantly, Gregorius is chained to a rock, the symbol of Peter, whose name means rock.[10]

After he's freed from the rock, Gregorius arrives triumphantly in Rome and walks in the shoes of St. Peter, the fisherman. Then, in line with Roman Catholic tradition, he inherits the papal title Vicar of Christ, who holds the key to heaven and may grant absolution to his parents. Christian symbolism and metaphor are abundant and obvious, while Freudian references to Oedipus are obscure and only discoverable by search.[11]

Mann's judiciously chosen title, *Der Erwählte*, is suited to its purpose, not solely because the hero is chosen to become Pope. He is chosen to become Vicar of Christ only after enduring suffering and humiliation in "imitation of Christ," and he enters the Holy City riding on a donkey. Nonetheless, although Mann's title seems more fitting to this symbolic role, the standard English title of the work abides by the title of the Lowe-Porter translation, *The Holy Sinner.* The cognomen, Chosen One, expresses the doctrine of election and the messianic prophecy of salvation and suffering sacrifice. In Martin Luther's German translation of Matthew 12:18, Jesus is "*erwählt,*" and in his translation of Isaiah 43:20, in which Matthew saw as a prophecy of Jesus the Messiah, the word is *auserwählt.* The gospel of St. Matthew proclaims that, in fulfillment of prophecy, Jesus is the Chosen One, the Son of God, the beloved servant, the man of sorrows, the "Lamb of God, who taketh away the sins of the world," and atones for the sin of Adam and Eve.

> **Martin Luther Version: Matthaeus 12:17-18:** *auf das erfüllet würde, was gesagt ist von dem Propheten Jesaja, der da spricht: Siehe, das ist mein Knecht, den ich erwählt habe, und mein Liebster, an dem meine Seele Wohlgefallen hat.*

> **King James Version: Matthew 12:17-18:** That it might be fulfilled which was spoken by Esaias the prophet, saying, Behold my servant, whom I have chosen; my beloved, in whom my soul is well pleased.

When *Der Erwählte* is translated literally, the meaning is clear; Mann's Gregorius, like Hartmann's Gregorius, is "a man of sorrows, and acquainted with grief." After long suffering, he remits the original sin of his parents, as Jesus remitted the original sin of Adam and Eve. The symbol of the fish itself is prominently exploited in *Der Erwählte* as a heraldic symbol. Clemens describes the knightly coat of arms that Gregorius adopts as he embarks on his *quête de preux,*:

> But the upper garment was actually cote armour, for there was an oval piece let in over the breast, with a fish embroidered on it. That, as the youth conceived, should be his crest on his travels, and I must say it is the only thing about his preparations which pleases me. For while the fish indicated that the traveller came from a fisherman's hut, it is also the symbol of the Christus and evidence that the wearer had grown up within the walls of the Church.

While incidentally akin to the Greek legend, the Gregorius legend is rooted deeply in medieval Europe; its moral lesson is presented not by a chorus of Theban elders but by a Benedictine monk. The Greek drama turns on the protagonist's hubris, his blindness to see his own contamination. By contrast, Gregorius is obsessed with guilt and humility. He is early made aware of his original contamination, and he accepts without hesitation the unintended guile of his second.

Clemens, with his piously moralizing outbursts, may seem at times naive, but he is no buffoon, and his story is not a lampoon. Hermann Hesse's priestly creation, the abbot Narcissus, may seem more sophisticated, but Mann's Clemens is also adept at intellectual discourse, and he is surprisingly attuned to the material world. Heresies spring from Clemens's mind as spontaneously as worms from the cheese of Domenico Scandella.[12] His interjections throughout the narrative are a mixture of skepticism, faith, and an irony that is not always incidental.

His protests of cloistered unfamiliarity notwithstanding, he describes the conventions of chivalric combat, political intrigue, and courtly love. He is amazingly forgiving toward the young lovers' sin of the flesh, inspired by passion,

> Poor children! Glad am I that I have naught to do with love, the dancing will-o'-wisp above the marsh, the sweet devil's torture. So they went on to the end. . . . But how outward alone was this order and how disorderly things were with the erring pair, the charming young folk, to whom I will so well, without being able to excuse them, and who truly through lust were fettered far closer still to each other than ever—out of all bounds they loved and that is why I cannot quite rid me of well-wishing for them, God help me!

Through Clemens, Mann alludes to Christianity's unacknowledged and uncomfortable debt—the pagan notion of divine incest.

Clemens mingled tones of reverence and skepticism, allowing Mann to approximate a medieval voice, and this is no mere parody but a means of achieving authenticity. Clemens's inner thoughts display the scholastic tradition of *disputatio*—the dialectical reasoning of scholasticism. Through Clemens, Mann can preserve elements of skepticism and irony. To be sure, Mann's attitude toward medieval Christendom, with its miracles and superstitions, is sometimes parodic, but never broadly slapstick. R. J. Schork notes that Mann was disappointed that some reviewers of *Der Erwählte* had failed to appreciate the gentle humor and tender appreciation he felt for the mysteries of the past.

> *Aber wenn es das Alte und Fromme, die Legende parodistisch belächelt, so ist dies Lächeln eher melancholisch als frivol, und der verspielte Stil-Roman, die Endform der Legende, bewahrt mit reinem Ernste ihren religiösen Kern, ihr Christentum, die Ideen von Sünde und Gnade.*
>
> [But if it mocks as parody the old and devout, the laughter is rather melancholy than frivolous, and the playful style-novel, the final form of the legend, retains with pure earnestness it religious kernel, its Christendom, the ideas of sin and saving grace.][13]

Mann shared similar thoughts with his friend Hermann Hesse, who had reflected on the legend for many years since his 1914 introduction to Grasse's translation of the *Gesta Romanorum.* Mann owned a copy of this edition, and he exchanged ideas with Hesse regarding his own novelized adaptation of the story, which adhered, however, to Hartmann's touchingly sympathetic version, stressing the sister's perpetual love for the brother and departing from the *Gesta Romanorum*'s unequivocal rape scene, in which the brother leaves his sister weeping bitterly and inconsolably.

Concerning Mann's version, Hesse wrote to the author in June of 1948: "It will suffice for most readers of this charming poem to reach the irony, but not everyone will recognize at first the earnestness and piety that stand behind these ironies and gives it its true high cheerfulness."[14]

Cheerfulness, indeed! The modern audience is predictably more receptive to the parodic elements of *Der Erwählte* than its bittersweet optimism. It is true many readers have appreciated the several "ironies" in this poetic novel, and significant that Hesse applied such terms as "*entzückend*" (charming) and "*Heiterkeit*" (cheerful) to its tragic and antisocial events. Swan and Hooper, the English translators of the *Gesta Romanorum,* describe the initial incest as a "violation of every law both human and divine." If there is anything "charming" to be discovered, it must reside in the innocent expressions of Sibylla, its principal female character, and its cheerfulness in the operatic quality of its final chorus of triumph over adversity. In the end, Gregorius is happily reunited with Sibylla, whose original sin he forgives by papal fiat, along with that of Wiligis, his long-suffering father. Clement regards the original incest in the fashion of the narrator of *Tristan und Isolde,* as if to say that an act of lovers' passion will ultimately sanctified by the God of Love.[15]

The author's sentimental regard for medieval mysticism came close to a recapitulation of the nostalgia and quasi-Christianity expressed in Wagner's later operas. Mann recaptured the mingling of the sacred and profane in Renaissance iconography and iterated by the pre-Raphaelites. The sentimental historicism of *Der Erwählte* resembled that of Matthew Arnold or Brooks and Henry Adams, who felt that Western civilization had peaked in the twelfth century and been in decline ever since. Although he disdained the religious and political conservatism of T. S. Eliot, Mann expressed at least an aesthetic admiration for medieval

Christian mysticism and intellectual appreciation for its doctrines of papal dispensation and vicarious atonement. Mann neither departed from nor did he distort the spirit of Hartmann's idea of redemptive love.

HANNA STEPHAN'S *DIE GLÜCKHAFTE SCHULD*

Hanna Stephan's wrote her own version of the Gregorius legend *Die Gluckhafte Schuld* twelve years before Mann. She was a well-established, if not an overwhelmingly famous, author. Carsten Bronsema and Eva C. Wunderlich have noted her prior handling of the material, but neither claims to have discovered any evidence, internal or external, that she influenced Mann. Both works retained the core medieval Gregorius legend plot and made significant alterations to its structure, adding and subtracting key episodes. In both iterations, Gregorius's mother eventually recognizes her son but the time, place, and consequences of the recognition scenes differ dramatically. Stephan's Gregorius discovers his identity immediately after the wedding but before consummation of the marriage; Mann's hero consummates the marriage, cohabits with his mother for three years, and impregnates her twice.[16]

Stephan and Mann declined to impress a Sophoclean or Freudian character on the narrative, and Stephan's plot is so constructed as to virtually preclude such an imposition. Her literary debt is clearly to medieval Christianity rather than Greek mythology, as can be inferred from her title, *Die Gluckhafte Schuld*—a German rendering of the Latin *felix culpa* (happy fault), an exclamation attributed to the historical Pope Gregory the Great and sung with the *Exultet* of the Roman Catholic Easter liturgy: "O happy fault, O necessary sin of Adam, which gained for us so great a Redeemer!"[17]

Stephan's narrative deviates from medieval tradition by eliminating the introductory episodes of the story, providing no depiction of the death of the twin siblings' father, and no interaction between them before or after the act of Gregorius's conception. A graphic description of that transgression, so important to all the medieval accounts, is absent from her rendition, and she allows for no speculation on whether it was rape or seduction. She begins her narration nine months after the original sin, setting it on the strand at the foot of the castle in Aquitaine, against the cry of seagulls and the portentous singing of fishermen at the work on mending their nets.

So too are knotted the nets
Of the Great Fisherman
We shall be caught
Who can escape?

Out of the mist of a receding fog, the shadow of a Crusader knight materializes. He carries a naked sword over the krupp of his saddle, and its shimmering pierces the pale daylight. He is ushered through the courtyard and passes through the ancestral hall, but he is not presented to the queen of the castle. A maid tells him she is convalescing, at which news he shows irrepressible shock and dismay: "She is young and morning-fair. So spoke her brother, and so too the knights and pages attest. How can sickness have touched her."

The queen is waiting in another chamber with an infant in her arms. Agape, her faithful servant and former nurse must deliver the message, "He who was your brother, and your spouse, and the father of your son, lies slain beneath the Cross."

In the dead of night, the queen and her servant wrap the child in rich fabric embroidered with "crown and cross, animals and birds and other colorful, beautiful images," carry him to the beach, and place him in a small, rudderless boat. Beneath his head is placed a tablet on which his mother has writtten,

Gregorius, thou boy fatherless,
Gregorius, thou boy motherless.
May the sea and the stony beach show pity for
Sister and brother, the poor unfortunates.
May the pure flood of waters show pity for
The pure child of its impure blood,
And so that the hearts of men may pity Gregorius
White is the silver at his feet, red at his head the gold.

The two women commit the vessel to the waves, and three days later, fishermen retrieve it and give the boy to the nearby monastery's abbot, who provides the boy with an education. Stephan's narrative is faithful to the story's medieval antecedents in that Gregorius passes his childhood youth among the fishermen and develops a poisoned relationship with his foster brother. On journeying back to the land of his birth, he inadvertently marries his mother, but at this point, Stephan deviates further from the medieval narratives. Immediately after the wedding ceremony, the queen recognizes the fabric of Gregorius's previously concealed garments as a product of her own hands. It is worth noting that, according to canon law, no marriage would have existed. Even without the obstacle of consanguinity, it would have been null and void due to lack of consummation. She recognizes her son's apparel, the same fabric she swaddled him in as an infant, and reveals the truth. Gregorius departs immediately on his quest for atonement despite having been prevented from committing the act of profanation.

Stephan preserves Gregorius's virginity, for she has destined him to be revealed as "*der Reiner* [the Pure One]."[18] The novella retains Christianity's central doctrine of inherited sin, notwithstanding Stephan's repeated references to her Gregorius's purity despite his conviction that he inherits his parents' guilt. Obsession leads him to assume the Christlike burden of the suffering servant. Gregorius offers himself in suffering servitude to a fisherman, who is discovered to be his grudge-bearing foster brother, who chains him to a rock, hurling the key into the sea. Three pilgrims, inspired by a vision and searching for "the Pure One," locate Gregorius and ordain him as the new pope. They miraculously retrieve the key to his chains from the belly of a fish, and Gregorius, on returning a second time to Aquitaine, begins immediately to work miracles. As he progresses through the streets, the dust turns to grass beneath his feet; wherever he passes, the trees bear fruit, and church bells ring joyously. Finally, on the thoroughfare, he encounters his mother, her queenly raiment cloaked beneath penitential garb, but mother and son recognize each other and embrace. Where things will go from there is left to the reader's imagination.[19]

– CHAPTER FOURTEEN –

TWENTIETH-CENTURY *VERWANDLUNGSMÄRCHEN*: KAFKA AND LESSING

GREGOR SAMSA, in Kafka's *Metamorphosis*, is a sacrificial animal, turned into an insect and forced to confront his situation. His life heretofore has been a sacrifice in support of his family, but ironically enough, the sequence of his sudden incapacity and slow death is also a sacrifice that liberates his family from their dependency on him. Central to the plot is its exploration of the brother-sister relationship. It may well be accidental that Gregor's name is a variant of Gregorius, and that Grete's name is a variant of Gretel, but their relationship does have analogues in the Gregorius legend and the Hansel and Gretel fairy tales. Their characters have cognates in traditional sister-brother stories, especially the Grimm fairy tales where the brother is trapped in an animal's body.

Grete's role is "Kafkaesque," for although she is several times perceived as a mere child, there is an early display of her cleverness, her womanly allure, and her powers of persuasion. "If only his sister were here! She was clever; she was already in tears while Gregor was still lying peacefully on his back. And the chief clerk was a lover of women, surely she could persuade him; she would close the front door in the entrance hall and talk him out of his shocked state."

Grete immediately usurps maternal responsibility as she becomes Gregor's food provider, beginning with a bowl of milk, then progressing to solid foods. The sister who offers foodstuffs is a recurrent motif in sibling narratives, beginning with Eve's offering Adam the apple. Gretel must feed Hansel and conceal his weight gain from the witch. Sieglinde Aarenhold plies her brother with cherries and chocolates during the opera intermission. After their return from the opera, Siegfried consumes a caviar sandwich and gulps down a glass of wine, grumbling that it is tasteless to serve red wine with caviar. She frets that he has had little more than bonbons since tea and presses him to take at least an additional peach, which he gruffly disdains.

Grete likewise experiences difficulty meeting Gregor's less refined but specific culinary preferences as an insect. She notes his lack of interest in the bowl of milk, his erstwhile favorite beverage, and learns that he prefers the garbage and table scraps she subsequently brings him. Before Gregor's metamorphosis, Grete is the sole person in the family who seems to appreciate him, and Gregor is the only one who regards her as anything but a useless child while the rest of the family recoils in horror. The mother faints at the sight of Gregor, and the father expresses his disgust by bombarding him with apples—yes, apples. In these scenes, Grete emerges stronger than her mother, whom she supplants, but her potential role as healer is never developed. The story resembles a parable of suffering and redemption with Grete as a mediatrix of Graces, but the sibling relationship deteriorates progressively after the mother's collapse. "'Gregor!' shouted his sister, glowering at him and shaking her fist. That was the first word she had spoken to him directly since his transformation. She ran into the other room to fetch some kind of smelling salts to bring her mother out of her faint."

Grete becomes increasingly exasperated with her brother, and she is the first family member to declare her abandonment of all hope. Gregor, by contrast, never loses his devotion to Grete, which is constant before and after his metamorphosis. This is revealed in the novelist's several references to Gregor's appreciation for Greta as an accomplished musician: "Gregor only remained close to his sister now. Unlike him, she was very fond of music and a gifted and expressive violinist, it was his secret plan to send her to the conservatory next year even though it would cause great expense that would have to be made up for in some other way."

Gregor had been hoping to reveal this plan to Grete at Christmas. He fantasizes about her willingly coming to stay with him in his room and bestowing tearfully thankful embraces while he kisses her on the neck. This fantasy is not devoid of amorous implications, but it does not imply prurience or violation. Christmas has already passed, however, along with any possibility of any affectionate embrace. Gregor's other remotely sexual fantasies are represented by the framed clipping on his wall of a woman in furs, reminiscent of Sacher Masoch's *Venus im Pelz* (Venus in Furs), which mirrors the increasingly masochistic relationship between Gregor and his sister. Elizabeth Hunter has observed hints of brother-sister eroticism bridging Kafka's *Metamorphosis* and Thomas Mann's sibling incest narratives, and relates masochism to "the increasingly aggressive stance adopted by Grete in the course of the narrative [that] associates her with the kind of dominant femininity suggested by the 'Pelzdame' motif."[1] To Hunter's observations, I would add that the culmination of brother-sister eroticism in *Wälsungenblut* occurs on an animal pelt.

Before his sudden and unexplained metamorphosis, Gregor is a good and faithful servant to his family, and thereafter he becomes the suffering servant of Isaiah 53:3: "He is despised and rejected of men; a man of sorrows, and acquainted with grief: and we hid as it were our faces from him; he was despised, and we esteemed him not."

Upon Gregor's death, Grete comments on his withered corpse, soon to be swept away like the desiccated remains of the Hunger Artist featured in another of Kafka's works. His prolonged agony is not without redemptive quality, for, as we have seen, Gregor's ordeal releases his family from their erstwhile pathological dependence upon him. They now plan to abandon their old house, which we now discover was chosen by him. Gregor, who has embodied and enabled his parents' flaws, eventually redeems them through his metamorphosis and death. The story ends with the family's celebrating their liberation with an excursion to the countryside, and "as if in confirmation of their new dreams and good intentions, as soon as they reached their destination Grete was the first to get up and stretch out her young body."

DORIS LESSING: *MARA AND DANN*

At least one reviewer has observed that Doris Lessing's post-apocalyptic novel, *Mara and Dann,* although set thousands of years in the future, can transport a reader's imagination backward in time to the primeval legend of Adam and Eve.[2] Norah Vincent, writing in *Salon*, refers to the main characters as "our surrogate Adam and Eve, although without much explication. This is not surprising, for if the novel makes any allusions to Genesis, they are obscure and discernable only with assiduous search. Religion does not conspicuously intrude into the thoughts or actions of the protagonists, and Lessing's abjurement of opportunities to exploit religious myth and metaphore places artistic limits on the world she creates."

Mara and Dann have committed no original sin; they are a prince and princess spirited away as small children from their parents' assassins, unaware of their royal identities. On reaching adolescence, they migrate north, across a drought-stricken continent of Africa, until they encounter survivors of their lost kingdom. The bond between them is strongly suggestive of the erotic, and Lessing teases the reader as she has them skinny-dipping together on one occasion and sharing a bed more than once, with Mara aware but not alarmed at one point by Dann's erection pressing against her body. As the novel reaches its climax, they are discovered sleeping naked in bed together by Felix, a self-appointed retainer, who, supported by his wife, Felissa, urges them to marry and regenerate the royal line: "Real royalty. We need the Royal blood. Your child would revive the Royal house, the Royal family. When people know there is a Royal couple back in the Centre, and Royal children, then they would support us, as they did in the past."

The prospect tempts Dann, and Mara admits she loves Dann more than Shabis, the lover whose child she will eventually carry. At an anticlimactic moment, the brother and sister share a brief but passionate kiss, but renounce the invitation to form a royal union. This is neither due to moral scruples nor Westermarckean indifference but partly in response to Mara's fortuitous discovery in a conveniently surviving scientific library of the deleterious effects of inbreeding.

Mara and Dann are as guiltless in their trials as Hansel and Gretel, to whom Sharon R. Wilson compares them in her article on "Lessing's Mara And Dann," with its "motifs of starvation, struggle for survival, cannibalistic greediness and archetypal characters in this novel." Furthermore, she recognizes its relationship to "the Grimms' 'Hansel and Gretel' . . . about abandoned, often incestuous, orphans trying to outwit ogres and find their way."[3] Mara courageously rescues Dann from a dungeon and nurses him back to health.

Wilson does not remark that the core pattern of Mara and Dann's saga, like that of Hansel and Gretel, follows the archetypal exile myth of Adam and Eve. Valenta Adami assumes that task in her scholarly article on the novel's "Mythic and Fairytale Elements," which addreses the novel's other inescapable element, "In particular, the theme of brother-and-sister incest is often related to stories about the origin of the human race or of a dynasty, just like in the case of Mara and Dann, who are asked to play a kind of Adam-and-Eve role of 'First Couple.'"[4]

Dann offers little resistance to temptation, especially after being separated from her for a spell, and more easily persuaded by flattery and the prospects of power and luxury.

> "You will think about our plan," ordered Felix.
> "We'll think about it," said Mara and stood up, and so did Dann, and they went to their rooms. There Dann said, violently, "They want me as a stud, and you as a brood animal."
> "That's about it," she said.
> Then his mood changed and he said, "I rather fancy the idea of being married to you, Mara.
> And all our little ones running about."
> "I would say they are a little insane," said Mara, "a little mad."
> "Perhaps we shouldn't be too quick to see everything as mad."
> She did not know what to say; she felt apprehensive.[5]

In this crisis, the Adam shows himself to be weaker and more susceptible to temptation than the Eve. Mara demonstrates, as she has throughout the novel, a decisiveness lacking in her Mercurial brother, to whom she delivers an ultimatum:

> "Dann, I'm leaving tomorrow, by myself if I have to."
> He whirled about, his face ugly with suspicion and with anger. "You can't leave. I won't let you."
> "Your marvellous plans depend on one thing. On me. On my womb."
> And she tapped her stomach. "And I'm leaving." He gripped her two arms and glared into her face.

> "Dann," she said softly, "are you going to make me your prisoner?" His hands did not lessen their grip, but they trembled, and she knew her words had reached him.
>
> "Dann, are you going to rape me?" He furiously shook his head.[6]

With these words, Mara forces the story past its long-postponed crisis, and later she explains why there is to be no original sin.

– CONCLUSION –

ORIGINAL SIN AND VICARIOUS GUILT

THE DISCOURAGING words of the *New England Primer,* "In Adam's fall, we sinned all," must have been lurking in my subconscious when, as a college freshman at Wayne State University in the fall of 1960, I raised my hand in Professor George Nakhnikian's philosophy 201 lecture to ask the naive question of vicarious guilt.[1] "What if God decides to punish another person for something I've done? Am I morally responsible if God punishes someone else for a sin I've committed?"

I was shocked and humiliated by his response, which seemed to me, after eight years of Catholic schooling, not merely impatient but frightfully blasphemous: "Any God who would do that can go to hell as far as I'm concerned!"

This withering retort by my much-admired professor left me feeling foolish for many years, wondering what had possessed me to introduce such an absurd notion as vicarious guilt. Nakhnikian seemed to dismiss my question as patently trivial and beyond reasonable consideration, but with over a half-century of reflection, I've realized what I might have said in response. In the realm of Christianity, the doctrine of vicarious guilt is as fundamental as the doctrine of vicarious atonement. The transference of guilt from original sin is why all the children of Adam and Eve are exiled from the Garden.

I cringed before Nakhnikian's emotional response and shriveled with embarrassment because I had not yet fully realized the degree to which religious mythology permeates American social and political culture. My high school survey of American history had not acquainted me with Thomas Jefferson's jeremiad on America's plenary guilt for slavery, its original sin: "I tremble for my country when I reflect that God is just: that his justice cannot sleep for ever."[2]

Four generations later, the awakened wrath of God descended on the country Abraham Lincoln inherited from Thomas Jefferson,

> Fondly do we hope, fervently do we pray, that this mighty scourge of war may speedily pass away. Yet, if God wills that it continue until all the wealth piled by the bondsman's two hundred and fifty years of unrequited toil shall be sunk, and until every drop of blood drawn with the lash shall be paid by another drawn with the sword, as was said three thousand years ago, so still it must be said "the judgments of the Lord are true and righteous altogether.

Vicarious guilt is felt today in a German nation that must bear the weight of Hitler's abominations. By rivers of Babylon, even the faithful must weep for the guilt of Israel's idolaters. In ancient Thebes, the abomination of one man brought down plague on an entire city. Vicarious guilt and vicarious redemption are the elements of justice.

But with original sin came the knowledge that wisdom and suffering are inextricably linked. The fruit of knowledge had little to do with "carnal knowledge." When our eyes are opened, we see our nakedness before the coldness of truth, our hopeless ignorance, our intellectual dishabille. Yahweh himself, like other gods and men, sees nakedness in his own image and likeness. The gods are constantly pursuing their lusts and cloaking their fears. We are like unto these gods Kronos and Uranos, Zeus and especially Yahweh—a jealous God who reflects our own discontent—arbitrary, capricious, the rapist of virgins who cares for nothing but his own glory, and whose wants can never be supplied. Behold, he is eternally tormented by his need for praise and scorned by his children; so often forgetful of their fear of the lord and so often neglectful in singing his praise, so often unmindful of his kingdom and his power and his glory. Thus, he "repents" of having made them and shows his wrath with fire and flood.

Since defiance of Him is futile, Satan was irrational when he "durst defy th'Omnipotent to arms" or, as Ben Jonson put it, "The devil is an ass." Satan's rebellion and its result were fixed from the moment of creation when all the sons of God rose among the stars and sang for joy. The book of Job says, "when the sons of God present themselves before the LORD, Satan comes also among them." Are Satan and his angels as happy as Blake declared them to be? Perhaps so. And perhaps Leibnitz was right in pontificating that their fates and ours are "all for the best."

Or perhaps Voltaire was correct in surmising that, at any moment, all our fortunes may suddenly be dashed:

> he will of the implacable Being who had punished Lot's wife for her curiosity, but preserved her scheming daughters and drunkard father, with their incestuous propensities. The justice of a silent and mysterious God struck Onan down without a hearing, but heard the remonstrance of Cain, and relented, then given him a special mark, and blessed him with a wife and permitted him to found a city.[3]

As we have seen, certain church fathers viewed these Old Testament believers as immature persons who, seduced by Satan, exposed themselves to the wrath of an omniscient parent. But the Genesis narrative does not indicate their discovery of nakedness was followed by any curse on sexual activity, despite the unfounded supposition of Augustine. Equally unsupported are John Milton's suppositions that Adam and Eve were sexually active before the fall or that they employed sex immediately thereafter as an analgesic balm. The "apple" was, if anything, an anti-aphrodisiac. The sibling incest taboo is instilled in toddlers, reinforced throughout childhood, and solidified at puberty. It was not lust but childlike curiosity that first prompted the disobedience of Eve and Adam, and Genesis does not say their sudden discovery of their nakedness had anything to do with sexual activity, only with the shock of recognizing their exposure, their childish attempts to hide their shame, and their fear of discovery. The story of Adam and Eve illustrates and subliminally reinforces the sexual taboo acquired in childhood and the dread of being "caught with one's pants down" by wrathful adult authority.

We might say that the fable is an allegory of the arrival of young adulthood, with puberty's uncertainties and discomforts. The eyes of young adults are opened as they acquire the fruit of knowledge, along with all the discontent accompanying civilized expectations. The fable prominently displays the loss of childhood's presumed innocence, symbolized by the acquisition of the adolescent's nakedness taboo. "Taboo," a word implied but not employed in the Genesis fable, does not indicate sexual indulgence but rather avoidance and anxiety. The word "knowledge" and its multilingual correlatives, whether in the Septuagint, the Tanakh, the Latin Vulgate, or the translations of Luther and King James, is ambiguous, and Adam and Eve's nakedness is an ambiguous symbol. There is, however, no ambiguity in the moral of a story that illustrates the terror of parental wrath and vengeance. The fable is a vivid example of a powerful and persistent tradition in the mythic, folkloric, and archetypal children's nightmares.

Adam and Eve's story illustrates the child's dawning awareness of the nakedness taboo and the shame and secrecy accompanying forbidden games with siblings and other playmates. This taboo is all the more powerful because it is mysterious and inexplicable in the infantile imagination. Before a child reaches puberty, the universal horror of sibling incest is firmly fixed as an aspect of the discomfort all societies manifest with sexual feelings in general, and this discomfort, persisting into adulthood, is amplified by the universal unease societies attach to human sexuality in their religion, politics, and law. Most societies have some form of nakedness taboo, but while human societies do not maintain uniform expressions of nakedness taboo across cultural boundaries, every society has a historical tradition of sexual taboos. Sexual taboos have proven to be variable according to time and place, but the sibling incest taboo gives every indication of being universal and perpetual. How then do we explain that, in the poetry of the ancient Near East, the love of siblings became a metaphor for the perfect, enduring, ideal expression of erotic love?

It is often said that when lovers address one another as brother and sister, as in the poetry of ancient Egypt and Song of Solomon, the purpose is to illustrate the permanence and depth of mutual affection. There is, nonetheless, a noteworthy ambiguity in this, as in all myths and metaphors. The poetic mythology of Apollo and Artemis in the *Homeric Hymns* is ambiguous but suggestive of consortship. Divine incest was normal among the gods of "classical" Greece, and the sibling marriage of Zeus and Hera is undisguised and unmistakable in Homer's *Iliad.* In Athens and Sparta, the marriage of half-siblings was allowed, and this was a prelude to the full-sibling marriage the Ptolemy dynasty adopted that usurped the rulership of Egypt but revived the pharaonic custom of royal incest. Sibling marriage made its appearance among Egyptian commoners as well, but the practice, which was forbidden under Roman law, became completely unthinkable with the Christianization of the empire and the subsequent rise of Islam. Hence there is no remnant of sibling marriage in modern Egypt.

Sibling incest is the original sin in the medieval Gregorius legend, which tacitly evokes the fable of Adam and Eve, who transmit their guilt to their offspring but, in that same act, generate their ultimate redeemer. So positive a result of romantic love between siblings has been rare in literature, notwithstanding the remarkable exceptions of Gower's "The Tale of Canace and Machaire," Richard Wagner's *Die Walküre*, and Thomas Mann's *Der Erwählte.* My original plan did not include devoting an entire chapter to Mann's *Der Erwählte,* but finally it dawned on me that its plot and symbolism directly and specifically recapitulate the fall and redemption of Adam and Eve. While the story's cognate in the Oedipus legend is obvious and unavoidable, its Christian emphasis is far more significant. Mann repeatedly returns to the theme of original and inherited sin. His allusions are not to the legendary ancient Greece, but to the biblical traditions of medieval Europe. And these are to be found not only in Genesis but in the Gospel of St. Luke, as becomes obvious when Sibylla meditates before a painting that depicts the angel Gabriel's announcement of Christ's *saintisme engendrement.*

I have shown how the nightmare of Adam and Eve's expulsion to the dark forest is recapitulated in the Grimm fairy tales of "Hansel and Gretel," "*Brüderchen und Schwesterchen,*" and "*Das Lämmchen und Fischchen,*" where a brother and sister are banished. These fables simultaneously cloak and reveal the subliminal contradictions in the trope of sibling romance that have found expression in the fables of archaic Greece and the love poetry of the ancient Near East. The depiction of sibling romance was sporadically recurrent in medieval literature and had a fitful reappearance early in the Romantic Movement, but contemporary audiences find it grossly disturbing. Wagner's presentation of the love scene between Siegmund and Sieglinde in *Die Walküre* can reliably evoke gasps of disapproval, for even persons who have no siblings of either sex may experience the Westermarck effect.

This study has been a brief exercise in the practice of literary criticism, sacrilegious when applied to the piously titillating legend of Adam and Eve. I deduce from that fable that there are no prescriptions for our times. Politics and the law obviously and inevitably reflect and influence attitudes toward sexuality and eroticism, especially when questions of violence, duress, and power relationships require answers, and this study does not evade such discussion. It addresses, for example, Amnon's brutal violation of his sister, Tamar, and reflects Gower's horror at the wrath of Eolus, so cruelly directed at Canace for her love of Machaire. But since the rhetoric of gender, sex, and culture so often has unpredictable legal and political consequences, and great potential for unintended mischief, I advocate no program for social change. I have limited myself to studying the sibling exile legend, with its rebellious and protective sisters.

If defiance of power was Eve's original sin, it was even more her justifying valor.

ENDNOTES

Introduction

1. Wilson Jeremiah Moses, *Black Messiahs and Uncle Toms: Social and Literary Manipulations of a Religious Myth,* revised ed. (State College: Penn State University, 1993), xiii.

2. Cicero, *The Nature of the Gods,* trans. H.C.P. McGregor (New York: Penguin, 1972), 151, 217.

3. See Andrew George, *The Epic of Gilgamesh: The Babylonian Epic Poem and Other Texts in Akkadian and Sumerian* (London: Penguin Books, 2000); George Smith, *The Chaldean Account of Genesis* (New York: Scribner, 1876). David Damrosch, *The Buried Book: The Loss and Rediscovery of the Great Epic of Gilgamesh* (New York: Henry Holt, 2006).

4. See "Gilgamesh" in Wayne R. Dynes, ed., *Encyclopedia of Homosexuality* (New York: Garland, 1990), 479.

5. James George Frazer, *The Golden Bough* (New York: Macmillan, 1922), 385. Those unfamiliar with the cruelty of Artemis and Apollo may consult the indexes of Edith Hamilton's perennial bestseller, *Mythology: Timeless Tales of Gods and Heroes,* 75th anniversary edition (New York: Little, Brown, 1998).

Chapter One: Divine Incest, Royal Incest, and the Sibling Exile Narrative

1. There are several available databases of the Aarne–Thompson–Uther Index. Also helpful is a site constructed by D. L. Ashliman, editor, "Hansel and Gretel and other folktales of Aarne-Thompson-Uther types 327, 327A, 327B, and 327C about abandoned children," revised February 11, 2023, https://www.pitt.edu/~dash/type0327.html.

2. The "happy fault" is retained in the Greek tradition of Iraneus and the *felix culpa* doctrine of St. Augustine.

3. Benjamin Franklin, "The Autobiography," in *Benjamin Franklin's Autobiography: An Authoritative Text, Backgrounds, Criticism,* ed. J. A. Leo Lemay and P. M. Zall (New York and London: Norton, 1986).

4. Rodigast was a decent enough poet to have endowed us with a sentence capable of bearing several meanings. I return to Rodigast's words elsewhere in this work and offer some possible translations at the recurrence of his name, but good poetry, such as this, can neither be translated nor paraphrased.

5. Joel Edmund Anderson, "Irenaeus of Lyon: Adam and Eve as Children, and the Greek Philosophical Concepts of Becoming and Being (Part 3)," Resurrecting Orthodoxy, November 19, 2015, https://www.joeledmundanderson.com/irenaeus-of-lyon-adam-and-eve-as-children-and-the-greek-philosophical-concepts-of-becoming-and-being-part-3/.

6. There is a tremendous amount of literature surrounding the idea attributed to Irenaeus, that Adam was not created perfect, *i.e.,* as an adult. For discussion of this position, see Edmund

Newey, "'God Made Man Greater When He Made Him Less': Traherne's Iconic Child," *Literature and Theology* 24, no. 3 (September 2010): 227-241, https://www.jstor.org/stable/23927237. Christopher R. Smith has found evidence that "for Irenaeus, Eve in the garden was actually prepubescent" in "Chiliasm and Recapitulation in the Theology of Ireneus," *Vigilae Christianae* 48, no. 4 (December 1994): 318, https://doi.org/10.2307/1584297. Cited by M. C. Steenberg, "Children in Paradise: Adam and Eve as 'Infants' in Irenaeus of Lyons," *Journal of Early Christian Studies* 12, no. 1 (Spring 2004): 1-22, https://dx.doi.org/10.1353/earl.2004.0016. None of this is to deny the rabbinical tradition recorded by Louis Ginzberg that Adam was created as a fully formed adult. See Ginzberg, *Legends of the Jews* (1909; repr. Adansonia Press, 2018), 31.

7. George Boas, *Primitivism and Related Ideas in the Middle Ages* (Baltimore: Johns Hopkins University, 1948), 15-18. Brian Murdoch, *The Apocryphal Adam and Eve in Medieval Europe: Vernacular Translations and Adaptations of the Vita Adae et Evae* (Oxford: Oxford University Press, 2009).

8. Richard Gilmore, *Bible History, Containing the Most Remarkable Events of the Old and New Testments, to Which is Added a Compendium of Church History for the Use of the Catholic Schools* (New York: Benziger Brothers, 1904), 9-10.

9. Ante-Nicene Fathers, *On the Apparel of Women,* Book 1, Vol. IV, https://www.tertullian.org/anf/anf04/anf04-06.htm.

10. William Blake, "To Nobodaddy," in *The Poetry and Prose of William Blake*, David B. Erdman, ed. (New York: Doubleday, 1965), 462.

11. Louis Ginzberg recounts a Jewish legend of God's taking counsel with his angels in the creation of man, and also describes the fall of rebellious angels. See Ginzberg, *The Legends of the Jews*, 51. Genesis 1 and 2 deliver two sequential creation narratives, but there is no mention of angels in either of these. Inconsistencies in the sequence of events and other discrepancies in the two accounts have puzzled some readers, but others have dismissed them as inconsequential. All readers seem to agree that God planted a garden and placed a subtle serpent within it. Christians assert that the serpent was either possessed by or an incarnation of Satan, whom they identify with the fallen angels and the dragon cast out of heaven in the Apocalypse. If any similar linkage or association ever sprang up in Jewish legend, it never became canonical. Nothing in Genesis associates the serpent with a fallen and perpetually irredeemable angel. The Satan of the Jewish Bible makes his first appearance in the Book of Job, where we see God taking counsel with him.

12. "Adam Lay Ibunden," author unknown, is a frequently anthologized late Middle English poem. For bibliographies addressing the various attributions of the exclamation, "O felix culpa," see Victor Yelverton Haines's article in *A Dictionary of Biblical Tradition in English Literature,* David Lyle Jeffrey, ed. (Grand Rapids: W. B. Eerdmans), 274-5.

13. Edmund Newey, "'God Made Man Greater When He Made Him Less,'" quotes Traherne.

14. Book of Jubilees, chapter 3, verse 15.

15. Smith, "Chiliasm and Recapitulation." Also see Steenberg, "Children in Paradise."

16. Otto Rank discusses the appearance in epic and folklore of the child who is doomed to be abandoned or exposed because of some perceived threat to the parents or to the cosmic order. See Otto Rank, *The Myth of the Birth of the Hero* (Mansfield Centre, CT: Martino, 2011). See also Joseph Campbell, *Hero with a Thousand Faces* (Pantheon Books, 1949) and Frazer, *The Golden Bough* (1890–1915).

17. Voltaire had great fun with the phrase translated as "one of us," which he interpreted as evidence that the authors of Genesis were polytheists.

18. Elizabeth Archibald, *Incest and the Medieval Imagination* (Oxford: Clarendon Press, 2001), 29 cites Gower, *Confessio Amantis,* Macaulay ed., Book 8: 68-70. Calmana, or Kalmana in the *The Seder HaDorot* or "Book of Generations" (1768) by Lithuanian Rabbi Jehiel Heilprin

(1660–1746). Medieval Christian scholar Peter Comesta gives Cain's wife that name in *Historia scholastica,* according to Brian Murdoch, *The Apocryphal Adam and Eve in Medieval Europe*, 221.

19. Genesis 12:14-16, King James Version.

20. Genesis 20:6-7, King James Version.

21. *Catholic Encyclopedia,* published between 1907 and 1912, is typical of scholarly sources in not resolving the question of Abram's ultimate truthfulness, but some Protestant evangelicals accept Abram's word that Sarai was his half-sister, for example, Ligonier Ministries, "Abaraham's Sister," https://www.ligonier.org/learn/devotionals/abrahams-sister.

22. Genesis 38:9, King James Version.

23. Augustine, *City of God,* Book XV, Chapter 16, "Of Marriage Beteen Blood Relations." Thomas Aquinas, *Summa Theologiae,* Second Part of the Second Part, Question 154, "The Parts of Lust," Article 9, Question 3.

24. This book is not rooted in late twentieth-century post-modernism but in more traditional approaches to literary history, although it recognizes the contributions of Stefani Engelstein. I attempt to understand each with an appreciation for the social and cultural circumstances of the authors who produced them. I have often acknowledgeed my indebtedness to Aristotle, Aquinas, and Freud and to the newer historicism of Marina Warner, Elizabeth Archibald, Ellen Pollak, Brian Murdoch, Stephen Greenblatt, and others.

25. One may compare this to story of the primal division of male and female from an original hermaphrodite in Plato's *Symposium.* For references to Genesis, see Henry Abramovitch, *Brothers and Sisters: Myth and Reality,* (College Station: Texas A&M Press, 2014), 10. Howard Schwartz, *Tree of Souls: The Mythology of Judaism* (Oxford University Press, 2006), 138. Also see Rabbi David Cooper, who cites the *Midrash Rabbah* at https://www.rabbidavidcooper.com/cooper-print-index/2010/11/8/2351-adam-and-eve-as-siamese-twins-n.html. Also see article by Rabbi David J. Meyer, "What the Torah Teaches Us About Gender Fluidity and Transgender Justice," Religious Action Center of Reform Judaism, September 20, 2018, https://rac.org/blog/what-torah-teaches-us-about-gender-fluidity-and-transgender-justice.

26. Doyle McKey, et al., "The Evolutionary Ecology of Clonally Propagated Domesticated Plants," New Phytologist 186, no. 2 (February 25, 2010): 318–332, https://doi.org/10.1111/j.1469-8137.2010.03210.x. Cloning of plants goes back to biblical times—check Romans 11:17, 24. Frank B. Sliisbury, "Biology of Cloning: History and Rationale," *BioScience* 50, no. 8 (August 2000): 636, https://doi.org/10.1641/0006-3568(2000)050[0636:BOCHAR]2.0.CO;2. I begin by dispelling the widely held oversimplification that "plants grow from seeds"—indeed many of them do, but quite a few have evolved the capacity for asexual (clonal) reproduction. Even before the origins of agriculture, about twelve thousand years ago, mankind has been observing wild plants performing feats of asexual reproduction. Cornell Video, "Introduction: A Historical Perspective," Cornell University, https://www.cornell.edu/video/history-of-plant-cloning-1-historical-perspective.

27. Adam and Eve's sibling relationship is more fully discussed in the following chapter, along with the traditions that present them as such, as well the supportive academic discourse.

28. G. Tachon, et. al., "Discordant Sex in Monozygotic XXY/XX Twins: A Case Report," H*uman Reproduction* 29, no. 12 (December 2014): 2814–2820, https://doi.org/10.1093/humrep/deu275.

29. Otto Rank, *Das Inzest-Motiv in Dichtung und Sage* (Leipzig: Franz Deuticke, 1912).

30. Peter Enns, *The Evolution of Adam* (Grand Rapids: Brazos Press, 2012). Peter Enns seeks to reconcile scripture with modern evolutionary theory by regarding Genesis as myth and metaphor. Stephen Greenblatt, *The Rise and Fall of Adam and Eve: The Story that Created Us* (London: Vintage, 2017) 92.

31. Jules Glenn, "Opposite-Sex Twins," *Journal of the American Psychoanalytic Association* 14, no. 4 (August 1966): 736–759, https://doi.org/10.1177/000306516601400405.

32. Marriage of three-year-old opposite-sex twins reported in *Coconuts* (Bangkok), November 19, 2015. Marriage of six-year-old opposites in *The London Daily Mail,* December 25, 2018, and *The Sun* (United Kingdom), December 25, 2018.

33. Louis Ginzberg, *The Legends of the Jews*, 33.

34. Rabbi David Cooper, "2351 Adam and Eve as Siamese Twins (N)," Rabbi David Cooper, November 8, 2010, https://www.rabbidavidcooper.com/cooper-print-index/2010/11/8/2351-adam-and-eve-as-siamese-twins-n.html. Also see Abramovitch, *Brothers and Sisters*, 10.

35. Robert Sungenis, "Creationism, Pope John Paul II, and the Case Against Theistic Evolution," Kolbe Center for the Study of Creation, 2021, https://www.kolbecenter.org/the-case-against-theistic-evolution/. According to Brian Harrison, the first Catholic who suggested that Adam and Eve may have been twins was J. Paquier in his book *La Création et l'Evolution, la Révélation et la Science* (Paris: Gabalda, 1932), 132. Paquier is cited to this effect by J. Gross, "The Problem of Origins in Recent Theology" in *Theology and Evolution*, ed. E.C. Messenger (London: Sands, 1950), 144. See Brian W. Harrison, "Did Woman Evolve From The Beasts? A Defence Of Traditional Catholic Doctrine," *Roman Theological Forum* 97 (January 2002): http://www.rtforum.org/lt/lt97.html.

36. "Jérôme Lejeune 1927–1994," Les Temoignages, 2004, http://trisomie.21.free.fr/jerome_lejeune_ang.htm.

37. Monozygotic twins are naturally occurring clones. "Natural clones, also known as identical twins, occur in humans and other mammals. . . . These twins are produced when a fertilized egg splits, creating two or more embryos that carry almost identical DNA." See National Human Genome Research Institute ,"Cloning Fact Sheet," National Institutes of Health, August 15, 2020, https://www.genome.gov/. For a study indicating DNA differences between monozygotic twins, see statement on research by the study's lead authors, Carl Bruder, Ph.D. et. al., "Phenotypically Concordant and Discordant Monozygotic Twins Display Different DNA Copy-Number-Variation Profiles," *American Journal of Human Genetics* (February 2008): https://doi.org/10.1016/j.ajhg.2007.12.011: "The presumption has always been that identical twins are identical down to their DNA. That's mostly true, but our findings suggest that there are small, subtle differences due to CNV. Those differences may point the way to better understanding of genetic diseases when we study so-called discordant monozygotic twins. . . . a pair of twins where one twin has a disorder and the other does not."

38. Monozygotic opposite-sex twins rarely occur, and result in the girl's manifesting abnormal development, *i.e.* Turner Syndrome. See J. H. Edwards, Tessa Dent and Jacob Kahn, "Monozygotic Twins of Different Sex," *Journal of Medical Genetics* 3, no. 117 (1966): https://doi.org/10.1136/jmg.3.2.117. G. Tachon, et. al., "Discordant Sex in Monozygotic XXY/XX Twins: A Case Report," 2814–2820.

39. Marcia Landy, "Kinship and the Role of Women in Paradise Lost," *Milton Studies* 4 (January 1972): 3–18, https://doi.org/10.2307/26395332.

40. Archibald, 244.

41. The alternative explanations offered by Freud and Edvard Westermarck for sibling incest aversion are discussed elsewhere in the present volume and surveyed along with other works, including those cited by Carl Degler, *In Search of Human Nature: The Decline and Revival of Darwinbism in American Social Thought* (Oxford: Oxford University Press, 1991) and Dwight W. Read, "Incest Taboos and Kinship: A Biological or a Cultural Story?," *Reviews in Anthropology* 43, no. 2 (June 2014), https://doi.org/10.1080/00938157.2014.903151.

42. Brian Murdoch, *Adam's Grace,* first edition (D.S. Brewer, June 2000), 59.

43. Margarita Stocker, *Paradise Lost* (New York: Macmillan, 1988), 53.

44. Quoted by Annette Volfing, in her commentary on *Heinrich von Mügeln: Der meide kranz; Münchener Texte und Untersuchungen zur deutschen Literatur des Mittelalters* 111

(Tübingen: Niemeyer, 1997), 377, note 15. Abramovitch refers to "Adam and Eve, twin brother and sister" in *Brothers and Sisters*, 10. Ellen Pollak, *Incest and the English Novel* (Baltimore: Johns Hopkins Unviersity Press, 2003), 42. Pollak also entertains an idea borrowed from Bolinbroke that Adam is Eve's father. Shannon Miller endorses Pollak's opinion that they are brother and sister in her *Engendering the Fall: John Milton and Seventeenth-Century Women Writers* (Philadelphia: University of Pennsylvania Press, 2008), 211. Ilona Nemesnyik Rashkow addresses the "obvious brother-sister/ spousal relationship of Adam and Eve" in *Taboo Or Not Taboo: Sexuality and Family in the Hebrew Bible* (Fortress Press, Minneapolis), 71.

45. Genesis 2:24, King James Version.

46. The etiological myth explaining the origins of marriage was probably a later addition to the original narrative, since Adam and Eve were created as one flesh, and even closer than fraternal opposite-sex twins. They were like those rare instances of twins who originate in a single zygote but diverge sexually. Opposite-sex "identical" twins are known to occur naturally in the human species, although with extreme rarity.

47. Robert Crumb's illustration of Genesis 2:24 shows a smiling Adam engaging a smiling Eve *a tergo,* but the biblical text has always implied much more than joyous copulation.

48. Sigmund Freud, *Totem and Taboo* (Hugo Heller, 1913), Robert Henry Codrington, *The Melanesians: Studies in their Anthropology and Folk-Lore* (Oxford: Clarendon Press, 1891), and Frazer *Totemism and Exogamy:A Treatise on Certain Early Forms of Superstition and Society* (Hamburg: Severus, 1910), 77.

49. Freud suggests that infantile sexuality conflicts with adolescent morality, and that civilization necessitates the suppression of incestuous impulses and produces anxiety and unease.

50. Bishop Richard Gilmore, *Bible History: Containing the Most Remarkable Events of the Old and New Testament* (Benzinger Brothers: 1935).

51. Sigmund Freud, *Das Unbehagen in der Kultur* (Vienna: Internationaler Psychoanalutischer Verlag: 1930).

52. The words of Professor Hayes in her Yale lecture were available on YouTube as late as early 2022.

53. Kyle Greenwood, "Tree of Knowledge," Bible Odyssey, June 20, 2017, https://www.bibleodyssey.org/articles/tree-of-knowledge/.

54. Genesis 9:23, King James Version.

55. John Savoie "'That Fallacious Fruit,' Lapsarian Lovemaking in 'Paradise Lost,'" *Milton Quarterly* 45, no. 3 (October 2011), 161-171, https://www.jstor.org/stable/24462010.

56. Pope Pius XI, "Casti Connubii," Dicastero per la Comunicazione, Libreria Editrice Vaticana, https://www.vatican.va/content/pius-xi/en/encyclicals/documents/hf_p-xi_enc_19301231_casti-connubii.html

57. Bronisław Malinowski, *Magic, Science and Religion* (Garden City, NY: Doubleday, 1985). Malinowski, *Sex and Repression in Savage Society* (Chicago: University of Chicago Press, 1987). Malinowski, *The Sexual Life of Savages* (Boston: Beacon, 1929).

58. Freud cited the report of Robert Henry Codrington, *The Melanesians*.

59. Malinowski, *The Sexual Life of Savages*, 332. Yishai Kiel, *Sexuality in the Babylonian Talmud* (Cambridge: Cambridge University Press, 2016), 146.

Chapter Two: Adam and Eve: The Urtext, and Milton's Paradise Lost

1. For a heavily footnoted summary of the question, see Rebecca Scharbach Wollenberg, "Did Ezra Reconstruct the Torah or Just Change the Script?" *TheTorah.com*, 2024, https://thetorah.com/article/did-ezra-reconstruct-the-torah-or-just-change-the-script.

2. An interlinear translation is available at Bible Hub, https://biblehub.com/interlinear/genesis/1-1.htm. Another is available at "The Complete Jewish Bible," Cahabad.org, https://www.chabad.org/library/bible_cdo/aid/8165.

3. "It has been largely accepted, however, that Milton's English Bible translation of choice was the King James, or Authorized, Version, first published in 1611, when he was just two or three years old." Jeffrey Shoulson, "Milton's Bible," from *The Cambridge Companion to Paradise Lost*, ed. Louis Schwartz (Cambridge: Cambridge University Press, 2014), 68–80.

4. See Christine Hayes, *Introduction to the Bible* (New Haven: Yale University Press, 2012), ix-x.

5. See Plato's *Symposium,* where Pausnias discourses on the complex character of Aphrodite.

6. Rabbi David J. Meyer, "What the Torah Teaches Us About Gender Fluidity and Transgender Justice," Religious Action Center of Reform Judaism, September 20, 2018, https://rac.org/blog/what-torah-teaches-us-about-gender-fluidity-and-transgender-justice.

7. Genesis 1:27, King James Version.

8. Ibid.

9. Kristen E. Kvam, Linda S. Schearing, and Valarie H. Ziegler, *Eve and Adam: Jewish, Christian, and Muslim Readings on Genesis and Gender* (Bloomington: Indiana University Press, 1999). Ronald S. Hendel, "Adam" in *Eerdmans Dictionary of the Bible*, ed. David Noel Freedman (Grand Rapids: Eerdmans, 2000). Alberdina Houtman, "The Development of the Adamic Myth in Genesis Rabbah," in *Religious Stories in Transformation: Conflict, Revision and Reception,* ed. Alberdina Houtman, et. al. (Leiden, Netherlands: Brill, 2016), 36-51.

10. L. R. Shero, "Plato's Apology and Xenophon's Apology," *The Classical Weekly* 20, no. 14 (January 31, 1927): 107-111, https://doi.org/10.2307/4388911. Gabriel Danzig, "Apologizing for Socrates: Plato and Xenophon on Socrates' Behavior in Court," *Transactions of the American Philological Association* 133, no. 2 (Autumn 2003): 281-321, https://www.jstor.org/stable/20054089. Gabriel Danzig, *Apologizing for Socrates: How Plato and Xenophon Created Our Socrates* (Lanham, MD: Lexington Books, 2010). Wilson J. Moses, *Thomas Jefferson: A Modern Prometheus* (Cambridge: Cambridge University Press, 2019), 364, 366. Bertrand Russell, *History of Western Philosophy* (New York: Simon and Schuster, 1945), 83.

11. Based on the research of Henry Ansgar Kelly, *Satan: A Biography* (Cambridge: Cambridge University Press, 2006), Henry Ansgar Kelly, *Satan in the Bible, God's Minister of Justice* (Wipf & Stock, 2017), and William Kent, "Devil," *The Catholic Encyclopedia* (1908), vol. 4. Second-century CE Christian apologist Justin Martyr was the first recorded individual to identify Satan with the serpent from the Garden of Eden was in chapters 45 and 79 of his *Dialogue with Trypho: A Conversation on Faith and Salvation.*

12. Some readers of the King James Bible read Genesis 3:15 as fortelling the coming of the Messiah. "And I will put enmity between thee and the woman, and between thy seed and her seed; it shall bruise thy head, and thou shalt bruise his heel." According to this interpretation, Jesus will crush the head of the serpent. But readers of the Douay-Rheims Bible interpret this to mean that the Virgin Mary will crush the serpent, as she does promininently in Roman Catholic paintings and statuary.

13. T. S. Eliot, *Milton: Two Studies*, (London: Faber and Faber, 1936). C. S. Lewis, *A Preface to Paradise Lost* (Oxford: Oxford University Press, 1961), 82. Stephen B. Dobranski and John P. Rumrich, eds., *Milton and Heresy* (Cambridge: Cambridge University Press, 1998).

14. Genesis 3:6, King James Version.

15. John Milton, *Paradise Lost*, Book IX, verse 1042.

16. Tamar Kadari, "Eve: Midrash and Aggadah," online editition of *The Shalvi/Hyman Encyclopedia of Jewish Women,* https://jwa.org/encyclopedia/article/eve-midrash-and-aggadah.

17. There is no biblical Urtext. The Hebrew Bible, as it exists today, is a reconstruction from several ancient languages, codified as the Masoretic Text between the seventh and tenth centuries CE. The present author is not a scholar of biblical languages and relies on the translations of King James, Martin Luther, and the Douay version, among others.

18. Carl Jung wrote the preface to R. J. Zwi Werblowsky, *Lucifer and Prometheus* (London: Routledge, 1952).

19. Genesis 3:12, King James Version.

20. Justin Glenn, "Pandora and Eve: Sex as the Root of All Evil," *The Classical World* 71, no. 3 (November 1977), 179-185.

21. Hesiod describes Athena's part in the clothing of Pandora in *Theogony Works and Days* along with the roles of Hephaestus, Aphrodite, the Graces, and other divinities in her creation.

22. See George F. Butler, "Tertullian's Pandora and John Milton's 'The Doctrine and Discipline of Divorce,'" *Christianity and Literature* 52, no. 3 (Spring 2003): 325–342, https://www.jstor.org/stable/44313233; Stella P. Revard, "Milton and Myth," in *Reassembling Truth: Twenty-First Century Milton,* ed. Charles W. Durham and Kristin A. Pruitt (Selinsgrove: Susquehanna University Press, 2003), 37. William E. Phipps, unimpressed by the tradition, attacks the "prevailing opinion" in "Eve and Pandora Contrasted," *Theology Today* 45, no. 1 (April 1988): 34–48, https://doi.org/10.1177/004057368804500104.

23. Tertullian, *Apparel of Women*, 197 AD.

24. Bruce Rosenstock, "Incest, Nakedness, and Holiness: Biblical Israel at the Limits of Culture," *Jewish Studies Quarterly* 16, no. 4 (2009): 333-362, https://www.jstor.org/stable/40753496.

25. Johan Huizinga, *Homo Ludens: A Study of the Play Element in Culture* (Boston: Beacon Press, 1955).

26. John S. Tanner and Justin Collings, "How Adams and Jefferson Read Milton and Milton Read Them," *Milton Quarterly* 40, no. 3 (October 2006): 207-219, https://www.jstor.org/stable/24465010.

27. Louis Ginzberg, *Legends of the Jews.*

28. The legend is a fictional representation of several attitudes present in Jewish, Muslim, and Christian traditions. Some storytellers have invented versions in which Eve was with Adam when she ate the apple, and others say she was alone. It is all a matter of what the storyteller chooses to convey. There is no Urtext of the story—all we have are the restorations and translations of this variously interpreted fictional narrative.

29. The Douay translation uses the plural, "you shall be as Gods." Luther, King James, and most others employ the singular.

30. Genesis 3:22, King James Version.

31. John Milton, *Paradise Lost,* Book IX, verse 1034-48. Ronald A. Veenker, "Forbidden Fruit: Ancient Near Eastern Sexual Metaphors," *Hebrew Union College Annual* (1999), 57-73, https://www.academia.edu/78115296/Forbidden_fruit_Ancient_Near_Eastern_sexual_metaphors. Brian O. Murdoch, *The Apocryphal Adam and Eve in Medieval Europe: Vernacular Translations and Adaptations of the Vita Adae et Evae* (Oxford: Oxford University Press, 2009). Philip C. Almond, *Adam and Eve in Seventeenth-Century Thought* (Cambridge: Cambridge University Press, 2008). Stephen Greenblatt, *The Rise And Fall Of Adam And Eve* (New York: Norton, 2017).

32. Heidi Hunter says that "most commentators regarded" Adam and Eve as siblings in her *Rereading Aphra Behn: History, Theory, and Criticism* (Charlottesville: University of Virginia Press, 1993), 154. Hunter's point is reiterated verbatum by Ellen Pollak, and fortified by Brian Murdoch and other scholars.

33. Lynda E. Boose, "The Father's House and the Daughter in It: The Structures of Western Culture's Daughter-Father Relationship," *Daughters and Fathers,* ed. Lynda E. Boose and Betty S. Flowers (Baltimore: Johns Hopkins University Press, 1989), 44–48.

Chapter Three: Eve's Promethean Defiance

1. Abigail Adams to Elizabeth Smith Shaw, in *Adams Family Correspondence*, Massachusetts Historical Society (2009), volume 9. Printed from Charles Francis Adams, ed., *"Letters of Mrs. Adams: The Wife of John Adams,"* 1848, 357–359.

2. Genesis 3:3, King James Version.

3. God's words to Adam have been loosely interpreted as meaning that if Adam ate from the Tree of Knowledge, God would deprive him and Eve from access to the Tree of Life; therefore, both of them were already dying on the day they ate from the Tree of Knowledge.

4. Romans 2:11, King James Version.

5. John Byron, *Cain and Abel in Text and Tradition: Jewish and Christian Interpretations of the First Sibling Rivalry* (Leiden, Netherlands: Brill, 2011), 11; Anglea Y. Kim, "Cain and Abel in the Light of Envy: A Study of the History of the Interpretation of Envy in Genesis 4:1-16," *Journal for the Study of the Pseudepigrapha* 12, no. 1 (2001): 65–84, https://doi.org/10.1177/095182070101200103.

6. This painting, almost twenty-three-feet long dominates a wall at the Musee d'Orsay in Paris. It is completely non-scriptural, and bears no relation to anything other than its supposed inspiration in Victor Hugo's poem "Conscience " in his collection, *La Légende des siècles.*

7. Genesis 4:5, King James Version.

8. Louis Ginzberg, *The Legends of the Jews.*

9. Genesis 4:11-12, King James Version.

10. Genesis 4:13-14, King James Version.

11. Genesis 4:15, King James Version.

12. C. G. Jung, *Part I: Archetypes and the Collective Unconscious,* trans. R. F. C. Hull, *Collected Works of C. G. Jung* (New York: Princeton University Press, 1980), 9:238.

13. The challenge of Immanuel Kant in *Was ist Aufklärung* was implicit if inadvertent in the *Areopagitica* of Milton, who obviously did not apply that maxim to Eden's Tree of Knowledge.

14. See Erich Auerbach's chapter, "Adam and Eve" in his *Mimesis: Dargestellte Wirklichkeit in der abendländischen Literatur,* ed. Herbert Read and Michael Fordham, trans. Willard R. Trask (Bern: Franke Verlag, 1946),142. My translation differs from Willard Trask; where he uses the word "unreflectingly," I choose the word "playfully," in accord with Mann's description of his work as playful. See his "Bemerkungen" in Thomas Mann, *Gesammelte Werke* in 13 Bänden (Frakfort: Fischer, 1974) 11:691.

15. Louis Ginzburg, *Legends of the Jews.*

16. Jung, *Part I: Archetypes*, 249.

17. Otto Rank, *Das Inzest-Motiv in Dichtung und Sage* (Leipzig: Franz Deuticke, 1912), 450–52, 557.

18. Ibid. See George Woodcock's appraisal of the Richter translation of Rank's *The Incest Theme* (1992) in "The Making of Books on Love," *The Sewanee Review* 102, no. 3 (Summer 1994): 506–510, https://www.jstor.org/stable/27546904. In Woodcock's assessment, with which I agree, "It is a curiously promising and unsatisfying book, long, prolix, and dogmatic, at times enlightening, but marred by its efforts to find so many of the sources of literary creativity in the group of incest complexes of which the most famous is named after Oedipus."

19. Genesis 4:3-6, Jewish Study Bible.

20. Woodcock, "The Making of Books of Love," 506–510.

21. Ibid.

22. William Graham Sumner, *Folkways* (London, 1906), 419-20, also see chapter XII, entitled "Incest." Although critical of missionary activity, Sumner was an ordained Episcopal

priest, who, according to his biographer, remained at least nominally active in the church until the end of his life, Harris E. Starr, *William Graham Sumner* (H. Holt, 1925), 543.

23. Charles Darwin, *The Variation of Animals and Plants Under Domestication,* vol. 2 (New York: Appleton, 1868).

24. Sumner's treatment of incest in *Folkways* does not address Darwin's biological-evolutionary theory of incest aversion but does contain several references to Edvard Westermarck's Darwinian hypothesis in *Human Marriage*. David H. Spain, "The Westermarck-Freud Incest-Theory Debate: An Evaluation and Reformulation," *Current Anthropology* 28, no. 5 (December 1987): 623-645, https://www.jstor.org/stable/2743359. Walter Scheidel, "Evolutionary Psychology and the Historian," *The American Historical Review* 119, no. 5 (December 2014): 1563–1575, https://www.jstor.org/stable/43698890.

25. Kara K. Walker, et al., "Chimpanzees breed with genetically dissimilar mates," *Royal Society Open Science*, 4, no.1 (January 2017), https://doi.org/10.1098/rsos.160422.

26. Freud, unlike his contemporaries Robert E. Park and Oswald Spengler, did not distinguish between culture and civilization. In rejecting this distinction, he resembled E. B. Tylor and T. S. Eliot, so Strachey translated *Das Unbehagn in der Kultur,* to suit some private ends, as *Civilization and its Discontents.*

27. Edvard Westermarck, *Human Marriage* (New York: Macmillan, 1901), 319. A survey of post-Darwinian literature and the incest taboo is presented in Chapter 10 of Carl Degler, *In Search of Human Nature: The Decline and Revival of Darwinism in American Social Thought* (Oxford: Oxford University Press, 1991).

28. Robin Fox, "Sibling Incest," *British Journal of Sociology* 13 (1962): 128-150.

29. Anise K. Strong, "Incest Laws and Absent Taboos in Roman Egypt," *SSRN* (April 27, 2003), http://dx.doi.org/10.2139/ssrn.1596967.

30. Fifty-three percent of the world population is nominally Christian or Muslim and presumably have some exposure to the Eden myth. Additional billions of people, even if they adhere to other religions, have been exposed directly or indirectly to the Hebraic, Indo-European, and Muslim religious mythologies, fairy tales, folklore, and superstitions.

31. Eran Shor and Dalit Simchai, "Incest Avoidance, the Incest Taboo, and Social Cohesion: Revisiting Westermarck and the Case of the Israeli Kibbutzim," *American Journal of Sociology* 114, no. 6 (May 2009): 1803–1842, https://doi.org/10.1086/597178. Shor and Simchai, "Exposing the Myth of Sexual Aversion in the Israeli Kibbutzim: A Challenge to the Westermarck Hypothesis," *American Journal of Sociology* 117, no. 5 (March 2012): 1509–1513, https://doi.org/10.1086/665522.

32. See for example, Markus J. Rantala & Urszula M. Marcinkowska, "The Role Of Sexual Imprinting and the Westermarck Effect in Mate Choice in Humans," *Behavioral Ecology and Sociobiology* 65 (2011): 859–873, https://doi.org/10.1007/s00265-011-1145-y; Shor and Simchai, "Incest Avoidance," 1803–42; Shor, "The Westermarck Hypothesis and the Israeli Kibbutzim: Reconciling Contrasting Evidence," *Arch Sex Behavior* 44, no. 8 (November 2015): 2139–2150, https://doi.org/10.1007/s10508-015-0558-5. Shor and Simchai conducted interviews with kibbutz-reared peers, concluding that, in opposition to what Westermarck suggested, many of them felt attraction toward same-age peers while growing up and almost none of them reported any feelings of sexual aversion toward peers.

33. Arthur P. Wolf's obituary in *Stanford News* of June 4, 2015, stated "Stanford anthropologist Arthur P. Wolf dies at 83; Wolf was known for his knowledge of early 20th-century Taiwan and as a scholar of the biological roots of incest avoidance." Arthur P. Wolf, "Westermarck Redivivus," *Annual Review of Anthropology* 22, no. 9 (October 1993): 157–175, https://doi.org/10.1146/annurev.an.22.100193.001105.

34. Arthur P. Wolf, *Sexual Attraction and Childhood Association: A Chinese Brief for Edvard Westermarck* (Redwood City: Stanford University Press, 1995); Arthur P. Wolf and

William H. Durham, ed., *Inbreeding, Incest, and the Incest Taboo: The State of Knowledge at the Turn of the Century* (Redwood City: Stanford University Press, 2004); Arthur P. Wolf and Chieh-Shang Huang, *Marriage and Adoption in China, 1845–1945* (Redwood City: Stanford University Press, 1980); Arthur P. Wolf, *Incest Avoidance and the Incest Taboos: Two Aspects of Human Nature* (Redwood City: Stanford University Press, 2014); Arthur P. Wolf, "Adopt a Daughter-in-Law, Marry a Sister-A Chinese Solution," *American Anthropologist* 70, no. 5 (October 1968): 864–874, https://www.jstor.org/stable/669753. References to studies critical of Wolf are in Dwight W. Read, "Incest Taboos and Kinship: A Biological or a Cultural Story?," *Reviews in Anthropology* 43, no. 2 (June 2014): 150–175, http://doi.org/10.1080/00938157.2014.903151.

35. Alan Richardson, "Rethinking Romantic Incest: Human Universals, Literary Representation, and the Biology of Mind," *New Literary History* 31, no. 3 (Summer 2000): 553-572, https://www.jstor.org/stable/20057619.

36. Jonathan Haidt, "The Emotional Dog and Its Rational Tail: A Social Intuitionist Approach to Moral Judgment," *Psychological Review* 108, no. 4 (2001): 814–834, https://doi.org/10.1037/0033-295X.108.4.814. Also see Edward B. Royzman, Geoffrey P. Goodwin, and Robert F. Leeman, "When Sentimental Rules Collide: 'Norms With Feelings' in the Dilemmatic Context," *Cognition* 121, no. 1 October (2011): 101–114, https://doi.org/10.1016/j.cognition.2011.06.006. Edward B. Royzman, Kwanwoo Kim, Robert F. Leeman, "The Curious Tale of Julie and Mark: Unraveling the Moral Dumbfounding Effect," *Judgment and Decision Making* 10, no. 4 (July 2015): 296–313, https://doi.org/10.1017/S193029750000512X.

37. Thomas Aquinas, *Summa Theologiae,* Article 9, reply to Objection 3.

38. Elizabeth Archibald, *Incest and the Medieval Imagination* (Oxford: Clarendon Press, 2001), 192.

39. Archibald, *Incest,* 26. Her citations are to Aristotle's *Historia animalium,* 9, 47 (631a21); for the comments on inbreeding see 6.22 (576a).

40. *The Summa Theologiae of Saint Thomas Aquinas,* trans. Fathers of the English Dominican Province, 2nd revised ed., online ed. (Kevin Knight, 2017), http://www.newadvent.org/summa/3154.htm.

41. R. Burtsell, "Consanguinity (in Canon Law)," in *The Catholic Encyclopedia* (New York: Robert Appleton Company, 1908), https://www.newadvent.org/cathen/04264a.htm.

42. Gerald J. Massey, "Medieval Sociobiology: Thomas Aquinas's Theory of Sexual Morality," *Philosophical Topics* 27, no. 1, *Zoological Philosophy* (Spring 1999): 69–86, https://www.jstor.org/stable/43154302. Similar to Massey, who reads Aquinas's attribution to incest as a "natural or quasi-natural inclination," Howard Kainz, a Catholic theologian, interprets Aquinas's views on incest as "borderline 'natural,' if it involves male-female intercourse, is nevertheless a grievous sin since it flouts the natural relationships proper to people connected by consanguinity or affinity." Howard Kainz, "Human Nature and Aquinas' Taxonomy of Sexual Sins," *Crisis Magazine,* July 20, 2012.

43. Sigmund Freud, *Das Unbehagen in der Kultur* (Vienna: Internationaler Psychoanalutischer Verlag: 1930).

44. Gregory C. Leavitt, "Tylor vs. Westermarck: Explaining the Incest Taboo," *Sociology Mind* 3, no. 1 (January 2013): 45–51, http://doi.org/10.4236/sm.2013.31008. E. B. Tylor, "On a Method of Investigating the Development of Institutions Applied to Laws of Marriage and Descent," *Journal of the Royal Anthropological Institute* 18 (1888): 245–269, https://doi.org/10.2307/2842423.

45. Westermarck's *History of Human Marriage* had gone through at least six editions before Freud challenged it. The relationship between incest aversion and inbreeding avoidance was among the topics problematized at a conference representing both the biological and sciences, and resulting in the publication of Arthur P. Wolf and William H. Durham's

"Inbreeding, Incest, and the Incest Taboo." Also see Delphine De Smet, "The Moral Psychology of Sibling Incest Aversion: Evolutionary Origins and Legal Future" (doctoral thesis, Ghent University, 2015), https://biblio.ugent.be/publication/5882077. Emile Durkheim offered a challenge to Westermarck, and Westermarck responded to both Durkheim and Freud with the valid argument that their positions were not empirically based. See J. P. Roos, "Durkheim vs. Westermarck: an Uneven Match," in *The New Evolutionary Social Science: Human Nature, Social Behavior, and Social Change*, eds. Heinz-Jurgen Niedenzu, Tamas Meleghy, Peter Meyer (Boulder: Paradigm, 2008), 135–146; Leslie A. White, "The The Definition and Prohibition of Incest," American Anthropologist 50, no. 3 (July-September 1948): 416-435, https://doi.org/10.1525/aa.1948.50.3.02a00020.

46. Peter K. Jonason and Laura K. Dane, "How Beliefs Get in the Way of the Acceptance of Evolutionary Psychology," *Frontiers in Psychology* 5 (November 2014), https://doi.org/10.3389/fpsyg.2014.01212.

47. Arthur P. Wolf, "Westermarck Redivivus," *Annual Review of Anthropology* 22 (October 1993): 157–175, https://doi.org/10.1146/annurev.an.22.100193.001105.

48. Debra Lieberman, John Tooby, and Leda Cosmides, "Does morality have a biological basis?: An empirical test of the factors governing moral sentiments relating to incest," *Proceedings of the Royal Society of Biological Sciences* 270, no. 1517 (April 22, 2003): 819–826, https://doi.org/10.1098/rspb.2002.2290.

Chapter Four: Serpent of Eden and Incest Avoidance

1. Barbara Walker, *The Woman's Encyclopedia of Myths and Secrets* (New York: HarperCollins, 1983), 907.

2. A giant serpent, the Drakon Ophiogeneikos (Dragon of the Serpent-Born) guarded a sacred grove of Artemis in northeastern Mysia. "Ophiogeneikos," Theoi Project, 2017, www.theoi.com/Ther/DrakonOphiogeneikos.html.

3. The King James version of 1611 substitutes "screech owl." "Harlot of God" concept found in Felicia Waldman, "From Demoness to God's Partner: The Astonishing Career of the World's First Feminist, Lilith," in *Jewish Studies Yearbook* (2009–2011), 99–106.

4. Mark Wayne Biggs, *The Case for Lilith* (Samson Books, 2010), 114. The Zohar also teaches that Lilith is the serpent who deceived Eve. Zohar 1:148a-148b (Vayetze: Passage 23) calls Lilith a "snake" and the "female of Samael." John K. Bonnell, "The Serpent with a Human Head in Art and in Mystery Play," *American Journal of Archaeology* 21, no. 3 (July-September 1917): 255–291, https://doi.org/10.31826/9781463220549-001.

5. Raymond Williams, *Keywords: A Vocabulary of Culture and Society* (Oxford: Oxford University Press, 1976), 184.

6. One finds frequent references to Freud's identification of the snake as a phallic symbol, but I have been unable to detect any in his major works. None of the neo-Freudian or pseudo-Freudian references I have so far located have provided me with a direct quotation in English or in German of his saying, "Sometimes a cigar is just a cigar." My searches for the serpent of Eden in Jung's writings have so far been equally fruitless.

7. Carl Sagan, *The Dragons of Eden: Speculations On The Evolution of Human Intelligence* (New York: Random House, 1977), 160 and 172. See Sherwood Washburn, *Ape Into Man; A Study of Human Evolution* (Boston: Little, Brown, 1973) on the primate snake-aversion thesis. Also see Arne Öhman and Susan Mineka, "The Malicious Serpent: Snakes as a Prototypical Stimulus for an Evolved Module of Fear," *Current Directions in Psychological Science* 12, no. 1 (February 2003): https://doi.org/10.1111/1467-8721.01211.

8. Quan Van Le, et. al., "Pulvinar neurons reveal neurobiological evidence of past selection for rapid detection of snakes," *Proceedings of the National Academy of Sciences* 110, no.

47 (October 28, 2013), https://doi.org/10.1073/pnas.1312648110. Anne E. Pusey, "Inbreeding Avoidance in chimpanzees," *Animal Behaviour* 28, no. 2 (May 1980): 543–552, https://doi.org/10.1016/S0003-3472(80)80063-7. Kara K. Walker, et al., "Chimpanzees breed with genetically dissimilar mates," *Royal Society of Open Science* 4, no. 1 (January 2017), https://doi.org/10.1098/rsos.160422.

9. Quan Van Le, et. al., "Pulvinar Neurons Reveal Neurobiological Evidence."

10. Edward O. Wilson, *In Search of Nature* (Washington: Shearwater Books, 1996): 20–28.

11. *Jewish Study Bible*, 834.

12. Jung merges the Lamia and the serpent with Eve as the temptress of Adam.

Chapter Five: Divine Incest, Royal Incest, and Brother-Sister Gods

1. Of course there are apocryphal texts that suggest God has a wife; see Raphael Patai, *The Hebrew Goddess*, 3rd enlarged ed. (Detroit: Wayne State University Press, 1990).

2. Fuminobu Murakam, "Incest and Rebirth in Kojiki," *Monumenta Nipponica* 43, no. 4 (Winter 1988): 455–463, https://doi.org/10.2307/2384797.

3. Walter Scheidel, "Evolutionary Psychology and the Historian," *The American Histrical Review* 119, no. 5 (2014): 1563–1575, https://www.jstor.org/stable/43698890.

4. Anise K. Strong, "Incest Laws and Absent Taboos," *SSRN* (April 27, 2003), http://dx.doi.org/10.2139/ssrn.1596967.

5. Sheila L. Ager, "The Power of Excess: Royal Incest and the Ptolemaic Dynasty," *Anthropologica* 48, no. 2 (2006): 165–186, https://doi.org/10.2307/25605309. Katja Lembke, "*Interpretatio Aegyptiaca vs. Interpretatio Graeca? Der Ägyptische Staat und Seine Denkmäler in der Ptolemäerzeit*," *Mediterraneo Antico* 15 (2012): 345–346, and P.M. Fraser, *Ptolemaic Alexandria* (Oxford: Oxford University Press, 1972), I:117-118; II:209-210, cited by Sergio Casali in Ovid's Canace and Euripides' "Aeolus": Two Notes on "Heroides" II, *Mnemosyne*, Fourth Series, Vol. 51, Fasc. 6 (December 1998), 700-710.

6. Keith Hopkins, "Brother-Sister Marriage in Roman Egypt," *Comparative Studies in Society and History* 2, no. 3 (July 1980): 303–354.

7. Anise K Strong, "Incest Laws and Absent Taboos."

8. Brent D. Shaw, "Explaining Incest: Brother-Sister Marriage in Graeco-Roman Egypt," *Man* 27, no. 2 (June 1992): 267–299, https://doi.org/10.2307/2804054.

9. Jane Rowlandson and Ryosuke Takahashi, "Brother-Sister Marriage and Inheritance Strategies in Greco-Roman Egypt," *The Journal of Roman Studies* 99 (2009): 104–139; Keith Hopkins, "Brother-Sister Marriage in Roman Egypt"; Anise K. Strong, "Incest Laws and Absent Taboos."

10. Genesis applies the Mosaic code retroactively to Onan's avoidance of siring children by his brother's widow, as prescribed in Deuteronomy 25:5-6. Genesis implicitly disapproves the homosexual predilections of the denizens of Sodom, later forbidden in Leviticus 18 and 20. Genesis makes no retroactive application of the Mosaic code to the incest of Abraham with his sister or the incest of Lot and his daughters, equally forbidden by the Mosaic code. See Tamar Kadari, "Lot's Daughters: Midrash and Aggadah," Jewish Women's Archive, February 27, 2009, https://jwa.org/encyclopedia/article/lots-daughters-midrash-and-aggadah.

11. David's status as a prophet is usually argued via reference to his authorship of the Psalms, sacred writings with scriptural status in both Christian and Jewish tradition. There are disputes as to whether David was the author of the Psalms, and there have been discussions among Christians and Jews as to whether David was actually a prophet. Many Chistians affirm his status as a prophet because he is identified as such by Peter in Acts 2:29-31 and by implication by Paul in Hebrews 11:32.

12. William H. Propp "Kinship in 2 Samuel 13," *The Catholic Biblical Quarterly* 55, no. 1 (January 1993): 39–53. Pierre L. Van Den Berghe and Gene M. Mesher, "Royal Incest and Inclusive Fitness," *American Ethnologist* 7, no. 2 (May, 1980): 300–317. William C. Sturtevant, "Royal Incest: A Bibliographic Note," *American Ethnologist* 8, no. 1 (February 1981): 186. On existence of a historical King David, see Baruch Halpern, *David's Secret Demons; Messiah, Murderer, Traitor, King* (Grand Rapids: Eerdmans, 2004). Israel Finkelstein and Neil Asher Silberman, *David and Solomon: In Search of the Bible's Sacred Kings and the Roots of the Western Tradition* (New York: Free Press, 2007).

13. Emil G. Hirsch, et. al.,"Incest," The Jewish Encyclopedia, JewishEncyclopedia.com. Also see Henry Abramovitch, *Brothers and Sisters: Myth and Reality,* (College Station: Texas A&M Press, 2014), on the implication of David's willingness to condone an incestuous royal marrriage.

14. 2 Samuel 13:19, King James Version.

15. Song of Solomon 8:1, King James Version.

16. Benjamin Edidin Scolnic, "Why Do We Sing the Song of Songs on Passover?" *Conservative Judaism Journal* 48, no. 4 (Summer 1996): 53–54.

17. Margaret Maitland, "Emojis vs. Hierogyphs: Why is Ancient Egyptian Writing Still Dismissed as Primitve almost 200 Years after its Decipherment?," The Eloquent Peasant (blog), June 2, 2015, http://www.eloquentpeasant.com/category/literature/.

18. Miriam Lichtheim, *Ancient Egyptian Literature: A Book of Readings,* Vol II, (Berkeley: University of California Press, 1976).

19. It has long been suggested that Solomonic literature was influenced by Zorastrianism. See Moncure Daniel Conway, *Solomon and Solomonic Literature* (Chicago: The Open Court Publishing Company, 1899). Emil G. Hirsh and Crawford Howel Toy in the article "Song of Songs," in *Jewish Encyclopedia* (2021-2022) have dated the Song to a period after the Persian occupation.

20. Song of Solomon 4:9-10, King James Version.

21. Song of Solomon, 5:1, King James Version.

22. Scolnic, "Why Do We Sing the Song of Songs," 53–54. Solomon B Freehof, "The Song of Songs: A General Suggestion," *The Jewish Quarterly Review* 39, no. 4 (April 1949): 399.

23. The encyclical issued in 1954 receives further mention later in these pages.

24. J. A. Phillips, *Eve: The History of an Idea* (New York: Harper and Row, 1984), 28, 35.

25. Marina Warner, *Alone of All Her Sex: The Myth and Cult of the Virgin Mary* (New York: Random House, 1976), 50–68.

26. Peter Howard, "Memorial Of The Queenship Of The Blessed Virgin," SpiritualDirection.com, August, 22, 2014, https://spiritualdirection.com/2014/08/22/memorial-queenship-of-blessed-virgin-mary.

27. Distinguished art historian Susan Foister has commented on the mingling of iconography in this painting. See Susan Foister, "Lucas Cranach the Elder: Cupid Complaining to Venus," *National Gallery Catalogues: The German Paintings before 1800*, National Gallery Company, 2015, https://www.nationalgallery.org.uk/media/16340/cranach-catalogue-cupid-complaining-to-venus.pdf.

28. Stephen D. Moore, "The Song of Songs in the History of Sexuality," *Church History* 69, no. 2 (June 2000): 328–349.

29. Moore, "The Song of Songs in the History of Sexuality," 341.

30. Moore, "The Song of Songs in the History of Sexuality." Shawn M. Krahmer, "The Virile Bride of Bernard of Clairvaux," *Church History* 69, no. 2 (June 2000): 304-327.

31. Peter Howard, "Memorial Of The Queenship Of The Blessed Virgin."

32. Raphael Jospe, "Regina Coeli: A Jewish Source?," in *Jewish-Christian Relations, Insights and Issues in the Ongoing Jewish-Christian Dialogue,* March 7, 2019; Revelation 12:1, King James Version.

33. Compare, for example, the Douay and King James versions at https://biblehub.com/drbc/genesis/3.htm. Julia Ward Howes's famous line, "Let the Hero, born of woman, crush the serpent with his heel," appears in "Battle Hymn of the Republic."

34. Bill Thayer, "Isis and Osiris by Plutarch," University of Chicago, https://penelope.uchicago.edu/Thayer/e/roman/texts/Plutarch/moralia/isis_and_osiris*/a.html.

35. Aaron J. Atsma, "Hera Myths," The Theoi Project, https://www.theoi.com/Olympios/HeraMyths.html.

36. Homer, *The Iliad*, trans. A.T. Murray (Cambridge: Harvard University Press, 1924).

37. Douglas Bush makes Pheobe and Artemis practically identical in the index to his *Mythology and the Renaissance Tradition in English Poetry* (New York: Norton, 1963). The only reference I have found to Artemis and Apollo as husband and wife is in a Theoi Project reference to a medieval source, *Commentary on the Iliad* by Eustathius of Thessalonica (c. 1115–1195/6)

38. Syncretism can be defined succinctly or endlessly problematized; it refers, in short, to the appropriation of one culture's religious aparatus by another, whereby the divinities, myths, religious sites, and rituals of one culture are taken over and reinterpreted in accord with the material and spiritual needs of another. It has long been a topic of scholarly exploration. Recent explorations include Anita Maria Leopold and Jeppe Sinding Jensen, *Syncretism in Religion: A Reader* (New York: Routledge, 2016); Eric Maroney, *Religious Syncretism* (London: SCM Press, 2006); and Hans Kloft, *Mysterienkulte der Antike: Götter, Menschen, Rituale* (Munich: C. H. Beck, 2010).

39. For Diana's evolution into a triple goddess, see C. M. Green, *Roman Religion and the Cult of Diana at Aricia* (Cambridge: Cambridge University Press, 2007). Cicero, *The Nature of the Gods,* trans. H. C. P. McGregor (New York: Penguin, 1972), 151, 217.

40. Robert Graves, *The Greek Myths* (New York: Penguin, 2017), 57.

41. Apuleius, *The Golden Ass,* trans. by A.S. Kline, Poetry in Translation, https://www.poetryintranslation.com/PITBR/Latin/Apuleiushome.php.

42. C. M. C. Green notes that the problem of Artemis's virginity was an "insurmountable problem. Venus/Aphrodite regularly renewed her virginity." *Roman Religion and the Cult of Diana at Aricia* (Cambridge: Cambridge University Press, 2007), 143. I refer elsewhere to the bath whereby Hera renewed hers.

43. Thomas Mann addresses this point in his novel, *Der Erwählte*. Marina Warner also develops the theme of Mary as bride of God in chapter eight of *Alone of all Her Sex* (Oxford: Oxford University Press, 1976). See also Barbara G. Walker's entries under Mary in Barbara Walker, *The Woman's Encyclopedia of Myths and Secrets* (New York: HarperCollins, 1983), 907.

44. "Hymn 27 to Artemis," *The Homeric Hymns and Homerica*, trans. Hugh G. Evelyn-White (Cambridge: Harvard University Press, 1914).

45. Alberta Randall, "Apollo And Artemis: Culture And Instinct," Silo Tips, May 21, 2017, https://docplayer.net/21792722-Apollo-and-artemis-culture-and-instinct.html.

46. H. J. Rose, A *Handbook of Greek Mythology* (New York: E. P. Dutton, 1928), 112–118. Graves, *Greek Myths,* 83–86.

47. Apollo is not prominently displayed in Frazer's *The Golden Bough,* but Artemis is divested of her virginity, as we see above. For Graves's treatment of Artemis and Apollo, see his *The Greek Myths*, 57. Apollo's representation as Adam may be compared to the representation of Hermes in Botticelli's *Primavera.*

48. Frazer's *The Golden Bough* recapitulates assertions in the 1890 edition. In all instances Frazer stresses Artemis's eastern origins and cognates, as well as her later merger with Roman fertility goddesses and fertility cults, consequently downplaying or questioning her virginity.

49. Jean Seznec, *The Survival of the Pagan Gods: The Mythological Tradition and Its Place in Renaissance Humanism and Art,* trans. Barbara F. Sessions (Princeton: Princeton University Press, 1953), 96. Edgar Wind, *Pagan Mysteries of the Renaissance* (New York: Norton, 1958), 73.

50. Bill Thayer, "Isis and Osiris by Plutarch."

51. In Asia Minor and Roman religion, Artemis was sometimes syncretized with fertility goddesses and earth-mother figures such as Demeter and Persephone, or with the moon goddess, Selene. Tobias Fischer-Hansen and Birte Poulsen, eds., *From Artemis to Diana: The Goddess of Man and Beast* (Chicago: University of Chicago Press, 2009). For Lemprière's entry under Diana, see *Lempriere's Classical Dictionary* (London: Bracken Books, 1984).

52. C. G. Jung, "King and Queen," *Collected Works of C.G. Jung*, trans. R. F. C. Hull (New York: Princeton University Press, 1980), 16:49.

53. Bill Thayer, "Isis and Osiris by Plutarch."

54. Walker, *The Woman's Encyclopedia*, 33, 61, 122.

55. Thomas Bulfinch, *The Age of Fable, or Stories of Gods and Heroes,* 2nd ed. (Boston: Sanborn, Carter, and Bazin, 1856), 280.

56. For Hera's restorative bath, see Sue Blundell, *Women in Ancient Greece* (Cambridge, MA: Harvard University Press, 1995), 25.

57. Bush, *Mythology and the Renaissance*; Seznec, *The Survival of the Pagan Gods,* 96; Wind, *Pagan Mysteries of the Renaissance,* 73. Luther's protests are quoted in Seznec, 96.

58. Apollo and Diana (c. 1526), Royal Collection Trust, https://www.rct.uk/collection/407294/apollo-and-diana.

59. Peter Paul Rubens, *Venus Wounded By a Thorn*, oil on canvas, USC Fisher Museum of Art, Los Angeles; Raphael Marco Dente, *Venus Removing a Thorn*, engraving, Metropolitan Museum of Art, New York; Pierre Audouin, *Venus Pulling a Thorn from her Foot,* etching with engraving, Royal Collection Trust, London; Jacquiot Ponce, *Venus Removing a Thorn from her Foot,* bronze sculpture, Victoria and Albert Museum, London.

60. John Milton, *Paradise Lost,* Book IX, verse 385–390.

61. Barbara G. Walker, *The Woman's Encyclopedia*, 289.

Chapter Six: Royal Sibling Incest and the Avuncular Transmission of Kingship

1. Friedrich Engels quotes Tacitus with some exaggeration and greater fidelity to Lehrbach in *The Origin of the Family, Private Property, and the State* (Chicago: Charles H. Kerr, 1902). See W. E. B. Du Bois, *Darkwater: Voice from within the Veil* (New York: Harcourt, 1920).

2. Alexander Boyle, "Matrilineal Succession in the Pictish Monarchy," *The Scottish Historical Review* 56, no. 161, (April 1977): 1–10. Nicholas Evans, "Royal Succession and Kingship among the Picts" *The Innes Review* 59, no. 1 (Spring 2008): 1–48. Livy, *Ab urbe condita.*

3. Tacitus remarked in *Germania* that the wife did not bring a dowry to her husband, but the husband to his wife.

4. Tacitus, *Germania,* chapter 20, Loeb: "Sisters' children mean as much to their uncle [avunculus, actually "mother's brother"] as to their father: some tribes regard this blood-tie as even closer and more sacred than that between son and father, and in taking hostages make it the basis of their demand, as though they thus secure loyalty more surely and have a wider hold on the family." Clair Hayden Bell, *The Sister's Son in the Medieval German Epic: A Study in the Survival of Matriliny* (Forgotten Books, 2018), 67–182.

5. William H. Propps, "Kinship in 2 Samuel 13" *The Catholic Biblical Quarterly* 55, no. 1 (January 1993): 39–53. James Marchand, "Germanic Kinship: A Truncated and Annotated Bibliography on Germanic Kinship," The Online Reference Book for Medieval Studies, https://the-orb.arlima.net/bibliographies/kinship.html.

6. In Elizabeth Archibald, *Incest and the Medieval Imagination* (Oxford: Clarendon Press, 2001), Archibald explores "the complex and changing definition of incest in the Middle Ages."

7. Archibald, *Incest,* 223 cites Mandach. André de Mandach, *L'Inceste et l'effondrement d'un monde: Tristan et Mordret*, ed. Giovanna Angeli and Luciano Formisano. Claude Evans,

"*Le personnage d'Yseut dans le Tristan de Béroul et les Folies de Berneet d'Oxford: une perspective inspirée par les textes irlandais et gallois,*" *Le Moyen Age* 111 (2005): 95–114.

8. My translation of André de Mandach and Eve-Marie Roth, "*Le triangle Marc-Iseut-Tristan : un drame de double inceste,*" *Etudes Celtiques* 23 (1986): 193–213.

9. Paul Schach, "Tristan And Isolde In Scandinavian Ballad And Folktale," *Scandinavian Studies* 36, no. 4 (November 1964): 281–297. Bart Besamusca and Jessica Quinlan, "Fringes of Arthurian Fiction," in Arthurian Literatire, ed. Elizabeth Archibald and David F. Johnson (Cambridge: Cambridge University Press, 2023), 220. Also see Norris J. Lacy, ed., "Tristram og Iomfru Isolt," *The New Arthurian Encyclopedia* (New York: Garland, 1996). Elizabeth Archibald has discovered several stories that are remarkably similar to the Danish Ballad in *Incest and the Medieval Imagination*, 141–144.

10. Annette Volfing, "Gottfried's 'Huote' Excursus (Tristan 17817-18114)," *Medium Ævum* 67, no. 1 (1998): 85–103.

11. Ibid. Joseph J. Duggan, "The Hero Roland and the Question of Intentionality," *Electronic Antiquity* 14, no. 1 (November 2012): 97–108.

12. J. Pycke, "(2) Gilles," in *Dictionnaire d'histoire et de géographie ecclésiastiques* 20 (1984): 1352–1355. For Wetti of Richenau, see Richard Pollard and Julian Hendrix, "Digital Devotion from Carolingian Reichenau and St. Gall," *Digital Philology* 1, no. 2 (2012): 292–302.

13. Barton Sholod, "Charlemagne and Roland: A Mysterious Relationship?," *Butlletí de la Reial Acadèmia de Bones Lletres de Barcelona* 31 (1966) 313–319.

14. Barton Sholod, *Charlemagne in Spain: The Cultural Legacy of Roncesvalle*s (Geneva: Librarie Droz, 1966), 27.

15. Sholod, "Charlemagne and Roland." William Oliver Farnsworth, *Uncle and Nephew in the Old French Chanson de Geste: A Study of the Survival of Matriarchy* (New York: Columbia University Press, 1913).

16. Joseph J. Duggan "The Hero Roland and the Question of Intentionality." For more on Charlemagne legend and incest, see Susan E. Farrier, ed., *The Medieval Charlemagne Legend: An Annotated Bibliography,* vol. 11 (Routledge Library Editions, 2019), entry 920. Jan M. Bremmer, "The Importance of the Maternal Uncle,"173–186 and "Fosterage, Kinship and the Circulation," 1–20.

17. Éric Vanneufville, *Charlemagne: Rome Chez les Francs* (France-Empire 2000), 16.

18. "*Enfin, je tenais à cette histoire 'd'amour intedit' n'ait rien avoir avec ce qu'évoque actuellement presque automatiquement le mot 'inceste', qui est ajourd'hui lié avant tout au viol et à pédophile,*" Interview, *Maisons d'ecrivains* #12 Critique, September 2010.

19. Thomas Mielke, *Karl der Groβe: Der Roman seines Lebens* (Emons Verlag, 2013). Hans-Jürgen Ferdinand, *Karl und die Frauen: Die Begierden Karls des Groβen* (Kern GmbH, 2015).

20. *"Dans les temps ancients, jeta-t-ell alors, c'est ton fils . . . C'est Rolandque serait le future roi des Francs . . . Et comme tu avais un fils avec le roi, qui on l'occurence est ton frere, c'est cet enfant-la qui serait le seul hériter . . . Voilà qui sont désormais les vrais rois: ceux qui descendent du roi et de la fille de sorveraineté dominante du clan de Mérovée. Un compromise entre la vielle loi et la transmission par les pères. Je réussis a rire. "Si je comprends bien, ce systèm est une incitation à l'inceste." Bertrande sourit. Ma réflection l'amusait. "Theroiquement, oui."* Laure-Marie Lapouge, *Moi, Ghisla, Soeur de Charlemagne*, (Albin Michel, 2010), 233, 237. There have been other novelistic treatments of the spurious Charlemagne incest legend, and Thomas Mielke manufactures a relationship between Charles and fictitiously named sister in his novel, *Karl der Groβe*, 1992

21. Barbara G. Walker, *The Woman's Encyclopedia of Myths and Secrets* (New York: HarperCollins, 1983), 122. Walker references the following sources: S. H. Hooke, *Middle Eastern Mythology* (New York: Penguin, 1963), 256; Gaston Maspero, *Popular Storiesof Ancient Egypt* (University Books, 1967), 121; and E. O. G. Turville-Petre, *Myth and Relgion in the North* (Holt, Rinehart, & Winston, 1964), 172.

22. C. David Benson, "Incest and Moral Poetry in Gower's 'Confessio Amantis,'" *The Chaucer Review* 19, no. 2 (Fall 1984): 100–109.

23. Archibald, *Incest,* 83.

24. David Herlihy, *Medieval Households* (Cambridge: Harvard University Press, 1986), note 4, 106.

25. James A. Schultz, "Medieval Adolescence: The Claims of History and the Silence of German Narrative," *Speculum* 66, no. 3 (July 1991): 528. Schultz cites Herlihy, *Medieval Households,* note 4, 106; Otto Borst, *Alltagsleben im Mittelalter,* 442; Richard Koebner, "*Die Eheauffassung des Ausgehenden Deutschen Mittelalters,*" *Archiv für Kulturgeschichte* 9 no. 2 (1911): 136–198, 279–318, especially 13, https://doi.org/10.7788/akg-1911-0202.

26. See William Kremer, "What Medieval Europe Did With Its Teenagers," *BBC News,* World Service, March 23, 2014.

27. The Harvard University Chaucer Website identifies this text as adapted from *The English Works of John Gower,* ed. G. C. Macaulay (London: Early English Text Society, 1900), 81-82. This should be compared to *The Complete Works of John Gower,* ed. G. C. Macaulay (Oxford: Clarendon Press, 1901), which presents the works in modern rhymed translations.

28. *The Complete Works of John Gower,* ed. G. C. Macaulay.

29. See Paul's epistle to the Romans.

30. John Gower, *Confessio Amantis,* Book III, 143-359, text adapted from: *The English Works of John Gower,* ed. G. C. Macaulay, 81-82. https://chaucer.fas.harvard.edu/pages/tale-canace-and-machaire.

31. Benson, 101.

32. Bullón-Fernández, "Confining the Daughter: Gower's 'Tale of Canace and Machaire' and the Politics of the Body," *Essays in Medieval Studies: Proceedings of the Illinois Medieval Association* 11 (1994), 75-85.

33. Eran Shor and Dalit Simchai, "Exposing the Myth of Sexual Aversion in the Israeli Kibbutzim: A Challenge to the Westermarck Hypothesis," *American Journal of Sociology* 117, no. 5 (March 2012): 1509–1513, https://doi.org/10.1086/665522.

34. Joseph J. Duggan, "The Hero Roland and the Question of Intentionality," *Electric Antiquity* 14, no. 1 (November 2010): https://scholar.lib.vt.edu/ejournals/ElAnt/V14N1/duggan.html.

35. Psalm 19:9, King James Version.

Chapter Seven: Gregorius: An Imitation of Christ, not Oedipus

1. The age of the twins is left to the imagination in various renditions of the fable. In some versions, they could be as young as ten, and in others, they are as old as seventeen. Since the sister is still youthful and ravishingly beautiful when she marries the seventeen-year-old Gregorius, one may presume she cannot be much past thirty.

2. "Thus also do those who disallow Adam's salvation gain nothing, except this, that they render themselves heretics and apostates from the truth, and show themselves patrons of the serpent and of death." St. Irenaeus, *Against Heresies,* Book 3, Chapter 23, cited in *New Advent,* Catholic Encyclopedia.

3. Brian Murdoch, *Gregorius: An Incestuous Saint in Medieval Europe* (Oxford: Oxford University Press, 2012), 37. Murdoch cites Yoav Elstein's estimation of sixty different versions, but Murdoch's bibliography approached at least twice that number.

4. "*La vaine recherche des 'origines' du récit et de ses liens (ou de son absence de liens) avec l'Œdipe antique.*" Anita Guerreau-Jalabert, "*Inceste et Sainteté: La Vie de Saint Grégoire en Français (XIIe siècle)*" *Annales* 43e, no. 6 (November-December 1988): 1291–1319.

5. Hartmann von Aue, *Gregorius: A Medieval Oedipus Legend,* trans. Edwin H. Zeydel and Bayard Quincy Morgan (Chapel Hill: University of North Carolina Press, 1955), 4.

6. Peter Kirby, "Tertullian," Early Christian Writings, 2025, https://www.earlychristian-writings.com/text/tertullian27.html.

7. Brian Murdoch, *Gregorius*, 144.

8. *Gesta Romanorum.*

9. Carl Keller, ed., *Die Mittelenglische Gregoriuslegende* (New York and Heidelberg: G. E. Stechert, 1914).

10. Milton, *Comus, a Masque*, (1634).

11. The anonymous Latin edition cited here is, Sine Nomine, *Gesta Romanorum,* fine Saeculo XIII aut principio Saeculo XIV (Widmannsche Buchhandulung, Berlin, 1872). Translated by Rev. Charles Swan, revised and corrected by Wynnard Hooper (London: Bell and Sons, 1905), Vol II, 142.

12. Grasse, *Geeste Romanorum* (1842, repr. Anaconda) Hesse ed., 77. *Gesta Romanorum,* Swan-Hooper, ed., 142.

13. Murdoch, *Gregorius*, 37.

14. Volker Mertens, *Hartmann von Aue: Gregorius, Der arme Heinrich, Iwein.* Deutscher Klassiker-Verlag, Frankfurt am Main 2004 (Bibliothek deutscher Klassiker, 189), 33.

15. Deuteronomy 23:10 states, "If one of your men is unclean because of a nocturnal emission, he is to go outside the camp and stay there." Leviticus 15:19 specifies that a woman shall be set apart during menstruation and whoever touches her shall be unclean until evening. Her bed and whatever she sits on shall be unclean, and whoever touches those things shall be unclean.

16. Buehne translation, *Gregorius,* 33.

17. A brother's duty to find a husband for his sister is a premise of Friedrich Schiller's poem, "Die Bürschaft."

18. Murdoch, *Gregorius.*

19. Hartmann, *Gregorius: Oder, Der Gute Sünder*, trans. Karl Pannier (Leipzig: Reclam, 1897), lines 400–402.

20. Murdoch, *Gregorius*, 37.

21. Jeremy Taylor, *The Whole Works of the Right Rev. Jeremy Taylor, D.D., with a life by Reginald Heber,* revised and corrected by the Rev. Charles Page Eden, 9:149. Taylor does not document the case, or comment on its remarkable similarity to the Gregorius legend.

22. Ibid.

23. Richard A. McCabe, *Incest Drama and Nature's Law, 1550–1700* (Cambridge: Cambridge University Press, 1993), 48–56. This work describes the attitude of Martin Luther regarding papal dispensations as well as the discomfort of the papacy in cases involving unknown incest and the powers of the pope in matters of dispensation. Also see Elizabeth Archibald, *Incest and the Medieval Imagination* (Oxford: Clarendon Press, 2001), 42, 141, 156, 194.

24. McCabe, *Incest Drama and Nature's Law,* 284.

25. *The Heptameron of Margaret, Queen of Navarre,* trans. from the text of Le Roux De Lincy (London: Society Of English Bibliophilists, 1904).

26. The editors of the cited 1904 edition of *L'Heptaméron* say the story was purported to be true but offered no documentation.

27. Ellen Pollak, *Incest and the English Novel* (Baltimore: Johns Hopkins University Press, 2003), 129, 138-139; Archibald, *Incest,* 141-143, 209, 249. Pollak cites Cholokian, *Rape and Writing in the Heptaméron of Marguerite de Navarre* (Southern Illinois University Press, 1991), 146, 263n64. Nicole Cazauran, "*La Trentième Nouvelle de L'Heptaméron*" in *Mélanges Jeanne Lods* (1978), 617–652.

28. *Eleanora; Or a Tragical but True Case of Incest in Great Britai* (Dublin: 1751).

29. Peter L. Thorslev Jr., " Incest as Romantic Symbol," *Comparative Literature Studies* 2, no. 1 (1965): 41–58, https://www.jstor.org/stable/40245694.

30. McCabe, *Incest Drama and Natuyre's Law.* 50-51.

Chapter Eight: Ford's 'Tis Pity She's a Whore

1. Angela Carter, *Granta* (1988), 184; quoted in Simon Barker, ed., *'Tis Pity She's A Whore* (Routledge, 1997), 105.

2. Elizabeth Charlebois, "*Romeo and Juliet,* and *'Tis Pity She's a Whore,*" *Shakespeare Bulletin* 24, no. 3 (Fall 2006): 96. Sidney R. Homan, Jr., "Shakespeare and Dekker as Keys to Ford's *'Tis Pity She's a Whore,*" *Studies in English Literature, 1500-1900* 7, no. 2 (Spring 1967), 269–276. Other essays and articles discussing relationships between the two plays are presented in Barker, *'Tis Pity She's A Whore,* 113–120, along with his own critical commentary.

3. Lisa Hopkins, ed., *'Tis a Pity She's A Whore: A Critical Guide,* Continuum Renaissance Drama Guides (New York: Bloomsbury,), 3

4. Barker, 137.

Chapter Nine: The Presentation of Nature in Sibling Narratives of the Eighteenth Century

1. George E. Haggerty, *Unnatural Affections: Women and Fiction in the Later 18th Century* (Bloomington: Indiana University Press, 1998), 26.

2. Stefani Engelstein, "Sibling Incest and Cultural Voyeurism in Günderode's 'Udohla' and Thomas Mann's 'Wälsungenblut,'" *The German Quarterly* 77, no. 3 (Summer 2004): 279.

3. Ian Higgins concurs with the opinion of several authorities who regard Swift as someone who avoided "the Extremes of *Whig*" and the "Extremes of *Tory,*" as Swift himself put it in his position statement of 1708, *The Sentiments of a Church-of-England Man.* See online supplement to *The Eighteenth-Century: Theory and Interpretation* (Vol. 53, 2012).

4. Tijana Miletic, *European Literary Imagination into the French Language: Readings of Gary, Kristof, Kundera, and Semprun* (London: Brill Academic, 2008), 237.

5. John Gower put it in *Vox Clamantis* line 793. Henry Morley, *English Writers*, Volume 2, Part 1 (General Books, 1867), 44.

6. Haggerty, 26.

7. Stephen D. Moore, "The Song of Songs in the History of Sexuality," *Church History* 69, no. 2 (June 2000): 328–349. Michael V. Fox, *The Song of Songs and the Ancient Egyptian Love Songs* (Madison: University of Wisconsin Press, 1985).

8. Tobit 7:11, Douay-Rheims Translation.

9. Tobit 8:4, Douay-Rheims Translation.

10. Tobit 14:8, Douay-Rheims Translation.

11. See the entry "Bible" at *A Montesquieu Dictionary*, published in the framework of research conducted on and around Montesquieu within the Institute for the History of Classical Thought (*Institut d'histoire de la pensée classique*, UMR 5037), http://dictionnaire-montesquieu.ens-lyon.fr/en/article/1367167406/en/.

Chapter Ten: Romantic Movement Extends Natural Law Arguments of Enlightenment

1. Peter L. Thorslev, "Incest as Romantic Symbol," *Comparative Literature Studies* 2, no. 1 (1965): 47.

2. Alan Richardson, "Rethinking Romantic Incest: Human Universals, Literary Representation, and the Biology of Mind," *New Literary History* 31, no. 3 (Summer 2000): 553–572.

Also see Richardson, *The Neural Sublime* (Baltimore: Johns Hopkins University Press, 2010), 111–115.

3. Thorslev, "Incest as Romantic Symbol," 41–58.

4. Ibid.

5. Ibid.

6. F.W. Bateson, "Byron's Baby," *The New York Review,* February 22, 1973. Catherine Turney, *Byron's Daughter* (Scribner, 1972). John Stewart Chapman, *Byron and the Honourable Augusta Leigh* (New Haven: Yale University Press, 1975).

7. Joseph W. Lew, "The Deceptive Other: Mary Shelley's Critique of Orientalism in *Frankenstein,*" *Studies in Romanticism* 30 (1991): 255–283.

8. Jean Willoughby Ashton, "Harriet Stowe's Filthy Story: Lord Byron Set Afloat," *Prospects* 2 (July 2009): https://doi.org/10.1017/S036123330000243X.

9. Harriet Beecher Stowe, *The Byron Controversy. From Its Beginning In 1816 To The Present Time.* (London: Sampson Low, Son, 1870), 290.

10. Carlos Baker, *Shelley's Major Poetry: The Fabric of a Vision* (Princeton: Princeton University Press, 1948), 152.

11. Percy B. Shelley, *A Discourse on the Manners of the Ancient Greeks Relative to the Subject of Love.* James Bieri, *Percy Bysshe Shelley: A Biography: Exile of Unfulfilled Reknown, 1816-1822* (Newark, DE: University of Delaware Press, 2005), 71, notes Shelley's abstract tolerance but also notes that he associates homosexuality with "pain and horror" and does not deny his "repeated expressions of revulsion." Jennifer Ingleheart, ed., *Ancient Rome and the Construction of Modern Homosexual Identities* (London: Oxford University Press, 2015), 18. *The Symposium of Plato, The Shelley Translation,* ed. David K. O'Connor (South Bend, IN: Saint Augustine's Press, 2002), 78, 86. Stefani Engelstein, *Sibling Action: The Genealogical Structure of Modernity* (New York: Columbia University Press, 2017), 79.

12. For speculation on Shelley's life at Eton and a defense of the practice of fagging, see John Cordy Jeaffreson, *The Real Shelley: New Views of the Poet's Life,* Vol. 1 (London: Hurst and Blackett, 1885). Robert Graves, *Goodbye to All That* (1929; Vintage ed., 1985), 249, 267–268, 272, 287, 289, 296, 314.

13. John Donovan, "Incest in Laon and Cythna: Nature, Custom, Desire," *The Keats-Shelley Review* 2, no. 1 (July 2013): 49, https://doi.org/10.1179/ksr.1987.2.1.49.

14. Richardson, *Neural Sublime,* 111. Percy B. Shelley to Maria Gisborne, *Letters of Percy Bysshe Shelley,* ed. F. L. Jones, vol. 2 (Oxford: Clarendon Press, 1964), 154. Quoted in Carlos Baker, *Shelley's Major Poetry: The Fabric of a Vision* (Princeton: Princeton University Press, 1948), 152.

15. John Taylor Coleridge, "Shelley's Revolt of Islam," *Quarterly Review* 21, no. 42 (April 1819), 460–471. Carlos Baker, *Shelley's Major Poetry: The Fabric of a Vision* (Princeton: Princeton University Press, 1948), 152; J. Andrew Hubbell, "'Laon and Cythna': A Vision of Regency Romanticism," *Keats-Shelly Journal* 51 (2002), 174–197, 186; Teddi Lynn Chichester, "Transsexualism in Laon and Cythna," *Keats-Shelley Journal* 45, (1996): 97; Brent Steven Robida, "Shelley's Delusive Flames: Self and Poetry in The Major Works" (PhD diss., University of Tennessee, 2016), 80, https://trace.tennessee.edu/cgi/viewcontent.cgi?article=5250&context=utk_graddiss; Michael Scrivener, "Shelley's Poetry and Suffering" *Commemorating Peterloo: Violence, Resilience, and Claimmaking during the Romantic Era,* (June 2019): 271–288, https://doi.org/10.3366/edinburgh/9781474428569.003.0013; Lorraine Anne Morris, "All That Faith Creates, or Love Desires: Shelley's Poetic Vision of Being" (PhD thesis, Durham University, 1999), http://etheses.dur.ac.uk/4602/; Anthony John Daniel Burns, "Sweet Degradation: the Persistence of the Gothic in Shelley's Representations of Love" (PhD diss., The University of Leeds, May 2004), 50; Fatbardha Doko, "Analysis of Revolt of Islam By P. B. Shelley," *Book of Proceedings 1st International Multidisciplinary Scientific Conference,* Tetova, Macedonia, May 26, 2018.

16. John Taylor Coleridge, "Shelley's Revolt Of Islam," 460–471.
17. John Cordy Jeaffreson, *The Real Shelley* (1885), 341–342 .

Chapter Eleven: Us Against the World: Exile and Animal Transformation Narratives

1. The author has employed several editions of the Grimm *Märchen*, including but not limited to Jacob Grimm and Wilhelm Grimm, *Kinder- und Haus-Märchen* (Berlin: Realschulbuchhandlung, 1812/1815) and (Göttingen edition, Verlag der Dieterichschen Buchhandlung,1857). Excursions into the publishing history of each of these narratives, while interesting, would have led to a much longer article and the possible addition of discursive footnotes.

2. *Das Entchen kam heran, und Hänsel setzte sich auf und bat sein Schwesterchen, sich zu ihm zusetzen. "Nein," antwortete Gretel, "es wird dem Entchen zu schwer, es soll uns nacheinander hinüberbringen." Das that das gute Thierchen .*

3. Originally written, *Ach, ich bitte dich, Brüderchen, trink nicht, sonst wirst du ein wildes Thier und zerreißest mich.*

4. "*Und der Vorhang im Tempel zerriß,*" [Luther's translation, Mark 15:38] "And the curtain in the temple was rent." [King James Bible, Mark 15:38].

5. *Abends wenn Schwesterchen müd war und sein Gebet gesagt hatte, legte es seinen Kopf auf den Rücken des Rehkälbchens, das war sein Kissen, darauf es sanft schlief. Und hätte das Brüderchen nur seine menschliche Gestalt gehabt, es wäre ein herrliches Leben gewesen.*

6. The 1812 version reads, "*Brüderchen und Schwesterchen waren wieder beisammen und lebten glücklich ihr Lebelang.*" The 1819 version states more precisely that they lived happily together for the rest of their lives, "*Schwesterchen und Brüderchen lebten glücklich zusammen, bis an ihr Ende.*"

7. "*Brüderchen und Schwesterchen lieben sich, aber ihre Stiefmutter ist böse. Als sie mit anderen Kindern Fangen spielen, verwandelt sie sie in ein Lämmchen und ein Fischchen. Als nach langer Zeit Gäste aufs Schloss kommen, lässt sie den Koch das Lämmchen schlachten. Doch das Fischchen schwimmt mit vor die Küche und hält mit dem Lämmchen traurig Zwiegespräch. Der Koch erschrickt, schlachtet ein anderes Tier und bringt das Lämmchen zu einer guten Bäuerin. Die war die Amme der Kinder. Sie führt sie zu einer weisen Frau, die sie segnet, dass sie wieder Menschen werden, und in ein einsames Waldhäuschen führt. Da sind sie einsam, aber glücklich.*"

8. Philip Clayton, "Conclusion: Biology and Purpose: Altruism, Morality, and Human Nature in Evolutionary Perspective," *Evolutionary Ethics: Human Morality in Biological and Religious Perspective*, ed. Philip Clayton and Jeffrey Schloss (Grand Rapids: Eerdmans, 2004). Edvard A. Westermarck's theory of universal sibling incest aversion in *The History of Human Marriage* (London: Macmillan, 1891) is surveyed in Arthur P. Wolf, *Incest Avoidance and the Incest Taboos: Two Aspects of Human Nature* (Bloomington: Stanford University Press, 2014). Also see Thomas O'Carroll, "Arthur P. Wolf: Incest Avoidance and the Incest Taboos, Two Aspects of Human Nature" *Sexuality & Culture* 21, no. 1 (March 2017): 323–329. For a literary study, see Stefani Engelstein, *Sibling Action: The Genealogical Structure of Modernity* (New York: Columbia University Press, 2017).

9. Stith Thompson discusses various motifs and themes, such as the magical bird, the fairy lover, and the symbolism of swans, in his *The Folktale* (Dryden Press, 1951).

Chapter Twelve: W. E. B. Du Bois, Thomas Mann, and the Aristotelian Narrative

1. The germinal idea of Du Bois's novel *The Quest of the Silver Fleece* (McClurg, 1911), was the essay, "Of the Quest of the Golden Fleece," in Chapter 8 of his *The Souls of Black Folk* (McClurg, 1903).

2. R. A. Judy, "Lohengrin's Swan and the Style of Interiority in 'Of the Coming of John'," *CR: The New Centennial Review* 15, no. 2 (Fall 2015): 211–257; Christopher Powers, "Figurations of Passage through 'Of the Coming of John,'" *CR: The New Centennial Review* 15, no. 2 (Fall 2015): 59–82. Russell Berman, "Du Bois and Wagner: Race, Nation, and Culture Between the United States and Germany," *German Quarterly* 70, no. 2 (1997): 123–135. Sieglinde Lemke, "Of the Coming of John," *The Cambridge Companion to W. E. B. Du Bois*, ed. Shamoon Zamir (Cambridge: Cambridge University Press., 2008), 37–47. Robert Gooding-Williams, *In the Shadow of Du Bois: Afro-Modern Political Thought in America* (Cambridge: Harvard University Press, 2008).

3. Elizabeth H. Pleck, *Celebrating the Family: Ethnicity, Consumer Culture, and Family Rituals* (Cambridge: Harvard University Press, 2000), 212.

4. Adena Spingar, *Uncle Tom: From Martyr to Traitor* (Stanford: Stanford University Press, 2018), 124.

5. Du Bois presented a contrasting ideal of Christian martyrdom in his biography, *John Brown.* For Du Bois on the figure of Uncle Tom, see his *The Souls of Black Folk*, for his figure of the Black Mammy, see his *The Gift of Black Folk.*

6. Isaiah 53:3, King James Version.

7. W. E. B. Du Bois's Promethean rock imagery in *Black Reconstruction in America, 1860-1880* (World Publishing Company, 1935), 670.

8. R. A. Judy, 211–257.

9. After the lovemaking in the original ending, Sieglinde asks Siegfried, "What about Beckerath?" Siegfried responds, "*Beganeft haben wir ihn,—den Goy* [We've put one over on him, the Goy]." This orginal ending is provided in the restored German edition, *Wälsungenblut* (Frankfurt: Fischer, 2008). Siegfried's response was changed in the limited edition of 1921, which reads "*dankbar soll er uns sein. Er wird ein minder triviales Dasein führen, von nun an* [He ought to be grateful to us. His existence will be a little less trivial from now on.]" This is the ending provided in the current standard English edition, Thomas Mann, *Death and Venice and Other Tales,* trans. Joachim Neugroschel (New York: Penguin, 1998), 84.

10. Alan Levenson, "Thomas Mann's *Wälsungenblut* in the Context of the Intermarriage Debate and the Jewish Question," in *Insiders and Outsiders: Jewish and Gentile Culture in Germany and Austria*, ed. Dagmar C. G. Lorenz and Gabriele Weinberger (Detroit: Wayne State University Press, 1994). S Hanno-Walter Kruft, *Alfred Pringsheim, Hans Thoma, Thomas Mann: Eine Münchner Konstellation* (Munich, 1993), 113–126. Klaus Pringsheim, "Ein Nachtrag zu 'Wälsungenblut,'" *Betrachtungen und Oberblick Zum Werk Thomas Manns*, ed. Georg Wenzel (Berlin [Ost]: Aufbau-Verlag, 1966), 253–268. Sander L. Gilman, "Sibling Incest, Madness, and the Jews," *Social Research* 65, no. 2 (Summer 1998): 401–433. Hans Rudolf Vaget, "*Sang réservé in Deutschland: Zur Rezeption von Thomas Manns Wälsungenblut*," *The German Quarterly* 57, no. 3 (Summer 1984): 367–376. John Whiton, "Thomas Mann's Wälsungenblut: Implications of the Revised Ending," *Seminar* 2, no.1 (1989): 37–48. Stefani Engelstein, *Sibling Action: The Genealogical Structure of Modernity* (New York: Columbia University Press, 2017). Thomas Mann, Brief an Maurice Martin du Gard, August 21, 1931, quoted in Jurgen Kühnel,"'Braut und Schwester bist du dem Bruder.' Der Geschwisterinzest in der Völsunga saga, bei Richard Wagner und Thomas Mann," 134–148. *Les Interdits, Médiévales,* 54, ed. Danielle Buschinger, Presses Du Centre D'études Médiévales Université De Picardie, Jules Verne, Amiens, 2012. "Nocheinmal 'walsungenblut'." *Gesammelte Werke in dreizehn Banden: Reden und Aulsat".* Frankfurt: S. Fischer, '974' 11: 557–560. Hanno-Walter Kruft, *Alfred Pringsheim, Hans Thoma, Thomas Mann: Eine Münchner Konstellation* (München 1993). Verlag Der Bayerischen Akademie Der Wissenschaften In Kommission Bei Der C.H.Beck'schèn Verlagsbuchhandlung München. Gloria Chasson Erlich, "Race and Incest in Mann's 'Blood of the Walsungs'" *Studies in 20th Century Literature* 2, no. 2 (1978): 20

11. Thomas Mann-Heinrich Mann, Briefwechsel 1900-1949, ed. Hans Wysling (1975), 26f., cited in Kruft, Verlag Der Bayerischen Akademie Der Wissenschaften In Kommission Bei Der C. H. Beck'schèn Verlagsbuchhandlung München. Translation, which is my own, does not preserve the ambiguities of the original.

12. Mann's description of the Pringshems in Kruft, 19. Also quotes Klaus Pringsheim, "*Ich fühlte mich wohl ein wenig geschmeichelt, als ich in einzelnen Zügen und Redewendungen des jungen Helden der Erzählung mich wiedererkannte - eher geschmeichelt gewiß als peinlich berührt,*" 19.

13. Peter de Mendelssohn, *Der Zauberer. Das Leben des deutschen Schriftstellers Thomas Mann* (Frankfurt: S. Fischer, 1975). Vaget, 309. Rudolf Brettschneider, "Die Entdeckung des 'Wälsungenblut,'" *Bücherstube* 1 (1920), 110–112.

14. Todd Kontje, "Thomas Mann's 'Wälsungenblut': The Married Artist and the 'Jewish Question,' *PMLA* 123, no. 1 (January 2008): 109–124.

15. Hermann Kurzke, *Thomas Mann: Life as a Work of Art,* trans. Leslie Willson (Princeton: Princeton University Press, 2002). In their discussions of Mann's *Wälsungenblut,* neither Stefani Engelstein's *Sibling Action* nor Sander Gilman's "Sibling Incest, Madness, and the Jews" is concerned with the sibling incest theme at the core of Mann's *Der Erwhählte.*

Chapter Thirteen: Thomas Mann's Der Erwählte

1. Ruth Clifford Engs, "St. Scholastica: Finding Meaning In Her Story" traditionally attributed to Pope Gregory the Great (c. 540–604), gives the story of Benedict and Scholastica: Book II, Ch. XXXIII. Digitalized for IUScholarorks Repository http://hdl.handle.net/2022/1853.

2. Christian Luckscheiter, "Ist es erwähnenswert, dass die Verführung im *Erwählten* umgedreht ist?" "Noch einmal Thomas Mann und die Intertexualitat am Beispiel des *Erwählten.*" Weimarer Beiträge: *Zeitschrift für Literaturwissenschaft, Ästhetik und Kulturwissenschaften* 61, no. (2015): 229–249.

3. Brian Murdoch, *Gregorius: An Incestuous Saint in Medieval Europe* (Oxford: Oxford University Press, 2012), 208 cites Hermann J. Weigand, "Thomas Mann's *Gregorius,*" in *The Germanic Review: Literature, Culture, Theory* 27, no. 2 (1952): 83–95, who traces Auerbach's influence on Mann.

4. See "A Letter from Thomas Mann to Hermann J. Weigand," *PMLA* 87, no. 2 (March 1972): 306–308.

5. "*Trutgespiel*" seems to be Mann's, Clemens's, or Sibylla's invention. Stephen Bronsema suggests "*Spielgeselle* [playmate]" in his University of Osnabruck dissertation (2005). I found the word "*trut*" in Gerhhard Köbler, Mittelhochdeutches Wörterbuch, defined as "*gespenstiches Wesen.*" Helen Elizabeth Hunter suggests "*trûtgespil*" means something along the lines of dear companion/playmate in her University of Birmingham dissertation (2014).

6. Milton, *Comus, a Masque*, (1634).

7. "The sons of God seeing the daughters of men, that they were fair . . . and also afterward, when the sons of God came in unto the daughters of men, and they bare children to them, the same became mighty men which were of old, men of renown."

8. Hebrew linguists uniformly interpret the name as meaning "man of God."

9. "Nine Worthies," in The Oxford Companion to English Literature, 7th ed., ed. Dinah Birch, 2009, https://www.oxfordreference.com/display/10.1093/acref/9780192806871.001.0001/acref-9780192806871-e-5450.

10. "That thou art Peter, and upon this rock I will build my church; and the gates of hell shall not prevail against it. And I will give unto thee the keys of the kingdom of heaven: and whatever you bind on earth shall be bound in heaven, and whatever you loose on earth shall be loosed in heaven." Matthew 16:18-19.

11. T. S. Eliot, *Milton: Two Studies by T.S. Eliot*, ed. Faber and Faber, 1968. C. S. Lewis, *A Preface to Paradise Lost* (London: Oxford University Press, 1961), 82. Stephen B. Dobranski and John P. Rumrich, ed., *Milton and Heresy* (Cambridge: Cambridge University Press, 1998).

12. For heresy, see Carlo Ginzberg, *The Cheese and the Worms* (Baltimore: Johns Hopkins University Press, 2013).

13. Cited in Anne Isabelle François, "Ein höherer Spaß Jeu et écriture dans L'Élu de Thomas Mann," Presses Universitaires de Bordeaux, 2010, Conditions d'utilisation, http://www.openedition.org/6540. Also see R. J. Schork, "Thomas Mann's Der Erwählte: A Monastic Mélange," *The German Quarterly* 58, no. 1 (Winter 1985): 49-67. Thomas Mann, "Bemerkungen zu dem Roman Der Erwählte, in Thomas Mann," *Gesammelte Werke in 13 Bänden*, vol. 11 (Frankfort: Fischer, 1974), 691.

14. "*Bis zum Erfühlen der Ironieen dieser entzückenden Dichtung wird es bei den meisten Lesern reichen, aber wohl nicht bei allen bis zum Erkennen des Ernstes und der Frömmigkeit, die noch hinter diesen Ironieen steht und ihnen erst die wahre, hohe Heiterkeit gibt.*" My translation, cited as Hermann Hesse to Thomas Mann, November 8, 1950, in Anni Carlsson and Volker Michels, eds., *Thomas Mann: Briefwechsel* (Frankfurt, 1999).

15. The pagan god of love appears in some versions of Tristan and Isolde, as does Cupid in Gower's Canace and Machaire.

16. Hanna Stephan, *Die Glückhafte Schuld* (München: Michael Bedstein Verlag, 1940). Eva C. Wunderlich "Zweimal Gregorius: Thomas Mann und Hanna Stephan," *The German Quarterly* 38, no. 4 (November 1965): 640–651. Carsten Bronsema, "Thomas Manns Roman *Der Erwählte:* Eine Untersuchung zum poetischen Stellenwert von Sprache," (PhD diss., Universität Osnabrück, 2005), 17.

17. Victor Yelverton Haines, *A Dictionary of Biblical Tradition in English Literature,* David Lyle Jeffrey ed. (Grand Rapids: W. B. Eerdmans).

18. In Stephan's version, the bride does not recognize her son's raiment until the night of the unconsummated wedding. In Hartmann's version, the bride notes the familiarity of Gregorius's apparel but suppresses that recognition due the influences of Satan.

19. Stephan, *Die Glückhafte Schuld*

Chapter Fourteen: Twentieth Century Verwandlungsmärchen: Kafka and Dunn

1. Helen Elizabeth Hunter, "Literary Uses Of Biblical Imagery In Hartmann Von Aue's *Gregorius*, Kafka's *Die Verwandlung*, And Thomas Mann's *Der Erwählte*" (PhD diss., University of Birmingham, 2014).

2. Norah Vincent, "Review of *Mara And Dann*: An Adventure by Doris Lessing," *Salon* (January 8, 1999). Valentina Adami, "Mythic and Fairy-Tale Elements in Doris Lessing's *Mara and Dann*," in *Law and the Humanities: Cultural Perspectives*, ed. Chiara Battisti and Sidia Fiorato (Boston: De Gruyter, 2020), 463–476.

3. Sharon R. Wilson, "Storytelling in Lessing's *Mara And Dann* and Other Texts," in *Women's Utopian and Dystopian Fiction*, ed. Sharon R. Wilson (Newcastle upon Tyne: Cambridge Scholars Publishing, 2013), 25.

4. Adami, 476.

5. Doris Lessing, *Mara and Dann* (New York: Harper Perennial, 1999), 375-376.

6. Lessing, 385.

Conclusion: The Romantic Movement Extends Natural Law Arguments of Enlightenment

1. *The New England Primer* was an American edition of the less frequently cited, *Protestant tutor instructing children to spel and read English, and ground them in the true Protestant religion [...]* (London: Ben. Harris, 1679).

2. Jefferson, *Notes on the State of Virginia,* https://avalon.law.yale.edu/18th_century/jeffvir.asp.

3. Voltaire, *Candide* (London: 1823).

ABOUT THE AUTHOR

Wilson Jeremiah Moses (1942–2024) received his doctorate in American Civilization from Brown University. One of the most distinguished scholars of African American Studies of his generation, he was a professor of history at Penn State for twenty-two years. He published nearly a dozen books, exhibiting a tremendous range in the history of ideas.

Not only did he write on Frederick Douglass, Alexander Crummell, W. E. B. Du Bois, Booker T. Washington, Marcus Garvey, Ida B. Wells, Ralph Ellison, Martin Luther King Jr., and Malcolm X, he also wrote on Thomas Jefferson, Enlightenment philosophy, economics, comparative ethnic studies, and American Christianity. It could be argued that a common thread of all his interests was the social and historical manipulation of literary and religious myths.

Born and raised in Detroit from the 1940s to 1950s, he came to maturity in the transition from the CIO labor to the modern Black freedom movements. His parents passed on to him HBCU and Catholic traditions of education. He studied literature at Wayne State University. Besides Penn State, he also taught at Brown and Boston Universities, SMU, University of Iowa, and lectured and researched in Britain, Germany, France, and Africa.